Advance Praise for

The Natural Step for Commu

As the signals of distress from our planet become increasingly shrill,
the best hope for a sustainable future in the US lies in enlightened local
leadership. *The Natural Step for Communities* illustrates, with clear and practical
examples, what localities are able to accomplish — from zip cars in Massachusetts,
to organic farms in Philadelphia, to co-housing in Detroit to restoring clam
beds off the coast of Maine. The book resonates with a critical understanding that
any true sustainable grassroots revolution depends not just on innovation but also
on a robust and vital democratic process. This book should be required reading for
every mayor, town manager and city planner in the U.S.

— Ross Gelbspan, author, *The Heat Is On: The Climate Crisis, The Cover-up,*
The Prescription and *Boiling Point*

In Whistler, we use the Natural Step framework to bring clarity to the issue of
sustainability. As we set out on the challenging course of applying the framework,
it is encouraging to see *The Natural Step for Communities* —
a useful applications guide, complete with inspiring success stories from
a growing network of progressive communities.
I urge all elected local officials to read this book.

— Mayor Hugh O'Reilly of Whistler

This is an important book for any community serious about the journey to sustainability.
It lays out a rigorously conceived, comprehensive and tested methodology for
sustainable community development. Its case studies breathe life into the sometimes
esoteric sustainability discussion. I highly recommend it.

— David Gershon, founder and architect of Global Action Plan's award-winning
EcoTeam Program, CEO of the Empowerment Institute and a leading expert
on environmental behavior change

A wonderful and timely resource. Written as a fireside chat with Sarah and Torbjörn, this book should be required reading for everyone from elected members and chief executives to infrastructure managers and service delivery staff in city governments; it will provide them with a glimpse of what we all need to head toward. Our planet and society depend on it.

— Eric Park, Sustainable Christchurch Leader, Christchurch City Council, New Zealand

The Natural Step for Communities is an extraordinarily readable volume that dispels the myth that sustainable community planning cannot be accomplished on a large and continuing scale. It challenges the reader by demonstrating the multitude of ways in which cities in North America and Europe are creating more environmentally secure futures. The book is written in a way that will allow its findings to be effectively communicated with decision makers, lay planners, and citizens. Our own community is exploring models for success that can be used to build such a community, and we will be keeping this volume by our side for inspiration.

— Steven A. Preston, FAICP, Deputy City Manager/Community Development Director, San Gabriel, CA

The Natural Step for Communities provides us with a compelling and inspiring collection of success stories, clearly demonstrating that it is possible to achieve economic, ecological and social goals at the same time, and in many different and innovative ways. Congratulations to Sarah James and Tjorbörn Lahti for showing us how the Natural Step framework can empower community planners to design and create more sustainable communities. They give us hope that real change is possible in our lifetime. This book is a must read for anyone serious about moving his or her community toward sustainability.

— Kelly Hawke Baxter, Chair, The Natural Step Canada

The Natural Step
for Communities

How Cities and Towns can Change to Sustainable Practices

SARAH JAMES & TORBJÖRN LAHTI

Foreword by Dr. Karl-Henrik Robèrt

NEW SOCIETY PUBLISHERS

Cataloguing in Publication Data:
A catalog record for this publication is available from the National Library of Canada.

Cover design by Diane McIntosh. Image: Comstock, RF.

Printed in Canada.

Paperback ISBN: 0-86571-491-6

Inquiries regarding requests to reprint all or part of *The Natural Step for Communities* should be addressed to New Society Publishers at the address below.

To order directly from the publishers, please add $4.50 shipping to the price of the first copy, and $1.00 for each additional copy (plus GST in Canada). Send check or money order to:

New Society Publishers
P.O. Box 189, Gabriola Island, BC V0R 1X0, Canada
1-800-567-6772

New Society Publishers' mission is to publish books that contribute in fundamental ways to building an ecologically sustainable and just society, and to do so with the least possible impact on the environment, in a manner that models this vision. We are committed to doing this not just through education, but through action. We are acting on our commitment to the world's remaining ancient forests by phasing out our paper supply from ancient forests worldwide. This book is one step towards ending global deforestation and climate change. It is printed on acid-free paper that is **100% old growth forest-free** (100% post-consumer recycled), processed chlorine free, and printed with vegetable based, low VOC inks. For further information, or to browse our full list of books and purchase securely, visit our website at: **www.newsociety.com**

NEW SOCIETY PUBLISHERS   www.newsociety.com

Dedication

To the Findhorn community, where my journey to
sustainability began.

— Sarah James

To all the children — those who are already born,
and those who will be born.

— Torbjörn Lahti

Contents

Acknowledgments

It is now clear to me that it takes a village to write a book. I want to thank my "village," without whom this book could not have taken form.

To Janet Bush for her encouragement and advice about writing a book in the first place. To Jean Mason and Ted Allen for several months of reading, editing, and their many helpful suggestions. To Kim and Ileana Jones, Carolyn Revelle, and Maggie Carvan for their editing help. To Robin Harper for digitizing photos, document formating, editing, and hours of patient word-processing instruction to a sometimes-trying student. To Eva Tasaki for her many hours of Swedish to English translation and research. To Eric Park, my fellow Sustainable Sweden tour member, for his prodigious notes that allowed me to check the accuracy of mine and fill in some gaps. To the Swedish municipal staffers who answered our requests for information and those who welcomed, informed, and introduced us to the eco-accomplishments of their municipalities in August, 2001. To our publishers, Chris and Judith Plant, for their endorsement and support of this book project, and our editor, Judith Brand.

To my cohousing community for their company during the writing process. To my mother, Sarah Meyer, for her continual love and moral support.

To Philip B. Herr, who developed the Swamp Yankee planning approach described in this book. He has been my planning partner, colleague, teacher, advisor, and has contributed inestimably to my qualifications for co-writing this book.

To Karl-Henrik Robèrt and the Natural Step framework, pivotal in my own sustainability paradigm shift. To the eco-municipalities of Sweden for all their accomplishments and for leading the way. And finally to my co-author, Torbjörn Lahti, who has been instrumental in the journeys of the eco-municipalities on the path to sustainability.

— *Sarah James*

I have had the fortune to meet so many thousands of wonderful and competent people from all over the world. And each of them has given me so much and deserves my deepest gratitude, even if it is impossible to mention them all by name. Nevertheless, I must mention a few: To my dear friend and colleague, Gunnar Brundin, for our common struggle in winning and losing battles. Together we started Esam and become co-ordinators of the Swedish eco-municipality network. To all other co-workers at Esam, including Michael Jalmby, Vivi-Ann Adamsson, Barbro Kalla, Lasse Andersson, Oscar Lonconchino, Mikael Brändström, Susanne Eriksson, Sara Andersson, Erik Westerberg, and Ira Sundberg. To my colleagues in Robertsfors, including Björn Eriksson, Carina Aschan, Sören Borrelid, Hans Lindgren, and Mats Karlsson. We are in the middle of a thrilling process, and I hope they will keep on believing in the possibility to do things no one ever has done before. And of course, my dear family who I love more than anything else: To my wife, Mona, for living with an incurable optimist for the last 26 years. It is her invisible work that has made it possible for me to do what I have done all these years. I'm eternally grateful for that. To my children: Andreas and his girlfriend Christina, Johan, and Sara; they have been used to having a father always working and traveling, but I know they accept and appreciate the reasons why. I'm grateful for their patience and acceptance living in a somewhat different family where material things and consumption have been of low value. They have grown up with sustainable development as a natural way of behaving and thinking. There are moments when I'm surprised they still believe in at least parts of what the "old man" says. To my co-author, who did the main part of the job: I'm impressed with what you have done. It's "almost good."

— *Torbjörn Lahti*

Foreword

We need role models in the world when it comes to community building around the greatest challenge of our time — to create an attractive sustainable society. Unlike many other attempts around the world these days, this struggle is key for civilization. There is no more decent and dignified task. In this game, while dealing with all the acute and demanding issues of the present, you must also keep the long term in sight. There is only one way of doing this. Amongst all possible opportunities that can be evaluated in the short term, only those opportunities should be considered that can serve as platforms for progress tomorrow. This requires leadership.

Obsolete leadership is all about demand and control. Modern leadership is the opposite and builds on engagement and shared responsibility. It is paradoxical, that when modern leadership is effective, the demands for quality of the whole community become higher, and the control of quality becomes more effective. Effective modern leadership builds on clear core values for community development and on clear principles for identifying decent and desirable outcomes for those communities. Effective leadership builds on encouragement of all individuals to take active part in the creation of the new.

The clearer and more decent the communicated core values and principles are, the less leaders need to make demands upon participants and to control the process with all its details. Clear core values and principles for dignified goals attract engagement, and the demands and the control occur where it belongs — where the actual change takes place.

At the 1992 Rio Summit, conference participants realized that the perfect scale for the creation of socially and ecologically sustainable role models in politics was the municipality level — close to people as it is. They consequently realized that the municipality holds the key to a sustainable world in its hand. Many municipalities have seriously taken up this challenge. In The

Natural Step organization, we are now working hard to make these municipality examples known throughout the world. And we want to say to all people who are actively part of this long and demanding endeavor — please hang in there! It's not easy, but there is no other way.

Two experts on community building around sustainability have written this book. The book is about the methodology of being intellectually strict at the same time as it talks about the spirituality and joy of understanding something together. It describes obstacles, it teaches clear thinking, and it respects the change agents who have to be bold enough to work in the front line of a new paradigm where nobody has been before. It adds in a wonderful way to other books in this field — books like *Collaborative Spunk* by Gayle Hudgens and *Dancing with the Tiger* by Brian Nattrass and Mary Altomare. It offers a clear path for all communities to embark upon the journey to sustainability and demonstrates that this is an achievable reality.

— *Karl-Henrik Robèrt*

Preface

Whom this book is for — what it is; what it isn't

This is a book for practitioners — people who work with, and for, city and town governments and the larger communities they represent — as well as anyone else interested in sustainable development. It is a how-to book about changing the way we do things, moving away from practices that are harming the earth and its inhabitants, including us humans. It offers a different approach — an approach that has demonstrated economic and social benefits as well as environmental ones. It gives examples of communities that have changed their practices and offers guiding principles and concrete steps to help other interested communities follow in their steps.

This is not an academic book, although we hope that students and their teachers will learn from it. Principles and steps for developing sustainable practices are based upon what has been learned from scores of cities and towns both in Sweden and in the United States. An academic approach to this subject might present several community change processes, evaluate their pros and cons, and present recommendations accordingly. This book goes right to the key principles and steps that we have found essential to successful community adoption of change proposals, be these master plans, sustainable development plans, or projects.

Nor is this book a compendium of sustainable development practices, although Part II does present many examples of strategies, projects, and actions undertaken by communities. With a few exceptions, the book does not dwell on the technicalities of any one project or technique, such as how "green roofs" are designed or how biogas fuel is generated. If a particular description whets the reader's appetite to learn more, as we hope will be the case, there is plenty of in-depth information now available elsewhere about virtually all of the sustainable development approaches mentioned here.

Much is also accessible through the worldwide web. We have tried, to the best of our ability, to provide brief explanations of new practices for a general understanding and to provide sources into which interested readers can delve more deeply.

Much of the material in Part II was collected during the August 2001 Sustainable Sweden tour. Sarah James was a member of that tour, organized and led by Torbjörn Lahti. Many of the sustainable projects and practices described here are presented in the form of stories that are as close as possible to the original words of local officials, community practitioners, designers, housing occupants, and business people in the eco-municipalities we visited on the tour. In describing these projects and practices, we take a role that is more like a storyteller or reporter and less like an evaluator or analyst. We primarily rely on the accuracy of our sources, although we have done our best to verify information where appropriate.

How the book is organized

The book is divided into three parts, through which the reader can travel in sequence or in any other order. Part I, Compass for Change, is about the concepts of sustainability and sustainable development and offers a clear framework of principles to use in coming to understand better these complex subjects. This framework is used by almost all of the Swedish communities described here. Part II, Practices That Changed, presents the sustainable development success stories of the Swedish community experiences. Part III, Steps to Change, is the how-to section that presents concrete steps and guiding process principles for how to move toward municipal and community change. Supplementing these are some soup-to-nuts community case studies whose experience provides examples of key steps and process principles.

A few more words about Part II, Practices That Changed. In developing a section such as this based upon actual community and municipal experience, there are two major approaches to organizing the material. One is to present comprehensive case studies of a few communities, describing their background, what they did, what they accomplished, what they learned, and what conclusions can be drawn from their experience. A second is to present their accomplishments and results organized by functional area — for example, results in housing, economic development, energy use, education, and agriculture. We have chosen a combination of these two approaches. Part II presents community results by functional topic area. This has allowed us to include more of the activities and results than space would have permitted using the in-depth case study approach. These topic areas also represent all policy and functional areas with which most cities, towns, and local government are concerned and which usually comprise the chapters of a comprehensive (master) plan. This method also allows readers interested in a particular subject, such as energy or housing, to go directly to their individual area of interest. Hence, the reader will find one community project, such as a biomass heating plant, described in the chapter on renewable energy and another project in the same community, for example, a school, described in the chapter on ecological education and schools. Comprehensive case studies are presented in Part III to illustrate the change processes of several communities and one business.

Why Swedish communities?

There are countless cities and towns around the world that have begun sustainable development projects and that have made major strides in such areas as reducing greenhouse gas emissions, adopting green building programs, increasing municipal recycling rates, or redeveloping brownfields sites. Why does this book concentrate primarily upon the experiences of Swedish communities?

First, the experience of many other communities carrying out sustainable development initiatives such as Curitiba, Brazil, or Chattanooga, Tennessee, has already been well documented and described. As far as we know, the experience of the more than 60 Swedish eco-municipalities so far is largely unknown and unrecorded. We believe their experience has much to offer communities across the world.

Second, these Swedish communities appear to be distinguished from their world counterparts by two characteristics. The Swedish eco-municipalities are changing to sustainable practices on an across-the-board basis. This means they are working to change all municipal and community practices concurrently, instead of, say, choosing an energy reduction program this year and a water quality protection initiative next year. This does not mean these municipalities are trying to do everything at once, which is of course not possible. Rather, it means they are taking a systems approach to change that takes into account that municipal practices and functional policy areas, such as energy use and water protection, are interrelated and affect one another. A systems approach to these two areas, for example, would assure that measures to protect water would not be ones that require vast amounts of energy, or correspondingly, that selected energy reduction measures would not be ones that could pollute water sources.

Another key difference that sets these communities apart from others implementing sustainable development lies in the type of process they are using to bring about municipal and community change to sustainable practices. These eco-municipalities have committed to a bottom-up, democratic approach of change to sustainable community practices. This means they involve citizens, businesses, and municipal employees right from the beginning in identifying a sustainable community vision and in designing strategies that advance toward that vision.

These two distinguishing characteristics — an across-the-board systems approach and a bottom-up participatory approach — are also keys to the extraordinary implementation success of these eco-municipalities. Herein lies the enormous contribution that these communities can make to others. The eco-municipalities of Sweden demonstrate how other communities can systematically reorient to sustainable practices in the broad range of municipal and community operations within several years.

Clarifying some terms

Throughout this book, the reader will encounter the terms *municipality, city, town, village,* and *community.* These terms do not always mean the same in Sweden and in North America. In both, the term municipality means the official government body of a particular locality. In the United States, city and town are largely interchangeable with municipality. For example, a sentence that said "the City of Seattle adopted a master plan" would refer to the official government of Seattle — its municipality. In Sweden, however, this is not the case. In Sweden, if one is referring to the official local government of a locality, one would almost always use the term municipality rather than city or town. (The Swedish word for municipality is *kommun.*) In this book, however, city and town are used as synonyms for municipality; that is, they refer to the official government of the locality and its area of jurisdiction. In this book, a village describes a smaller settlement area within a municipality that does not have its own local government structure but rather is governed by the larger municipality.

The term community presents more challenges, as it can mean many things to many people. We use it to refer both to the municipal government and to the broader population of citizens, businesses, and interests that exist within the boundaries of that municipality. Eco-municipalities (*eko-kommuner* in Swedish) refers to a specific group of Swedish municipalities that have made a special commitment to sustainable change and who are part of a national association of eco-municipalities. They will be explained in more detail at the beginning of Part II of this book. Those in Sweden who coined the term *eko-kommun* commonly translate this label into English as eco-municipality instead of eco-community to make it clear that the commitment to sustainability is an official municipal policy, even though broader local interests beyond the municipal government share that commitment.

The reader also will encounter the terms sustainability, sustainable development, green, and ecological throughout this book. It is not always easy for people to understand or differentiate among these concepts, and many people who use these terms do not use them with clarity. In this book, sustainable, green, and ecological are used as synonyms and hence should be considered interchangeable. Part I is devoted to presenting and explaining the concepts of sustainability and sustainable development, including the trouble that people have describing it, and offering a framework to guide the reader in understanding these terms as we use them.

Transferability: Why are Swedish cities and towns valid exemplars for North American ones?

There are certainly differences between Swedish and North American communities. The political perspectives of their national governments, particularly when it comes to the environment and sustainable development, differ hugely at the beginning of the third millenium. For example, the national government of Sweden has set environmental goals for the entire country and expects municipalities to develop local plans to work toward these goals. The Swedish national government provides funding and technical resources for local environmental initiatives and planning for sustainable development. By and large, with some notable exceptions, the national government of the United States has to date done neither.

Sweden also is part of the European Union that offers yet more resources for local municipalities interested in planning for and implementing sustainable development initiatives. Further, all municipalities in Sweden have signed onto, in some form or fashion, the United Nations' model local sustainable development action plan known as Agenda 21. This plan, created in the 1992 United Nations Conference on Environment and Development in Rio de Janeiro, is being used by communities around the world, with the notable exception of the United States, as a guide to sustainable development. For reasons that might take another book to describe, many people in the United States do not even know what Agenda 21 is. This is not to suggest, however, that communities in the United

States are not working toward sustainable development. On the contrary, a great many U.S. communities have begun some effort in this direction.

Despite these notable differences, which might help explain why Swedish community change toward sustainable development is further along than that in the United States, there are some significant similarities. The first and foremost lies in the area of municipal independence and autonomy. Although the Swedish government has set national environmental goals, has endorsed Agenda 21 as a sustainable development guide, and supported local sustainability initiatives with funding and other resources, it is up to local municipalities to adopt and implement these goals. Herein lies the common bond between Swedish and United States municipalities where home rule is the modus operandi, and city and town planning, land use, and community development are largely under local municipal authority instead of national authority.

The experience of the cities and towns described in this book offers hope and concrete evidence that broadbased community change toward sustainable practices is possible. We hope that their experience, and the lessons we can learn from them, will inspire others around the world to do the same.

The Bumblebee That Changed the World

Övertorneå — the first eco-municipality in Sweden

In the mid-1980s, the little town of Övertorneå (Eu-vehr-tawr'-neh-aw) in northern Sweden received a national prize as the Municipality of the Year. In his speech at the award ceremony, a prominent county official, Councilman Jan-Olof Hedström, compared Övertorneå to a bumblebee. As lore has it, the famous aeronautic engineer Sikorsky hung a sign in his office lobby that reads: "The bumblebee, according to our engineers' calculations, cannot fly at all, but the bumblebee doesn't know this and flies."

This was the regional and national establishment's view of Övertorneå. Changes were happening in the town outside the envelope of what was then regarded as business-as-usual community development. The municipal government and its larger community had made a commitment to develop in a way that was in harmony with nature. Övertorneå residents and town officials sought a win-win-win relationship between humans, society, and nature. Residents and officials were coming to understand that investing in ecological approaches to meet community needs could also bring about an economically positive future. To characterize its transformation, Övertorneå began to call itself an "eco-municipality."

Övertorneå was discussing and practicing ideas such as mobilizing people, taking a bottom-up approach to community planning, collaborative community development, cooperating across department and industrial sector boundaries, investing in local culture, and taking into account the local informal economy. Such ideas were foreign to conventional Swedish town planning and community development practices at that time. What the regional and national establishments could see, without understanding why, was that these strange ideas evidently produced remarkable results — for example, over 200 new business enterprises producing several hundred jobs in a small town of barely 6,000 inhabitants. These county and national agencies considered new jobs and businesses to be the most important indicators of successful community development.

BACKGROUND

Övertorneå was located in the Swedish region hardest hit by the 1980 economic recession that brought about a 20 percent regional unemployment rate and subsequent out-migration. Övertorneå's population dropped 25 percent from its level 30 years earlier. Apathy and lack of trust in the future typified local attitudes. Social experts predicted the region was doomed to die, since no possible solutions were apparent.

In this seemingly hopeless situation, Övertorneå and its municipal government decided to explore what other future scenarios might be possible besides the prevailing bleak view. This decision was the town's first step toward becoming Sweden's first eco-municipality. It also was the first step toward changing both the perceived negative future and the actual negative conditions of hard economic times and population loss. In the six years following this decision, over 200 new companies in Övertorneå developed and prospered. These new enterprises included organic farms, beekeeping, fish farms, sheep husbandry, and eco-tourism enterprises.

Key to these successes was widespread community participation. The citizens of Övertorneå took on their own community development work to become the town they wanted. Over 600 residents took part in special study circles discussing regional development issues and

Figure 0.1: This idyllic scene of Övertorneå countryside belied its former depressed economy and community spirit.

future possibilities. Out of these study circles emerged village development associations that took charge of the ideas sprouting and gradually taking form. The ecological perspective blossomed in a municipal government investment in biofueled district heating, support for ecological farming such as farmer education and municipal purchasing of organic foods, establishing a "health home" and building an ecovillage to attract new families. Över-torneå's municipal government and town planner held continual training events and seminars explaining the ecological perspective to citizens, businesses, farmers, and the other interests in Övertorneå, gradually raising the community's awareness of the importance of ecology and the environment. New postsecondary education courses, elementary school education, and childcare taught with an eco-perspective started up. Marketing and outreach of this emerging "eco-region" brought about a surge of tourist interest and subsequent birth of new tourist-oriented businesses.

At the same time, local culture was undergoing a renaissance. Revival of the local Finnish minority dialect, establishment of a local theater, and start-up of music groups, among others, brought about a cultural revolution in Övertorneå and its region where pessimism transformed into trust in the town's future, its traditional culture, and its development potential.

The transformation continues to this day. Övertorneå currently has the lowest incidence of sicknesses in Sweden, measured by the proportion of absence of long-term illness, as one example. The community's good health is considered to be due in large measure to consistent municipal investment that supports public health.

The municipality of Övertorneå has become 100 percent free of fossil fuel use in its municipal operations and is working for community independence from fossil fuel as a heating source by 2010. The town has converted all five of its oil-based village heating plants to wood pellet-burning facilities. The town government and many citizens have purchased cars that run on ethanol, a grain-based alcohol, instead of gasoline. Now there are ethanol gas pumps in town. The town has made all public transportation available at no cost. This decision increased public ridership by 700 percent. The town designed and constructed new schools based upon ecological principles.

News of Övertorneå's transformation spread throughout the country over the next several years. Inspired in part by Övertorneå's small village revitalization, a national rural movement of 3,300 similar village development groups evolved, where hundreds of thousands of village inhabitants began to take part in developing their communities in the direction of a future they wanted.

In the early 1990s, scores of other Swedish cities and towns signed onto the idea of becoming an eco-municipality. At the same time, similar eco-community development was going on in Norway, Denmark, and Finland. Collaborations among these Nordic eco-cities and eco-towns brought about a combined Nordic eco-community presentation at the 1992 United

Nations Conference on Environment and Development, held in Rio de Janeiro. This conference, also called the 1992 Rio Summit, established an action plan for local sustainable development that has come to be known as Agenda 21. Much of the contents in this world guide to local sustainable development emerged from the Nordic eco-municipality contributions to the Summit, when many conference participants realized that they offered one of the few serious examples of sustainable community development in the Western world. Thus, the United Nations' world guide to local sustainable development urges communities to begin to work in the same manner as Övertorneå began to work ten years earlier.

Since the 1992 Rio Summit, all municipalities in Sweden have begun local development work using this United Nations sustainable development guide. More than sixty of these cities and towns have declared themselves as eco-municipalities. The eco-municipality concept also has spread to other countries, such as Japan and New Zealand. The little bumblebee that couldn't fly has evidently influenced matters far outside its own boundaries!

COMPASS FOR CHANGE: THE NATURAL STEP FRAMEWORK FOR SUSTAINABILITY

CHAPTER 1

Introducing and Using the Natural Step Framework

Why a framework?

For starters, why is a framework of sustainability principles needed? For those already interested in community adoption of sustainable development, there are plenty of good examples out there now. These include green building programs, walkable New Urbanist communities, transit-oriented development, smart growth approaches, climate change initiatives, bike trails, electric buses, solar panels, windmill energy, and sustainability indicators. Why not just pick one or more of these and get to work making them happen in a given community? Scores of cities and towns in North America and around the world have already completed these types of environmental initiatives and sustainable development projects.

But what happens when committed and well-intentioned people can't agree on what sustainability or sustainable development means, let alone how to move in these directions? What about communities where local officials and citizens really don't understand, or care, what sustainability means in the first place, or why we all need to think about it?

Or, how about those situations in communities where environmental, social, and economic initiatives and goals conflict? Do we use limited public funds to protect diminishing open space or to build affordable housing for those in need? Do we save the forests, spotted owls, fish, or the jobs of the loggers and fishermen who depend on these resources?

Then, some cities or towns have adopted an environmental practice in one branch of government, only to find another department operating at cross-purposes. For example, one New England community became one of the first in the region to adopt a municipal integrated pest management policy aimed at reducing and eventually eliminating the use of chemical pesticides in public parks and school recreation fields. Within months of doing this, another branch of local government sprayed most of the city with pesticides in an effort to kill mosquitoes that might be carrying the West Nile virus.

Next, there are the cases where an environmental initiative in one area has created unsustainable conditions in another area. An example of this is the well-intentioned effort, begun in the 1970s' oil "crisis," to construct buildings in a more energy-efficient way. And so we did — creating public and private buildings so airtight and well-insulated that they sealed us in with substances like volatile organic compounds emitted from carpets and pressboard cabinets, mold and dirt in air ventilation systems, all of which contribute to what is now known as sick building syndrome. Solving one problem while quite unintentionally creating another.

So, debates and arguments occur in trying to define what is sustainable. Issue-oriented or project-oriented sustainable priorities can conflict. Community actors can work at cross-purposes. We solve one environmental problem, only to create another. Many citizens and local officials still are not aware of the seriousness of what is happening at the global level or do not understand how this is directly related to the well-being of their own communities. Those who are aware often feel paralyzed and helpless in the face of seemingly overwhelming trends. These minefields can impede or stop the journey to community sustainability or even one well-intentioned project initiative.

Consider the case of a soccer team. All players on that team have their own roles and responsibilities. Each player may be doing something very different from the next on the field at any given second. Often, players have no idea what will happen next. If there were no shared understanding about the goal of the game, or the rules of play, there would be chaos on the field.[1]

So it is with a community team. The municipal government of a community, for example, has team members that can include public works, roads and highways, administration, purchasing, planning, conservation, recreation, fire and safety, public health, planning, code enforcement, community development, economic development, education, and housing.

The larger community team includes citizens from many walks of life, neighborhoods with their own special character, businesses of many shapes and sizes, public and non-profit institutions. Team members have their own set of responsibilities, activities, functions, areas of authority — sometimes regulatory authority — within the municipal government and the larger community.

If there already exists a shared set of playing rules in municipal government, these are usually implicit and have more to do with rules and expectations about budgetary constraints, public service provision, and politics than how to move toward a common desired future. In a way it is no wonder that city government, town government, and community affairs in general can often seem, if not actually be, chaotic.

Just suppose, for a minute, that all the departments, boards, and agencies of a city or town, and all the sectors of the larger community have a common vision about a sustainable community future and a shared understanding about a new set of playing rules for how to get there. Even though these "team members" carry out widely differing functions, responsibilities, and activities, their differing functions, like those of soccer players with differing positions and responsibilities, are aimed toward the same end goal.

What type of vision and playing rules can possibly bring this about?

> Dr. Karl-Henrik Robèrt, founder of the Natural Step, coined a motto about the Natural Step approach to sustainability — "Find fundamental principles of indisputable relevance, and thereafter ask the advice of others on how to apply them."

Introducing the Natural Step framework

A LITTLE BACKGROUND

It was this type of chaos on the playing field within the scientific and environmental communities and a single-issue approach to handling environmental problems that led a group of scientists in Sweden to seek a better way. In 1988, Dr. Karl-Henrik Robèrt, a practicing clinician and specialist in cancer research, contacted other members of the Swedish scientific and environmental community. He asked these scientists and professionals to join him in an open dialogue about the bigger picture — what was happening that was unsustainable — and to help develop a set of principles that could guide human action toward a more sustainable path regardless of the starting point.

Together, they developed an educational manuscript of basic principles of science and natural law that could serve as a basis for scientific agreement and societal cooperation. Over the next year, the dialogue broadened to include government officials, business leaders, trade union representatives, members of national non-profit organizations, entertainers, and eventually the King and Queen of Sweden. Some fruits of this expanded circle were a TV program and a tape-and-booklet mailing to every household in Sweden. This experience prompted Robèrt to coin a phrase for the modus operandi and overall motto of the Natural Step approach — "Find fundamental principles of indisputable relevance, and thereafter ask the advice of others on how to apply them."[2]

In his continuing journey to outline basic conditions that needed to exist for a society to be sustainable, Robèrt encountered a man who he later described as his multi-disciplinary mentor — Karl-Erik Eriksson — and his brilliant physics student John Holmberg.[3] Eriksson was a professor of theoretical physics at Chalmers University in Göteborg; Holmberg was a doctoral student studying materials flows. These three individuals, who were to collaborate closely in the evolution of the basic system conditions, came together at a 1990 conference in Orsa, Sweden. This conference was also the first gathering of the Swedish eco-municipalities, described in Chapter 4. Combining understanding of thermodynamics with knowledge of the biological conditions necessary for life, Robèrt, Holmberg, and Eriksson developed the model for a sustainable society that is the basis for the fundamental principles or system conditions for a sustainable society.[4] These principles, further developed by Robèrt and Holmberg, are the centerpiece of the Natural Step framework for sustainability.

To understand the basis for those principles, it helps to first move back and take a look at the bigger picture — what is happening at the global level that is unsustainable.

LOOKING AT THE BIG PICTURE

At the global level, two trends are converging. On the one hand, natural systems of the earth are deteriorating, and the rate of this deterioration is increasing. Since 1945, 11 percent of the Earth's vegetative surface has been degraded. The loss of species is estimated to be the sixth most massive extinction in Earth's history. The world's supply of freshwater and its ecosystems have been seriously diminished.[5]

At the same time, population and consumption are rising exponentially, and disproportionately in the developed versus the developing worlds. Population is growing faster than food supplies in 64 of 105 developing countries. In the next 25 years, over one-third of the world's population will experience severe water shortage.[6] Twenty percent of the world's population now consumes 70 percent of its material resources and holds 80 percent of world wealth. The ecological footprint of the average citizen in the United States is 24 acres (9.7 hectares), compared to that of the average world citizen's footprint of 5.6 acres (2.8 hectares)[7]

These two trends — declining natural systems, and rising population and consumption — are like two sides of a funnel that are converging upon each other. The time available for stabilizing these trends — the margin for action — is diminishing. And it is not known at what point irreversible effects will occur.

THE FOUR SYSTEM CONDITIONS FOR SUSTAINABILITY

The Swedish colleagues worked to identify what human activities were unsustainable over time and flaunted basic laws of physics, biology, and ecology. Based upon a clearer understanding of these unsustainable trends, agreement emerged about four conditions that all need to be met in order for a society to be sustainable. These system conditions, as they have come to be called, are as follows:[9]

1. **In the sustainable society, nature is not subject to systematically increasing concentrations of substances extracted from the Earth's crust.**

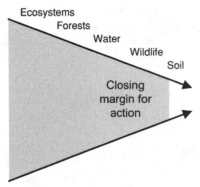

Deteriorating living systems

Ecosystems
Forests
Water
Wildlife
Soil

Closing margin for action

Population & Consumption

REASON: Human society mines and brings into use substances from below the Earth's surface. These substances include heavy metals, such as cadmium, lead, mercury, minerals such as phosphorus, and fossil fuels. These substances and their emissions, such as carbon dioxide and nitrogen oxide created by burning of fossil fuels, have been steadily accumulating both in human society and nature at levels far greater than their natural occurrences. Because these metals and minerals are elements, they cannot break down further. Many of these substances, such as mercury, lead, and cad-

Figure 1.1: The funnel of converging trends[8]

mium, already are known to be toxic.

While scientists argue about the toxic levels of other heavy metals and minerals, no one argues that natural systems, including humankind, can withstand continually increasing concentrations of these substances. The first law of thermodynamics says that energy can neither be created nor destroyed. The same goes for matter in normal chemical reactions. In practical terms this means we can't get rid of anything. Once these heavy metals and minerals are out and about in society, they are here to stay.

2. **In the sustainable society, nature is not subject to systematically increasing concentrations of substances produced by society.**

   REASON: Human society also has been manufacturing synthetic substances — chemicals and other compounds that do not occur in nature — faster than these materials can be broken down. The U.S. Environmental Protection Agency now lists over 70,000 chemicals that are in common use.[10] Many of these chemicals are persistent, meaning they do not break down easily or quickly, and they can spread far from their places of origin. For example, chemicals used to make flame-proof furniture upholstery are also known to interfere with brain and thyroid development and are found to be increasing exponentially in the flesh of Arctic seals, porpoises, crabs, and fish.[11]

   Synthetic chemicals also are accumulating in our own bodies. According to the U.S. Environmental Protection Agency, every U.S. citizen's fatty tissue contains at least 700 chemical contaminants.[12] To study the toxicity of the interactions of just 25 chemicals would require over 33 million experiments at a cost of about US$3 trillion.[13] To study the interactions of 11,000 chemicals would require 10^{3311} experiments,[14] a number greater than that of all the stars in the galaxies. Is it really feasible, then, to wait for scientific research to discover which and what combinations of those tens of thousands of chemicals are responsible for the many cancers, reproductive disruptions, and species extinction?

3. **In the sustainable society, nature is not subject to systematically increasing degradation by physical means.**

   REASON: Human activity also is breaking down natural systems — land, water, forests, soil, ecosystems — by depletion and destruction faster than these natural systems can renew themselves. Nearly one-half of the Earth's original forest cover has been lost. Two of every three species is estimated to be in decline.[15] Already, the demand for fresh water exceeds the world's supply by 17 percent.

   While we enjoy nature in the form of trees, open space, forests, babbling brooks, and singing birds, we often forget that nature also is our life-support system. It is the green plants, vegetation, trees, and ocean algae that produce the oxygen we breathe, absorb the carbon dioxide we give off, and produce the sugars and carbohydrates — through the process of photosynthesis — that are the basis of all the food we eat. The green cells of plants are the only cells in nature that can convert the sun's energy to these life-sustaining substances.

4. **And, in the sustainable society, people are not subject to conditions that systematically undermine their capacity to meet their needs.**

    REASON: If people around the world cannot meet their basic human needs, the first three system conditions will not be met. For example, farmers in Brazil will keep burning the rainforest if they cannot meet their needs for subsistence any other way. The control of 80 percent of the world's wealth and resources by 20 percent of the population is an unstable condition that can lead, if it is not already leading, to social unrest and conflict. This inequality will continually undermine achievements toward the first three conditions.

    The basic human needs — air, water, food, shelter — should take precedence over provision of luxuries. Within our communities, our needs include a means of livelihood, mobility, equal treatment, equal access, safety, participation in decisions that affect our lives, the right to peaceful enjoyment of life, and a connection with nature. They also include a need for psychological and spiritual connection and meaning.[16]

    Needs cannot be substituted for one another. For example, having a roof over our heads will not satisfy our body's need for water. Having enough water to drink does not meet our need for shelter. In the same vein, having a "monster house," SUV, TV and CD player in every room, and expensive running shoes cannot substitute effectively for unmet needs in other areas.

New "playing rules"

Four guiding objectives emerge from the system conditions of the Natural Step that, used together, can help a city, town, or region systematically develop policies and practices toward sustainability. Please see these guiding objectives on the next page.

While action in the direction of any one of these objectives is good, it is those practices that simultaneously move in the direction of all four that can be relied upon to truly move toward sustainability. Applying all four objectives in generating a plan of action or strategy for a particular context or topic area essentially assures that a systems approach will emerge for that topic, as opposed to a single-issue or project-oriented approach that may solve one problem but create others.

DEVELOP POLICIES AND PRACTICES THAT ULTIMATELY ...

Guiding Objective[17]	Type of Practices
1. Eliminate our community's contribution to fossil fuel dependence and to wasteful use of scarce metals and minerals.	Transit and pedestrian-oriented development; development heated and powered by renewable energy; mixed-use development; public transit, alternatively fueled municipal fleets; incentives for organic agriculture that minimizes phosphorus and petrochemical fertilizers and herbicides.
2. Eliminate our community's contribution to dependence upon persistent chemicals and wasteful use of synthetic substances.	Healthy building design and construction that reduces or eliminates use of toxic building materials; landscape design and park maintenance that uses alternatives to chemical pesticides and herbicides; municipal purchasing guidelines that encourage low- or non-chemical product use.
3. Eliminate our community's contribution to encroachment upon nature (e.g., land, water, wildlife, forests, soil, ecosystems).	Redevelopment of existing sites and buildings before building new ones; building "from the inside out" development and infrastructure policies; open space, forest, and habitat preservation; reduced water use and recycling of wash water; sewage treatment by plants.
4. Meet human needs fairly and efficiently.	Affordable housing for a diversity of residents; locally based business and food production; using waste as a resource; eco-industrial development; participatory community planning and decision making.

The Natural Step system conditions and four guiding objectives provide a compass for reorienting human actions from unsustainable directions to sustainable ones. Using these objectives as a compass, we can change course to actions that can level out the converging and unsustainable trends of the funnel and eventually move to restorative actions.

Planning by objectives — a little demonstration

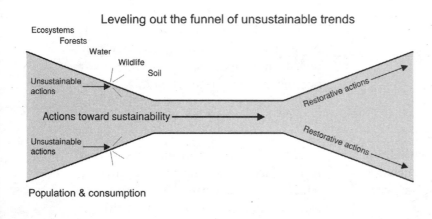

Figure 1.2: Leveling out the funnel of unsustainable trends [18]

So, that is the framework. Now, how do you go about using it to guide action? How can you get from the level of these objectives to specific action toward sustainability in a specific area?

The best way of answering this question is to see for yourself.

As an experiment, invite a group of colleagues or neighbors over to have a short brainstorming session on one or more particular topics or areas of interest. Examples of such topics might include: household living choices, office purchasing policies, designing or renovating a home or building, or a hypothetical strategic plan for sustainability in your particular field of interest and influence.

Taking one of these topics at a time, or splitting into groups that each address a different topic, pose each of the four sustainability objectives in turn as a question for that topic. For example, in what ways can household choices reduce wasteful dependence on fossil fuels, scarce, toxic metals such as cadmium, mercury, and minerals such as phosphorus? Reduce dependence upon persistent chemicals? Reduce encroachment upon nature? And in what ways can a household meet human needs — its own, and the needs of others — more fairly and efficiently? (You will, of course, need initially to give your friends an introduction to the four objectives and/or system conditions and some background about them). When everyone is done — particularly if different groups are working on different topics — it is interesting and elucidating for all to hear what other topic groups have come up with.

By going through this exercise, you have completed in miniature a process already performed by large and small corporations, as well as citizens and municipal employees in small towns and large cities. These corporations and communities have used this framework as a guide to figure out what steps they need to take to move in the direction of sustainability. What you have just experienced is also a microcosm of the second part of the Natural Step approach to sustainability that combines use of the four system conditions framework with a strategic planning process for organizational change and decision making. This strategic planning process, known as the A-B-C-D analysis, is discussed in Part III.

After you do this exercise and hear what people have come up with, some observations about the use of this framework might reveal themselves to you. First, how relatively quickly and easily people — normal, everyday people with perhaps no more than average knowledge and expertise in a given topic — can develop action ideas for that topic that are aimed in the right direction.

You might also observe that the sustainability objectives, and probably most of the strategies the participants have generated from them, address issues at their root — or through an upstream approach — as opposed to a downstream approach. A downstream approach to dealing with hazardous chemicals, for example, might be to focus on how to manage their storage and disposal. An upstream approach would be to find alternatives to use of those chemicals in the first place.

Then, you might notice how the collection of actions for a particular topic, when taken as a whole, starts to look remarkably like a comprehensive approach to moving that topic in the right direction. That is, an approach that goes beyond addressing just one aspect of the topic. For example, in the case of a household, looking at ways to reduce dependence upon fossil fuels might encourage that household to go beyond a single focus on home energy efficiency to a larger array of actions that might include choices to drive less, switch to eco-cleaners, plant trees, and recycle more solid waste.

Next, you could also observe how the same set of objectives (or system conditions) has been used in very different contexts — in this example, household decisions, office purchasing policies, home construction or renovation. Applying the objectives to each topic or context has generated, in each case, a very different set of action strategies. However, while these strategies differ widely among themselves, they are aimed in the same direction.

This is a practical demonstration of taking a systems approach to change — very different from dealing with issues on a one-by-one basis. You and your neighbors or colleagues just applied a set of basic first order principles to a range of complex function areas and came up with a set of strategies that, while differing widely among the topic areas, are aligned in the direction of a common set of sustainability objectives. You and your colleagues just experienced a planning approach that might be called planning by objectives — sustainability objectives.

Why useful for municipalities?

A city or town and its municipal government are complex systems. Municipal governments preside over a wide range of functions, services, planning, and regulatory activities. In the service category, municipalities usually are in charge of solid waste disposal, street and road maintenance, recreation and park maintenance, among other responsibilities. Some municipalities have water departments or electricity-generating facilities, or both. In the planning category, municipalities have responsibility for setting policies for present and future land use, transportation, economic development, location of infrastructure (roads, water, sewer), housing, natural and cultural resources, among others. In the regulatory category, municipalities have the authority for guiding land use and development — both the location and quality of that development. In the United States, municipalities

A municipal government and the community it serves are complex systems.

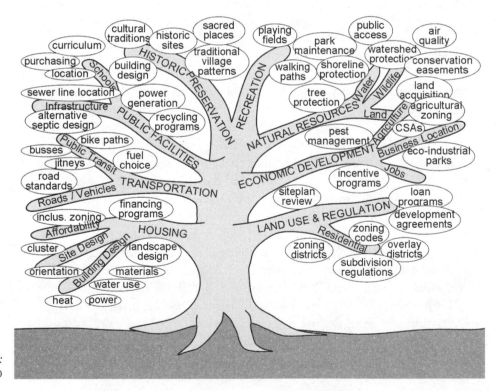

Figure 1.3:
A municipality "tree".[20]

— with some notable exceptions[19] — have the primary authority for guiding and regulating land use and development.

An image of a tree can help us to get our minds around that complexity and to begin thinking about how to bring change to the complex system of a community. The limbs of the tree might represent the different service, planning, and regulatory areas of that city or town. The branches and leaves could depict the countless functions and actions that are taken by the various departments, boards, and agencies within those areas. For example, housing development policy might be one limb. On that limb are branches that represent differing components of housing development, such as building design, site design, and affordability. And then on those branches are found the many leaves, specific tools and techniques that affect those components of housing development, such as cluster design or inclusionary zoning.

Is it any wonder that local government can seem chaotic and fragmented from time to time?

Now, how about trying to introduce change into this complex collection of the countless activities and policies — the branches and leaves? What

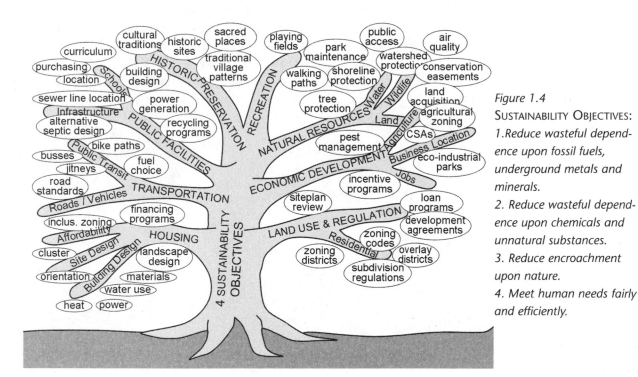

Figure 1.4

SUSTAINABILITY OBJECTIVES:
1. Reduce wasteful dependence upon fossil fuels, underground metals and minerals.
2. Reduce wasteful dependence upon chemicals and unnatural substances.
3. Reduce encroachment upon nature.
4. Meet human needs fairly and efficiently.

happens if we tried to change each leaf and branch one-by-one? How long would this take? Would it even be feasible?

If the tree is thirsty or ill, we apply treatment not to each leaf or branch but at the roots. The remedy then would travel up the trunk, out the limbs, and throughout the entire tree system. If we want change toward sustainable practices to occur throughout the system of limbs, branches, and leaves of a municipality and the community it serves, the best place to begin is at the level of the roots and the trunk — the starting point for policy direction and decision making. We can make this happen through planning by sustainability objectives.

Taking this approach means that the sustainability objectives are used as a compass that guides planning and decision-making processes for every limb and branch of municipal government — municipal departments, agencies, and regulatory boards. In this way, these objectives can guide the countless and diverse policies and practices that are the leaves of the municipal tree. As the trunk, these objectives can align the limbs, branches, and leaves of our municipal tree toward a common goal — a sustainable community. In this way, municipal departments and boards can work together as a team toward that common goal, with the shared playing rules discussed at the beginning of this chapter. Using a shared set of sustainability objectives can also help reduce conflicts and arguments between department policies and practices — the branches and leaves of the tree.

Some remarkable changes toward sustainable practices in communities that use new playing rules is the subject of Part II. Just exactly how a community might go about doing this is the subject of Part III.

CHAPTER 2

Sustainability: The Trouble We Have Talking About It

There are now many definitions, conceptual models, and sets of principles that characterize the idea of sustainability. How does the Natural Step framework relate to them? How is the Natural Step framework for sustainability different from, or alike, other models? Can it be combined with other sustainability conceptual models and tools? Why are any of these questions of relevance to towns and cities and the practitioners who work within, and for, them?

Let's start with the last question first. Why should practitioners — people interested in implementing sustainable development in communities — be concerned with varying definitions and conceptual models of sustainability? Can't we all just get on with it?

Well, of course, yes, we can just get on with it. But remember from our earlier discussions some of the minefields that can beset the path to implementation of sustainable development. One such obstacle is getting stuck in arguments about what sustainable development is and what sustainability means. This can come from an inability to get beyond current philosophical definitions of sustainability, relying upon vague definitions of sustainable development, or using sustainable development as an unspecified label to mask unsustainable activities — otherwise known as green-washing.

Philosophical and conceptual definitions of sustainability

When we first introduce the concept of sustainability to someone who is unfamiliar with it, we often are pressed to come up with a 25-word-or-less sound bite that can get the idea across to that person quickly and succinctly.

Frequently used for this purpose are some common philosophical character-izations such as the Brundtland Commission definition or the commonly used "three-legged stool" image that characterizes sustainability as the merg-ing of environmental, economic, and social objectives.

These general concepts are useful because·they quickly convey some key differences in how to look at decisions and activities. The Brundtland Commission definition of sustainability reminds us that our present-day actions have long-term results, and that what we do in the present will affect the future well-being of our children and grandchildren. Using the three-legged stool image to explain the concept of sustainability helps connect con-ceptually separated tracks of environmental action, economics, and social welfare in our thinking process. For example, if one leg of the stool is miss-ing, the stool will collapse.

As useful as these concepts are in introducing the idea of sustainability, we still need direction for how to actually go about changing to more sustain-able courses of action from where we are at present.

ALTERNATIVE LABELS FOR SUSTAINABILITY

In well-intentioned efforts to present and package sustainability concepts in an understandable way, substitute names have been offered to replace the terms sustainability or sustainable communities — for example, the term liv-able communities. Whatever the name substitution offered for the desired state may be, there still remains the job of figuring out how we get there from here. At some point, we have to get down to the business of figuring out precisely how we can make sure that our children and grandchildren inhabit a livable world or how we actually combine economic, ecological, and social objectives in one project or plan. So, even with alternative labels, such as livable communities, we still need a mental model to guide the change process toward it.

GREEN-WASHING

Another minefield stemming from unclear or differing understandings of sus-tainability is the growing practice of "green-washing." This means labeling conventional development as sustainable development for a particular pur-pose, such as attracting funding. This practice is easier to pull off when there is no pre-agreement about a definition of sustainable development or when the definition is vague. Or, invoking the mantra of sustainable development may be an attempt to deflect attention from aspects of a project or business that are environmentally or socially unsound. For example, a business that

BRUNDTLAND COMMISSION:[1] Sustainable development ... meets the needs of the present without com-promising the ability of future generations to meet their own needs.

showcases environmentally beneficial practices in one area of its operations could deflect public attention from other activities such as use of sweatshop labor. Installing solar panels on the building might serve to enhance the public image of a gambling institution, diverting attention from the social costs of its revenue source. Using a precise set of scientifically based principles such as the Natural Step framework to define sustainable development and applying these to all aspects of operations can help deter the practice of green-washing.

TALKING FROM DIFFERENT LEVELS

Another obstacle to a clearer understanding of sustainability and sustainable development is the confusion of sustainability principles with sustainability policies, strategies, actions, or tools. Examining some of the arguments about what sustainability means frequently unearths this type of mix-up.

"Promoting economically self-sufficient communities" or "encouraging green development," for example, are policies and strategies that — to go back to our tree image — are found at the level of the branches. This means that while they may be appropriate sustainability strategies for one or two limbs of the tree, such as economic development or building design, the policy or strategy may not make sense when applied to other departments. For example, "promoting economically self-sufficient communities" may be an appropriate goal for a municipal planning and economic development department but may not make much sense as a policy goal for a public works department.

Further confusion is often brought about through using sets of overlapping principles to guide a change process. For example, the green building program of an agency includes one "principle" to encourage use of environmentally preferable products and another "principle" to enhance indoor air quality. While these are certainly worthy goals, does not using environmentally preferable products contribute to enhanced indoor air quality? And do either of these "principles" help guide program designers to understand what "environmentally preferable" means or how "enhanced indoor air quality" is achieved and by how much? These are the types of confusions that can lead potential implementers of sustainable practices to discount the entire idea of sustainability as a viable guiding vision.

When one seems to be mired in debates and confusion about the meaning of sustainability and sustainable development, it can help to determine from what level the debaters are speaking. Are they speaking at the level of strategies or actions — for example, should we spend money on open space preservation or affordable housing? Is one person advocating a tool, for example, ecological footprint analysis or sustainability indicators, or, rather, advocating guiding principles for moving toward sustainability such as the Natural Step system conditions? These types of debates may make it seem as if these models were competitive or contradictory, but they are simply perspectives from different levels within the overall picture.[2]

SUSTAINABILITY: LEVELS OF APPROACH

Tools
(indicators, ecological footprint, life cycle assessment, environmental management systems).

Results & Impacts of Actions

Process principles
(social principles, investment, & political strategies)

Actions
(eg. density incentives for green buildings, replacing oil burner with geothermal heat system)

Context-specific strategies for achieving sustainability objectives
(eg., green building design, using waste as a resource)

Principles & objectives for a favorable outcome, i.e., a sustainable society
(eg.,The Natural Step system conditions; four sustainability objectives)

Philosophical vision of a sustainable society
(eg., Bruntland Commission definition; 3-legged stool concept)

The **ecosphere** and the **laws** by which it operates
(eg., the laws of thermodynamics, species interdependence)

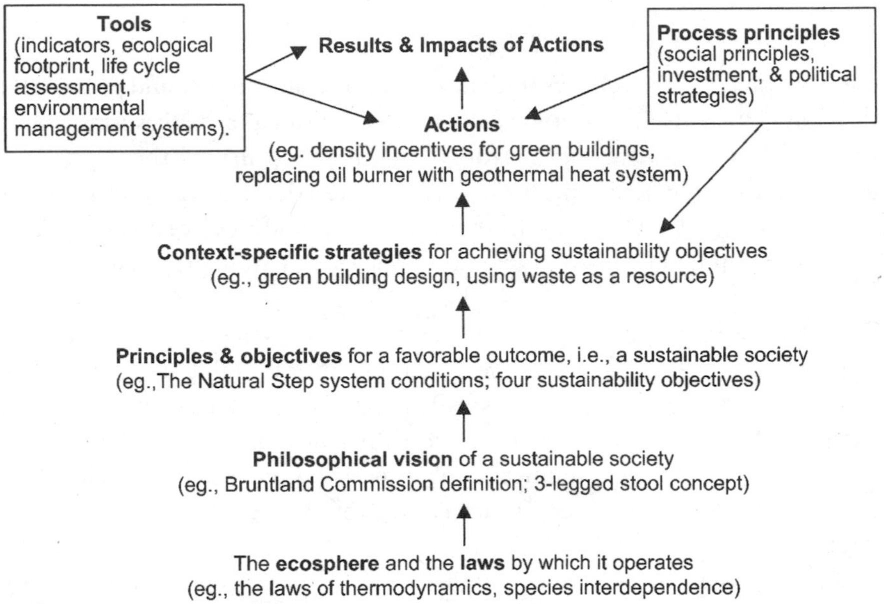

Figure 1.5: Sustainability: Levels of Approach

This section, Compass for Change, has focused on sustainability *principles and objectives* and how these can be used to achieve context-specific strategies. The next part, Practices that Changed, will present examples of *strategies, actions, and results* — the successful outcomes of the Swedish eco-municipalities. The last part of the book, How Communities Can Change, will present a *process* for successful strategies, actions, and results.

OTHER SUSTAINABILITY MODELS

Studying a range of sustainability models, although potentially confusing, can enrich and deepen understanding, stimulate creative thinking, and help us look at old problems in new ways. Some of these models tend to mix principles and strategies, philosophy and process, or use principles that overlap with each other. The different levels of approaches illustrated in Figure 1.5

can help in applying these differing models and principles and bring clarity to discussions about sustainability in general.

Here are some snapshots of a few of those models. We leave it to the reader to explore these and other models more deeply and determine what levels of approach to sustainability their model components address.

Ahwahnee principles

The Ahwahnee principles consist of about two dozen items that promote walkable, compact community design, and regional and implementation strategies to reduce urban sprawl. They were developed by a group of New Urbanist designers and presented to an audience of local government officials at a 1991 conference held at the Ahwahnee Hotel in Yosemite. They have been used by cities such as Pasadena and San Jose, California, and in a U.S. Department of Housing and Urban Development publication.[3]

Hannover principles

These nine principles, co-developed by architect Bill McDonough, are aimed at the built environment but are also applicable to a range of contexts including business and planning. They were developed as a set of guiding design principles for the 2000 World's Fair in Hannover, Germany, intended to deepen the design community's understanding of the issues inherent to green design, as opposed to an issue checklist approach. They have been adopted as guiding principles for sustainability by such organizations and agencies as the International Union of Architects and the U.S. General Services Administration (GSA).[4]

CERES principles

The CERES principles are ten guiding principles of the Coalition for Environmentally Responsible Economies — a group of businesses and corporations devoted to practicing environmental stewardship in their business operations. They have voluntarily adopted these principles as a commitment to environmental protection on an ongoing basis. Investors and others use these principles as a set of criteria to assess corporate environmental performance.[5]

AtKisson principles

Alan AtKisson, author of *Believing Cassandra*, has identified seven principles in his book for developing a new life perspective and crafting a path toward sustainability. Either individuals or organizations can practice these principles.[6]

CHAPTER 3

The Natural Step Approach: Why Is It Useful?

Figure 3.1: Scandic Hotels, with facilities throughout Scandinavia and Europe, moved from bankruptcy to a leading market position through changing to sustainable practices with the Natural Step framework as a guide.

A concrete example: Scandic Hotels

Corporations and communities around the world are using the Natural Step framework to bring about across-the-board change to practices that are sustainable throughout their policies and operations. One of these businesses is a Swedish-based hotel chain called Scandic Hotels.

In the early 1990s, Scandic was on the verge of bankruptcy. The company's board of directors hired a new CEO to try to steer the company back to economic health. This CEO had heard of the Natural Step approach and asked Karl-Henrik Robèrt to address Scandic's top management staff. Shortly afterward, Scandic embarked on a company-wide education program, introducing the Natural Step framework to thousands of its employees throughout the company's departments and locations. Over the course of the next few months, teams of employees in all departments worked to apply the Natural Step framework to

their particular department's functions and practices, making over 1,500 suggestions for how those practices could be reoriented to meet the four system conditions. Less than a year after Karl-Henrik Robèrt met with Scandic's management staff, the company began carrying out the action plans created by its own employees, guided by the four system conditions of the Natural Step. One example was plan for completely refurbished guest rooms that met the system conditions. Staff suggestions included changing to furniture and furnishings made from all-natural materials instead of plastic and synthetic ones and to natural wood floors instead of synthetic carpeting; wastebaskets to separate types of rubbish; and a temperature regulator for the shower to reduce waste of hot water.

Through this overall reorientation of its operations to sustainable practices, Scandic also was able to change its financial bottom line from red to black. It is now one of the most successful hotel chains in Europe. Its experience in finding that sustainable practices also make for sound business practices, and financial gain has been echoed by companies, such as Sånga Säby Conference Center and the Interface Company. Scandic's reorientation to sustainable practices, using both the Natural Step framework and a democratic, bottom-up implementation process, mirrors the Swedish eco-municipalities' approaches and the how-to strategy described in Part II.[1]

Other companies that have used the Natural Step framework to guide change toward more sustainable practices include McDonald's of Sweden, Electrolux, Mitsubishi Electric, IKEA, and the Collins Pine Company.

Cities and towns around the world have adopted the Natural Step framework and are using it as a guide to reorienting to sustainable practices. Christchurch, New Zealand, has adopted the four system conditions as their guiding framework and is presently in the process of implementing it. A Japanese city and town have done the same. The Whistler community in Canada is reorienting to sustainable practices with the Natural Step framework as a guide.[2] The City of Santa Monica, California, has used sustainability objectives based upon the Natural Step to integrate sustainability policies throughout its General Plan. And over 60 municipalities in Sweden — whose accomplishments are discussed in the next part of this book — have adopted the Natural Step framework and have brought about across-the-board changes toward sustainability.

Figure 3.2: Hotel staffers came up with this guest room wastebasket design to make it easy for guests to separate recyclables and organic waste from their trash.

Advantages at a glance

There are by now many definitions, frameworks, and sets of principles that can help deepen our understanding of what sustainability means and why it is important. While each of these models provides important perspectives about a challenging topic, the four guiding objectives of the Natural Step approach provide a particularly useful sustainability framework for municipalities and the communities they serve.

DEALS WITH COMPLEXITY

A municipality and its community are complex systems. The various departments, boards, agencies, and land use and planning policies generate countless actions and day-to-day decisions that can go in either sustainable or unsustainable directions. This complexity often results in actions or policies that can work at cross-purposes or compete with each other. It resembles how a sports team might behave if there were no agreement among the players about the rules or objective of the game. This complexity and potential for chaos, conflict, and competition among policies challenges us to go beyond the one-issue-by-one-issue, or piecemeal, approach in changing toward sustainable practices. As a set of first order objectives that can provide guidance whether they are applied in a land use, economic development, public works, or for that matter, any context, the Natural Step framework can serve as a new set of playing rules. These new rules can help guide the countless municipal and community team players to work from their differing starting points toward a common goal — a sustainable community.

TAKES AN UPSTREAM APPROACH

While well-intentioned, many municipal initiatives to improve the environment and community well-being are measures that focus on the downstream side of problems. For example, in dealing with hazardous materials, cities and town regulations customarily focus on regulating onsite storage or disposal of toxic substances. As important as these measures are, they do not address the continually increasing introduction of hazardous chemicals into our homes, businesses, bodies, and ecosystems.

The Natural Step framework helps us look for upstream approaches, such as finding alternatives to using toxic chemicals in the first place. Transportation policies often focus on mitigating the problematic effects of increasing traffic — better access management, installing more lanes or traffic lights. While these measures are important, they do not address steadily increasing trip generation that over time will require more and more lanes and traffic lights and access management. Use of the Natural Step framework challenges us to find ways of reducing that traffic in the first place. Even recycling programs, as beneficial as they are in re-using and diverting waste from landfills and incinerators, address the downstream end of the waste problem. The Natural Step framework prods us to find ways to reduce that waste in the first place and even come to think about it in a new way — as a resource by which our needs can be met more efficiently while encroaching less on nature.

USE AT ANY LEVEL, IN ANY GEOGRAPHIC REGION

As helpful as many of the current sustainability models are, it is challenging to find one that could be applicable to any city or town in any geographic region of North America or the entire world. The Natural Step framework can be used equally well by a regional or state government or agency as by a local municipality and even a national govern-ment. As first order principles, the Natural Step framework lends itself as a guide to sustainable action in all of these contexts and more. A densely packed city of millions and a village of 200 people each can use the Natural Step framework to design and guide a change process toward sustainability. A desert commu-nity in Arizona can use it just as easily as can a mountain town in Colorado, Canada, or a tra-ditional New England village. Further, each of these dramatically differing communities, while using the same framework of principles, can generate their own strategies that, while they move in the same direction, fit their own context, geography, and political situation. The form of those strategies might be voluntary or mandatory. They might involve use of "car-rots" or use of "sticks." The Natural Step framework allows its user to design a self-determined, situation-appropriate path toward sustainability — but a path that is assured of moving in the right direction.

THE NATURAL STEP SYSTEM CONDITIONS [3]
In the sustainable society, nature is not subject to systematically increasing:
1. concentrations of substances extracted from the Earth's crust
2. concentrations of substances produced by society
3. degradation by physical means
and, in that society,
4. human needs are met worldwide.

RESULTS IN ACROSS-THE-BOARD CHANGE

When the Natural Step framework is used as a guide throughout all depart-ments, agencies, boards and policies of a municipality, it can result in across-the-board change to sustainable practices. This is very different than the one-by-one issue approach that is more commonly used in cities and towns that have undertaken sustainability initiatives, as well-intentioned and worthy as these are. Using the Natural Step framework as the trunk of the municipal tree as would happen, say, if the top officials voted to adopt it as a guide for the entire city or town, can allow that "medicine for change" to flow through the limbs, branches, and leaves of the municipal tree, helping to align all the countless department land use and other policies in the same sustainable direction. This means that reorientation to sustainable practices can ripple through the entire complexity of operations and planning approaches of a city or town, aligning these to complement each other, rather than to work at cross purposes, and addressing conflict among competing priorities at an upstream, rather than downstream, point. This type of an approach could be called a systems approach.

THE FOUR SUSTAINABILITY OBJECTIVES

1. Reduce wasteful dependence upon fossil fuels, scarce metals and minerals that accumulate in nature.
2. Reduce wasteful dependence upon chemicals and synthetic substances that accumulate in nature.
3. Reduce encroachment upon nature.
4. Meet human needs fairly and efficiently.

Derived from the Natural Step system conditions.

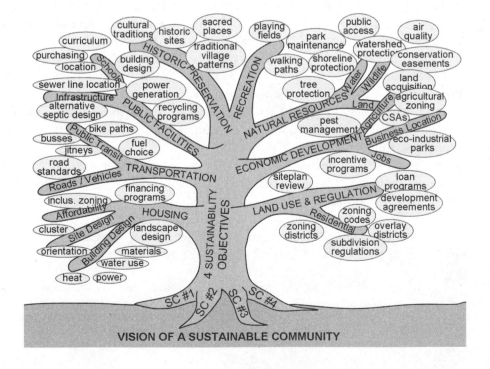

Figure 3.3: Guiding the municipal system

DEMONSTRATES SUCCESS

All this might sound like pie-in-the-sky dreams if it were not for the scores of cities and towns in Sweden, businesses, and organizations that have achieved these very results. These pioneering eco-municipalities and businesses show us that using the Natural Step framework to bring about across-the-board reorientation to sustainable practices is not a pipe dream, but an achievable reality. The next section of this book, Practices That Changed, will demonstrate those results.

PRACTICES THAT CHANGED

II

CHAPTER 4

The Eco-municipalities of Sweden: A Little Background

Throughout Sweden, more than 60 communities have made radical, across-the-board changes toward the "true north" of sustainability and used the Natural Step framework as the compass.

Some of these communities are cities with populations over 500,000; some are villages of about 300 inhabitants. Some are grappling with the demands of growth — how best to meet needs and service demands for mobility, solid waste disposal, heat, power, and social services for elders and those in need. Some have struggled to cope with declining populations, when young people leave to find better jobs and a more exciting lifestyle in an urban center. Some are older industrialized cities seeking ways to absorb waves of immigrants with different cultures and languages.

Others in remote rural areas have undergone economic depressions where almost one-half the population cannot find work. Some are seeking ways to recognize basic rights and culture of indigenous minorities — the Sámi people. Some have been working to preserve historic neighborhoods and buildings in the onslaught of new development.

So what do these seemingly disparate communities dealing with varied economies, sizes, and circumstances have in common? From radically different starting points, each has embarked on a journey to become a sustainable community.

What does this mean? For one thing, each of these cities, towns, and villages has made a collective commitment to sustainable change and has officially adopted the Natural Step framework to guide the process. For another, each municipality has committed to a democratic, participatory change process involving citizens and municipal employees. These two commitments also qualify a city or town to become a member of the national association of eco-municipalities, known in Sweden as SeKom. The results have been remarkable — change occurring throughout all municipal and community functions. Results include drastic reductions in fossil fuel use; up to 90 percent recycling rates of solid waste; healthy, ecological buildings; restoration of threatened native wildlife; and transport alternatives to gas-powered vehicles. These communities represent 20 percent, or one-fifth, of all the municipalities in Sweden. And all this has happened in the last 15 years.

In 1990, a pivotal conference took place in Orsa (Uh'shah), Sweden, bringing together municipal officials, environmental experts, and others to discuss what an ecological future society might look like. From this event emerged the first association of Swedish cities and towns that became eco-municipalities. The Orsa conference was also the meeting ground for the individuals who were to become the primary designers of the Natural Step conditions for a sustainable society — Karl-Henrik Robèrt, John Holmberg, and Karl-Erik-Eriksson — and the event that brought the Natural Step framework into the sphere of municipalities.

Since then, over 60 cities and towns have joined to support each other and work for change at the national level. Of course, other cities and towns in Sweden and elsewhere in the world have undertaken sustainable development initiatives. What distinguishes these eco-municipalities from their counterparts is that they have embarked upon an across-the-board, systematic approach to changing to sustainable practices.

For example, eco-municipalities have educated thousands of their employees about unsustainable environmental and social trends and the reasons why new local practices are essential for helping to change these trends. These municipalities have engaged community citizens —sometimes, entire villages — in planning and revitalization initiatives toward sustainability. These community initiatives have found locally suited ways to reduce use of fossil fuels, metals and minerals, chemicals, encroachment upon nature, and to meet human and community needs fairly and efficiently. Eco-municipalities have developed city or town master plans that integrate sustainability objectives throughout the range of planning policy areas.[1] Most of these communities have involved every aspect of town or city government in the change process. Most have established ongoing education, management systems, and monitoring programs to make sustainable practices part of business-as-usual in municipal service provision and community planning.

Four generations of eco-municipalities

In 1983, the town of Övertorneå, the "bumblebee that changed the world," became the first eco-municipality in Sweden. Three years earlier, the Finnish town of Suomussalmi (Suh'ohmoh-sahll'my) had become the first eco-municipality in Scandinavia. These two communities, both struggling with economic and social depression, became the first generation of eco-municipalities to integrate ecological, social, and economic action to shape their community's future.

What sets these particular communities apart from their counterparts in Sweden and elsewhere is that they have embarked upon an across-the-board, total approach to sustainable change.

Between 1990 and 1992, 14 more towns picked up the idea, becoming the second generation of eco-municipalities. All 16 communities agreed, at the 1990 Orsa conference, to work on a common vision-led development strategy that identified sustainability objectives for community issues. Each municipality would develop its own three-year action program, develop demonstration projects, and carry out employee and public education to raise ecological awareness throughout their communities and municipal governments. The work of these municipalities, presented at the 1992 World Conference on Environment and Development in Rio de Janeiro, helped shape that conference's local sustainable development planning guide known as Agenda 21.

Between 1993 and 1998, 55 cities and towns became the third generation of Swedish communities to adopt the eco-municipality concept. Several municipalities applied for joint funding for sustainable development projects in trade, industry, housing, and building. During this period, all eco-municipalities adopted the Natural Step framework as their defining guide for sustainable development.

In 1995, eco-municipality representatives met to form SeKom, the national association of eco-municipalities in Sweden. Since then, SeKom's membership has increased to over 60 cities and towns — the fourth generation of eco-municipalities. Through SeKom, Swedish eco-municipalities have made connections with sister communities in Estonia, and 20 Estonian communities have since adopted the eco-municipality concept. SeKom has helped develop municipal strategies for environmentally friendly purchasing and local sustainable development implementation. The organization also has established a national technical assistance center for eco-municipality change processes and projects.

Towns and cities in Norway and Denmark also have begun eco-municipality journeys. While their definitions of this term may differ, they all are working toward developing sustainable communities with their municipal governments as the development engine.

At the beginning of the third millenium, a fifth generation of eco-municipalities is applying a systems management approach to integrating sustainable practices throughout their municipal governments and larger communities. The stories of two such municipalities, Sundsvall and Robertsfors, are presented in Part III.

The Swedish eco-municipalities and the results of their successful adoption of sustainable practices are the subject of the next ten chapters. These practices include renewable energy sources, ecological housing, solid waste reduction, and increased recycling, organic agriculture, protection of biodiversity, and support of sustainable business practices. How they accomplished this — the change process and keys to its success — is the story in Part III.

CHAPTER 5

Changing to Renewable Energy Sources

In a sustainable society, nature is not subject to systematically increasing concentrations of substances extracted from the Earth's crust.
The Natural Step framework's System Condition #1[1]

Introduction: Why switch?

The burning of fossil fuels, such as oil, coal, and natural gas that are extracted from below the earth's surface, is steadily building up carbon dioxide and other greenhouse gases, such as sulfur and nitrogen dioxide, in the atmosphere far beyond their normal levels. The effects of these concentrations, for example, climate change, melting polar ice caps, rising sea levels, are now readily apparent to all those who are willing to see them. Local communities around the world also are experiencing the effects of fossil fuel burning in the form of air pollution, linked to spiraling increases in asthma and breathing disorders. Since September 11, 2001, another effect is now apparent — the link between fossil fuel dependence, the threat of terrorism, and national and community security.

Communities, particularly those in colder climates, have become heavily dependent upon burning fossil fuels for heat and for power. Reducing this dependence requires a combination of steps, including reducing the need for energy in the first place and seeking alternative energy sources that are renewable and, ideally, locally derived.

Communities around the world already are seeking out and using energy sources that are alternatives to fossil fuels. This chapter highlights a few of the steps taken by Swedish eco-municipalities, large and small, to change from fossil fuels to alternative and local sources of energy, accomplishing significant reduction in fossil fuel dependency. Two strategies used by these exemplar communities are demonstrated here — harnessing the energy of the wind and sun, and using waste as a resource.

In Sweden, municipal governments are responsible for providing power and heat to housing, businesses, and institutions within their jurisdictions. Over one-half of Sweden's 289 municipalities supply this heat through district heating systems. District heating systems usually deliver heat in the form of steam or hot water that is pumped through a system of underground pipes to homes and commercial buildings. In 1981, over 85 percent of all district heating systems in Sweden used oil or coal as an energy source. By 1993, the proportion of district heating systems using oil had dropped to 23 percent.[2]

Two strategies toward sustainable development: harnessing the energy of the wind and the sun, and using waste as a resource.

Harnessing the energy of the wind and the sun

FALKENBERG: WIND AND SUN HELP TO HEAT AND POWER A CITY

About Falkenberg

The city of Falkenberg (Fahl'ken-beryh), with a population of 39,000, sits on the scenic and windy coast of Halland County in southwest Sweden. Its twelve miles of seacoast attracts an additional 40,000 seasonal residents and tourists in summer. Its seaport transfers about a million tons of goods per year. Falkenberg features a compact, historic town center, the largest brewery and cheese manufacturer in the country, and a history of freshwater salmon-fishing dating back to the 1600s. The city also is home to a renowned bargain clothes factory outlet that attracts between 15,000 and 20,000 shoppers per year. This outlet and its customer base also generate business for other regional companies.

Falkenberg has been implementing a municipal plan for sustainable development since 1995. To raise community awareness about sustainable development, the city has reached out to schools, daycare centers, and businesses through forums, workshops, seminars, and the media. City officials decreed that all municipal departments should adopt and implement sustainable development goals. The city trained 2,000 staff — 60 percent of all municipal employees — in the Natural Step approach to sustainable development.

Falkenberg city planners use sustainable development objectives as guidelines for city planning. For instance, planning policies discourage location of shopping centers outside urban areas and encourage closer living and working relationships to reduce driving and support community life. Planners conduct environmental assessments prior to land use decisions. Falkenberg has excelled in protecting soil quality, an area where policies in food production, industrial development, and public health intersect. Falkenberg also uses green purchasing policies, buying municipal supplies, such as paper, cleaning agents, and office equipment, that are made of recycled materials, have low or no toxic chemical content, and which can be recycled in turn.

One Falkenberg goal is to become the cleanest community in the country in terms of its water and air. Toward this end, the city has reduced its fossil fuel use for generating heat and power through two remarkable renewable energy projects — a state-of-the-art windmill farm and a field of solar collectors.

Falkenberg's windmill farm

Falkenberg has developed a windmill farm of ten 660-watt wind turbines that produce a combined 12.5 gigawatt hours of electricity per year, an average power output of 1.43 megawatts (MW). This amount of electricity can completely heat and power 600 homes for a year. In Falkenberg, this represents five percent of all households in the city. The ten wind turbines sit on agricultural land leased from local farmers. In exchange, the farmers receive three percent of the wind electricity value, which comes to about US$2,000 per turbine per year. The city established a non-profit cooperative that now owns the wind farm. City residents and businesses can join the cooperative for about US$500 a year per household, then buy electricity at one-half the going market price. Non-members can still buy wind-generated power but must pay full market price.

The new wind farm allowed the city to reduce by 12.5 gigawatt hours the amount of coal-generated electricity it previously had purchased from Denmark. The total cost of the windmill farm was about US$650,000. The city was

Falkenberg's goal is to have the cleanest air and water of all municipalities in Sweden.

Figure 5.1: Falkenberg's 10-turbine wind farm provides electricity to co-op owners at one-half the market price.

able to procure a government subsidy for 15 percent of this cost. The city's payback for this investment is just under nine years. The windmill farm is expected to run between 25 to 35 years with good maintenance. About 90 percent of the wind turbine parts can be recycled and reused at the end of their useful life.

Falkenberg's solar array

In 1989, Falkenberg constructed and put into operation what was at that time the largest array of solar collectors in the world. Covering over an acre of land, the solar array, now the eighth largest in the world, generates 1.8 gigawatt hours of electricity per year. The solar array also heats water that supplies the city's district heating system. Heat generated by the solar collectors is carried to the central heating plant through a network of pipes, then passes through a heat exchanger to a 290,000-gallon water storage tank. Hot water for the district heating system is then piped from the top of the tank. Wood-fired boilers and a gas-fired back-up system can reheat storage tank water if it is too cool for the district heating system.[3]

Overall, Falkenberg, whose homes, businesses, and institutions use about 350 gigawatt hours of electricity per year, now generates about 30 percent of this from renewable energy sources.[4]

Figure 5.2: The City of Falkenberg's Energy Department has converted its fleet to electric cars. The slogan on this car says in Swedish "This car runs on clean wind power."

Figure 5.3: Falkenberg's solar array provides 1.8 gigawatt hours of electricity per year to city consumers.
Credit: Falkenberg Energi

KANGOS VILLAGE: "IT DOESN'T HAVE TO BE HIGH-TECH"

About Kangos

Kangos (Kahn'-gos) is a village of 330 inhabitants within the municipality of Pajala (Pah'yah-lah), far in the north of Sweden. Like other rural communities, Kangos had lost many residents to the jobs and more abundant living choices of the country's urban centers. As its population dwindled, Kangos faced the closing of its school and local post office. Many remaining residents could not find work and means to support their families.

In the late 1990s, Kangos villagers agreed to take part in a project to define a future for their village that people wanted, as opposed to a future forced upon them by trends seemingly beyond their control. The slogan for this initiative was: "Who decides our future?" Villagers realized that if they didn't decide what their future should be, others would decide it for them. And it might not be good.

The villagers embarked upon a revitalization initiative, deciding that this should occur in an ecologically sound way. This decision and the work that followed it gave birth to between 30 and 40 new eco-enterprises. As one example, the villagers decided to develop a small resort center that could thrive upon the region's steady stream of fishermen, hunters, and tourists coming in the warmer months to enjoy the region's bountiful natural resources and beauty. About 60 villagers formed a non-profit organization to develop and eventually manage the center. They bought 56 acres of land for about US$25,000 nine miles north of the village. Using local materials and their own time and labor, Kangos villagers built this center, board by board and building by building. Volunteers contributed countless work hours. County jobs council funding allowed the hiring of three unemployed villagers to work full-time on building construction.

The resort center, completed in 2001, features a large main building for conferences and weddings. A fishing area has been developed at the far end of the property. Four rental cabins for tourists were constructed and brought to the site from a nearby village. These cabins each have two beds, cooking facilities, and a woodstove. A sauna was constructed, of course, next to the river. The main building also houses a "honeymoon suite," which, according to local lore, is contributing to an increase in school enrollment. The economic future for the center looks promising. In its first two weeks of operations, the center garnered 30 guest-nights.

Villagers realized that if they didn't decide what their future should be, others would decide it for them. And it might not be good.

Choosing Renewable

An ecological goal for the Kangos resort center is for 100 percent self-sufficiency in heat and power. Solar panels are being installed to generate electricity onsite; woodstoves provide heat. And, villagers came up with a down-home solution to heat the swimming pool. The sun heats water for

Figure 5.4: Kangos villagers built this eco-resort center as part of their village eco-revitalization.

Figure 5.5 Swimming pool water is heated by the sun while passing through rubber hoses attached to the building's roof, demonstrating that renewable energy solutions don't always have to be high-tech ones.

the pool via rubber hoses installed on the main building's roof, demonstrating, among other things, that alternative energy solutions are not always costly or high-tech.

For more about the eco-revitalization of Kangos village, see Chapter 9.

Waste as a resource: Biomass

The growth and care of Westernized human society mostly follows a linear pattern that can be called take-make-waste. This means taking resources from the earth, making things out of them, wasting a lot of those resources in the

process, and then throwing these fabrications "away," creating further waste.

In nature, recycling is the rule. Each component of a natural cycle becomes the food, or resource, for the next. In a forest ecosystem, plants and berries are the food for some animals and birds. These creatures become the food for other creatures. The droppings and bodies of all these creatures become food for the microbes and nematodes of the earth, whose soil then nourishes the plants, and on it goes. Except for the energy that is lost in any change of state, everything is used.

Eskilstuna, Degerfors, and Övertorneå are just a few of the Swedish eco-municipalities, and others around the world, who are turning waste into a resource. In doing so, they have created a win-win-win strategy: reducing dependence upon fossil fuels, gaining savings in both reduced energy and landfill costs, and contributing to the greater health of the environment and their residents through reduced emissions.

In nature, recycling is the rule.

About Eskilstuna

The city of Eskilstuna (Ess'-kils-teu'-nah) is part of the rapidly developing Greater Stockholm region. It is a 60-minute train ride from Stockholm and the Stockholm airport. This metropolis, called the Mälardalen region, has a market area of three million people, with a growing service and commerce sector. Eskilstuna was once an industrialized city with a population of about 130,000. Through loss of factories and jobs, the city's population dropped to about 90,000. As of 2001 however, due to the changing trends of the larger region, Eskilstuna has grown rapidly. About 20 percent of its population now are refugees who speak several different languages.

HOW THE ESKILSTUNA CHP BIOMASS PLANT WORKS

The plant super-heats water at high pressure, converting it to steam in a boiler heated by wood by-products. Part of the steam runs a turbine and alternator that generate electricity. The remaining steam, together with heat recaptured from waste gases, is condensed back into water and sent into the district heating system, where it is piped to residential homes and businesses. A generator creates high-voltage electricity for transmission, so there is no need for a step-up transformer. This further reduces energy loss. The plant can produce a maximum 39 megawatts of electricity on the coldest winter day. The city's average daily

▶

Eskilstuna began its sustainable development action program in 1997, coordinating this program with its general (master) plan. For many years, Eskilstuna, which did not have its own electricity-generating facility, purchased power from outside sources. Four years after it began its sustainable development program, Eskilstuna is producing its own power, up to about 25 percent of the city's total requirements.[5]

Eskilstuna's CHP biomass plant

A major boost to Eskilstuna's self sufficiency in power generation and reduction in fossil fuel dependency was its construction of a state-of-the-art combined heat and power plant (CHP) run entirely on biomass fuel. The biomass fuel consists of by-product cuttings from timber or lumber, sawdust, bark pulp, branches, and chippings from the wood-processing industry.

Eskilstuna's CHP Plant now produces 95 percent of the city's heating in winter, cooling in summer, and 25 percent of the city's electricity requirements. This heat and power plant serves 25,000 multi-family units, 3,000 single-family homes, and all commercial buildings. The plant operates at a high efficiency rate of 90 percent, meaning that 90 percent of the fuel's energy content is used. In contrast, conventional power plants usually burn oil, coal, or natural gas at efficiency rates less than 35 percent.[6]

The CHP Plant is producing about 180 gigawatt hours of electricity and 330 gigawatt hours of thermal energy (heat). Consumer cost for biomass-fueled district heating has remained constant since the switch from fossil

Figure 5.6: Eskilstuna's power plant, fueled only by wood by-products, provides heat and electricity to all businesses and 28,000 homes in the city.

requirement for electricity is about 150 megawatts, so the electricity supplied by the plant is about 25 percent of the city's total needs.

Highly efficient flue gas scrubbers reduce sulfur dioxide and nitrogen oxide emissions to very small levels. Energy is extracted from exhaust gases with electrostatic precipitators, then the gases pass through water scrubbers. The plant can produce up to 700 gigawatt hours of power per year with a capacity of 20 megawatts. Heat is pumped to homes and buildings through a 60-mile network of pipes that carry hot water to those buildings, then return that water to the plant for reheating. [7]

fuels. Eskilstuna offers the tenth-lowest price for district heating in the country. Since 1997 when the plant went on-line, the city has reduced its consumption of fossil fuels for heating by 38 percent. The cost for the plant was about US$45 million. The city was able to obtain funding through the national government for 25 percent of the cost.

According to an Eskilstuna official, in 1980, most power plants in Sweden used 80 percent fossil fuels and 20 percent other sources to generate power. Today these ratios are reversed. Of the 150 Swedish municipal district heating systems, 30 percent now use biomass fuel.

About Degerfors

The town of Degerfors (Deh'gehr-fosh) is about a two-hour train trip from Stockholm. Its population of 10,500 inhabit an area of about 40 square miles (about 104 square kilometers). Degersfors is situated in the Bergslagen (Behryhs'-lah-ghen) district, the steel-producing region of Sweden. The literal translation of Bergslagen is "the place where they have broken the mountains to make steel." Mines, steel works, and iron foundries dot the area. Much like Eskilstuna, Degerfors has lost population, businesses, and jobs over time. Many abandoned buildings and factories line the river running through the town. Younger people left Degerfors for jobs in urbanized areas, leaving the older residents. The burden of paying for municipal services, including eldercare, was falling on fewer and fewer households.

During the 1990s, Degerfors undertook a sustainable development initiative that included economic development, sustainability education, and a green building program. Over 85 percent of the Town's 1,000 employees took part in sustainability education seminars introducing the Natural Step framework. The town ran similar seminars for its citizens. As of 2001, between 35 and 40 percent of the 10,500 Degerfors population — over 4,000 people — have learned about the Natural Step framework. Degersfors citizen education demonstrates how changing to sustainable practices can provide household economic and social benefits as well as ecological ones. For example, household heating costs can be lowered through converting from fossil fuel to biomass-produced heat. The town is updating its ten-year general (master) plan, using the Natural Step framework as its guiding objectives.

Degerfors converts to biomass

In 1997, Degerfors completed conversion of its fossil-fueled district heating system to one that now uses biomass fuel. One year later, the town's greenhouse gas emissions had dropped by 30 percent. Heating costs per household have declined significantly since that conversion, relieving financial burdens borne by hard-pressed Degerfors households.

Journey to freedom from fossil fuels: The town of Övertorneå

About Övertorneå

In the early 1980s, Övertorneå envisioned a future where the town was 100 percent free of fossil fuel use for energy and power. Like many other Swedish municipalities, Övertorneå operates a district heating system that provides heat to 2,500 homes and public buildings including schools and eldercare facilities. The town operates five heating plants, one located in each of its five largest villages. All these burned fossil fuels. The town also runs a public bus system and a fleet of cars, vans, and trucks for its municipal staff. All Town buses and cars ran on petroleum-based fuel. Switching to an alternative to fossil fuels posed an enormous challenge for the municipality.

Övertorneå converts

One by one, over several years, the town converted the burners in its five heating plants to furnaces that use biomass — wood pellets or wood chips — readily available by-products from nearby forest-based and lumber industries. As of fall 2000, an eldercare center, public health center, and swimming pool in the community were converted to biomass heating. By spring 2001, two schools had been switched over to wood-based fuel, with three more schools and another eldercare facility converted by fall 2001.

By late fall 2001, all municipal buildings, schools, eldercare and day-care facilities, and heat plants in Övertorneå had become independent of fossil fuels in their heating and operations. With the conversion of its fleet of buses and staff vehicles to biofuels, such as ethanol, at

In 2001, Övertorneå realized its vision of becoming 100 percent free of fossil fuels in its municipal operations.

Figure 5.7: This is one of the five village heating plants that the town of Övertorneå converted from fossil fuel operation to biomass fuel.

Figure 5.8: Wood pellets, a by-product of the regional timber industry, now fires this furnace in one of Övertorneå's village heating plants.

the close of 2001, Övertorneå realized its vision, formed over 15 years earlier, of achieving 100 percent freedom from fossil fuels in municipal operations.

This was not only an ecological success story for Övertorneå, but a financial success as well. The town's oil consumption dropped by 132,000 gallons (about 500,000 liters) per year. Just after all facilities were converted to biofuel use, the price of oil almost doubled to US$89 per barrel. The overall cost of the town's elimination of fossil fuels as an energy source was about US$375,000. The payback time for this investment was between two and three years.

Waste as a resource: In Umeå, garbage becomes power

About Umeå

Umeå (Euh'-meh-aw) is a city of about 100,000 people in northern Sweden. It is a university community, where a population of 20,000 students has spurred Umeå's metamorphosis from an old-fashioned town to a major regional educational and cultural center. It is one of the fastest-growing cities in the country, and its average citizen age is 35 years. One-half of Umeå's population comes from other regions of Sweden, and another ten percent come from other countries. This means, among other things, new ideas are always flowing into the community.

Historically and presently, Umeå is a place where different cultures meet. It is often described as the best city in the country to live and has the highest degree of resident satisfaction. Umeå residents call their community the "capital city of the north." Umeå combines the advantages of a big city with

HOW A VILLAGE BIOMASS HEAT PLANT WORKS

Wooden pellets for fuel are stored in a silo tower with a feed into the burner system. It takes between 10 to 20 minutes to fill the tower with wooden pellets. Once the silo is filled, it can provide enough energy for the domestic hot water and heating needs of village homes during the three to four summer months. In the winter, a silo-full of pellets provides heat ▶

the atmosphere of a small town. As one Umeå official advises, it is important to preserve this attribute in city planning.

Umeå originally developed as a trade center. Sámi people, known to many Westerners as Lapplanders, traveled to this region as they herded their reindeer from winter to summer feeding places. A lively across-the-sea trade developed among the Swedes, Finns, Russians, and the Sámi. When the municipality of Umeå was officially founded in 1622, there were about 200 inhabitants. In the late 1800s, the city became an industrial center, resulting in, among other things, the devastation of its forests. Umeå developed such a bad environmental reputation around the country that a particular term came to describe the city's poor behavior toward the environment — *Baggböleri* (Bugg-beu-ler-ee').[9] In 1960, the founding of Umeå University, which for years was the only university in northern Sweden, spurred the city's transition to its present status as a regional cultural and education center. Umeå now offers many festivals and cultural events, such as jazz, chamber music, film, and the only opera north of Stockholm. Baggböleri has been replaced by high environmental awareness among Umeå citizens and throughout their municipal government.

In the early 1990s, Umeå's municipal government worked to make that environmental awareness official. The city's governing Executive Council adopted goals for sustainable development and established a coordinating group with representatives from six municipal departments to make those goals a reality. Over the next two years, 50 department supervisors received training about the importance of a healthy environment and sustainable development practices to ensure this. City officials decreed that one working day be set aside to spread this message through all city departments. Included in these environmental training sessions were all employees of Umeå Energi, the city's municipal energy department that owned and operated the city heating plant.

Umeå's Dåva plant, which operates at an astonishing 99.5 percent efficiency rate, is fueled entirely by the city's own solid waste.

for the village for about one week. One hundred buckets of pellets, when burned, creates one bucket of ashes. Because the ashes come from 100 percent wood, they can be composted, so there is zero waste. These wooden pellets burn at an 85 percent efficiency rate, compared with a 65 percent efficiency rate for industrial oil, according to the town's energy coordinator. [8]

Umeå's energy crisis

Also in the 1990s, the city of Umeå was growing rapidly and found itself facing an acute power shortage. It became clear that the city's oil-burning power and heat-generating plant, built in the 1960s, was not going to be able to do the job of meeting the increased power demand. Instead of converting or retrofitting the older plant, Umeå officials decided to construct an entirely new facility with greater capacity to both service the increased demand and significantly reduce the city's dependence upon fossil fuel and emission of pollutants. The source of the plant's energy would be the city's own solid waste. Since increasingly strict national regulations were in the works to prohibit dumping of burnable waste and organic waste at landfills, the plant would provide solutions to several problems.

Enter the Dåva power plant

The Dåva power plant, Umeå's win-win solution for its energy crisis, has become known as the world's most energy-efficient and environmentally acceptable waste-burning power plant. Approvals and permits were obtained for Dåva in 1997 to replace the city's oil-burning plant. Construction on Dåva began in February 1998, and the plant went on-line in August 2000. Costing close to US$80 million, the Dåva plant is the single largest environmental project ever undertaken by the city of Umeå. Of its 65 MW of power produced, 55 MW provides district heating for 25,000 homes — 90 percent of all city households. The remaining 10 MW goes toward electricity production. The plant operates at an astonishing 99.5 percent efficiency rate. (As mentioned, a conventional power plant usually operates at between 35 to 45 percent efficiency).[10]

The Dåva plant is fueled entirely by the city's own solid waste. Municipal solid waste is collected, compressed, and stored in wrapped blocks near the plant. Household waste, business and industry waste, building materials, organics, food, plastic, rubber — all are fair game to fuel the plant, with the exception of metal and hazardous substances. Solid waste that cannot be remanufactured into new products has a fuel value that is higher than most biomass fuels, such as wood pellets or wood chips, according to Umeå Energi officials. The energy recovered from these substances is one form of recycling. The solid waste otherwise would be dumped in the city's landfill, creating more environmental degradation, in turn costing the city more to rectify. All solid waste materials are, of course, locally obtained, virtually eliminating the city's cost for importing fuel from afar. Solid waste haulers pay about US$28 per ton to dump at the power plant — far less costly than

Figure 5.9: The city of Umeå's Dåva plant provides heat and electricity to city businesses and residents, running entirely on the city's own solid waste.

Figure 5.10: Among other benefits, using its own solid waste for fuel has dramatically reduced Umeå's costs for fuel purchase and for landfilling city trash, shown at left, located near the plant.

dumping at the local landfill. The Dåva plant is also designed to burn biomass — material such as wood chips, pellets, or other wood by-products.

During Dåva's first year of operation, Umeå's fossil fuel use for heating dropped by 80 to 95 percent from its previous level. Electricity used as a form of heating energy has disappeared entirely in Umeå. Due to its state-of-the-art power generating and environmental cleaning systems, Dåva receives 3,000 to 4,000 visitors a year from round the world. The European Union, corporations, and international organizations are studying Dåva as a model for how to recapture and use the embodied energy in solid waste that would otherwise be lost.

Umeå's decision to build the Dåva plant was a multi-win solution — always a good sign that an action is aimed in the right direction. That decision drastically reduced fossil fuel use, greenhouse gas emissions, and fuel costs for the city, while meeting the energy needs of its expanding population. The decision dramatically reduced high environmental and financial costs of hauling and dumping the city's trash, and related increasing landfill encroachment.

The Swedish national energy scene: a snapshot

Between 1981 and 1993 in Sweden, oil dropped from 83 percent to 12 percent as a fuel source for district heating.[12] Stemming from a national referendum in the 1980s, Sweden is also gradually phasing out its dependence upon nuclear power to generate energy. The national government's target environmental objectives include clean air, protection of the ozone layer, limited influence upon climate change, and an environment safe from radiation.[13] Changing to locally developed renewable energy sources is seen as a key strategy toward meeting these national objectives.

NORTH AMERICAN EXAMPLES

District heating systems

According to surveys, over 3,000 district heating systems are operating in the United States. Municipalities that are operating district heating systems

---

HOW THE DÅVA PLANT WORKS

A steam boiler, fired by the burning of solid waste, produces electricity and heat. Two purification systems, one dry, one wet, clean the potential emissions. Combining these systems provides the best of both techniques. The dry purification system is good at collecting particle substances, such as heavy metals, mercury, and carbon dioxides. There is no opportunity for these substances to bypass the system. The wet system involves three scrubbers that wash the outflows with balsam. These scrubbers remove substances, such as hydrochloric acid, and convert sulfur to gypsum — a product that is used to make wallboard. Wastewater is further purified with a double treatment system condenser. Gas is cooled with water, and this water is reused as washwater for the wet scrubbers. Limestone removes 90 percent of acidic substances from the washwater. Ammonia (NH2) is extracted and goes back into the furnace. Heavy metals, such as cadmium, are precipitated through ▶

include Eugene, Oregon; Lansing, Michigan; Fairbanks, Alaska; and Jamestown, New York. Boise, Idaho, and San Bernadino, California, use geothermal heat as a renewable energy source to fuel their district heating systems.[14] In Canada, district heating systems that use biomass as a heat source are operating in Prince Edward Island, Quebec, and in a Cree-owned and operated system in Oujé-Bougoumou.[15]

Renewable energy

Since 1984, the municipally owned electric department of Burlington, Vermont, has provided electricity to city residents and businesses through a generating plant powered by wood chips, bark, and sawdust, eliminating an annual need for 360,000 barrels of fuel oil.[16] The Burlington Electric Department has been working with other city agencies and a nearby universi-ty to develop a district heating system using heat generated from this biomass power plant. Since forests cover 75 percent of the state, biomass is a logical source of renewable energy for Vermont. State agencies and organizations are helping to build capacity in Vermont's regional planning commissions to assist the development of local biomass district energy systems.[17]

The municipal electric department of the Town of Hull, Massachussetts, (pop. 11,000), has generated electricity from wind power since the early 1980s. Recently, the Town replaced its twenty-year-old windmill with a state-of-the-art wind turbine that generates enough electricity for 250

sand filters and combined with sulfur to make a more innocuous substance, such as cadmi-um sulfide. Excess water not reused is diluted and sent to the Umeå River. Eight megawatts of power are extracted by compressor heat pumps and reused, saving additional power costs. Before leaving the chimney, the flue gasses are cooled to between 50 to 60 degrees Celsius. Slag, a solid residual product from the waste incineration is quality-assured for use as a road aggregate material, saving the use of natural gravel for this purpose. Natural grav-el is another diminishing natural resource in Sweden that has been targeted for conservation. Overall, state-of-the-art cleaning systems have radically reduced greenhouse gas emissions, such as sulfur and nitrogen oxides and carbon dioxide, far below the emis-sions of the former oil-burning plant, as well as below the standards set by Sweden's environmental court. [11]

❖

homes. The new turbine, whose installation cost about US$300,000, will save Hull taxpayers about US$50,000 a year, repaying the town's investment in six years.[18]

Denver, Colorado, and Newton, Massachussetts, are among the municipalities that are promoting the use of solar energy throughout their jurisdictions, with assistance from the U.S. Department of Energy's Million Solar Roofs Program. In Newton, the mayor, board of aldermen, planning department, school system, chamber of commerce, and a citizens environmental organization have joined forces to bring about the installation of 500 solar power systems in public buildings, businesses, and private homes.[19]

In the United States, one-third of all electricity consumers are now able, if they choose, to purchase renewable energy through green pricing programs offered by utility companies or through independent suppliers.[20] As an example, the City of Santa Monica, California, recently signed an agreement with its power supplier that to purchase electricity that is 100 percent generated from renewable energy sources.

CHAPTER 6

Getting Away from Fossil-fueled Vehicles: Transportation and Mobility

If per capita automobile driving were the same in China as ours [in the U.S.] is today, China would consume the world's total gasoline production.
— Ray Anderson, *Mid-Course Correction*[1]

Introduction

Being able to get around easily and affordably to conduct the affairs of one's life is a central need no matter where one lives — in a large city, in a small town, in the rural hinterlands. Those of us who are able to do so often take it for granted. Those who are not able to do so understand better its necessity.

In the United States, the car and the fossil fuels used to power it have become central to society — or seemingly so. It has also become apparent in recent years that fossil-fueled cars, trucks, and other vehicles are contributing hugely to the conditions that are causing global warming, climate change, and deteriorating air quality in many parts of the country and the globe. Transportation's generation of carbon dioxide emissions is the fastest growing source of this greenhouse gas that accounts for 21 percent of the world's total production.[2] Central to the increasing concern with sprawl development in the United States is the automobile's role in society that shapes people's living and location choices, transportation policy, land use, business location decisions and operations, and, what is becoming increasingly apparent, foreign policy and national security.

Reducing dependence upon fossil fuels, as one of the four sustainability objectives, challenges us to understand, and then change, the complex network of factors that support the burning of fossil fuels by vehicles. One part of this network is patterns of land use and development that give people no other choice but to get in their cars and drive to work, food, and other people and places in their communities and beyond. Having no other means to move around, such as the ability to walk, bike, or take affordable, easy public transportation, reinforces the necessity to drive. When no other fuels are available to power those cars beside fossil fuels, fossil fuels will be used to power the cars. If people can only purchase cars that run on fossil fuels, these are the cars that people will drive.

Fortunately, increased understanding of this complex network fostering transport dependence upon fossil fuels plus efforts to lessen its grip are occurring even in the United States, where consumption of fossil fuels for driving and vehicle miles per person traveled per year is unparalleled in the world.[3] Among these efforts, the eco-municipalities of Sweden are working to bring systematic change to the interconnections of transportation and mobility. This chapter presents two examples of systematic and innovative city approaches that encourage people to move around other than via private, fossil-fueled cars.

Eskilstuna: Designing a transport system based on nature's principles

The City of Eskilstuna is changing its entire transportation approach to one based upon the eco-cyclic principles of nature. (The reader learned about Eskilstuna in Chapter 5.) The City is concurrently re-evaluating its approaches to traffic, land use, public transportation, emissions control, bicycle travel, noise abatement, business development, fueling, and municipal vehicles.

To accomplish this, Eskilstuna is using four eco-cyclic principles, similar to the Natural Step framework, as a policy guide. The city is developing approaches to the issues listed above to bring them into harmony with these principles. In using a principle-guided approach, Eskilstuna is working to assure that land use, business development policies, public transit, and municipal transportation policies all operate as a system whose parts will all work together toward reduction of fossil fuel use for mobility needs. The eco-cyclic principles guiding the city's transportation program are that:

- Extraction of finite resources must be minimized
- Release of substances that are difficult to break down must cease
- The physical conditions for nature's cycles must be preserved

- Extraction of renewable resources must not be greater than their ability to renew.

PICTURE OF EXISTING CONDITIONS

A first step in the program's development was to obtain a clear picture of Eskilstuna's current transportation and environmental situations, in particular, what city policies and actions were violating these eco-cyclic principles. The city learned that the total motor vehicle distance traveled within its boundaries was 3,800 miles per person per year. Total distance traveled in and out of the city center was 3,000 miles per person per year. Every day, there were 100,000 car, train, bicycle, bus, and walking trips to and from the city center. The city found that its stream of out-commuters was equivalent to the stream of in-commuters — about 10 percent in each case. One positive finding was that train travel in and out of the city had increased from 6 percent to over 25 percent between 1993 and 1998. Eskilstuna found that its carbon dioxide emissions from transportation sources were about equal to the national average in Sweden, but about 50 percent higher than that of a rival city also working to reduce emissions levels. One astonishing study finding estimated that vehicle traffic in Eskilstuna was wearing off about 15 tons of asphalt from roads on an average winter day and 100 tons of particles were wearing off the tires of privately owned cars. The city also learned that it dispensed 550 tons of road salt during the winter months of a given year.

SIX TARGET AREAS

Following its inventory of traffic and environmental conditions, Eskilstuna decided to concentrate on six areas of transportation policy. First, a community planning initiative is examining the relationship between land use and traffic generation. Other efforts are in the works to make the city more bicycle-friendly and to improve its public transportation. Other target areas include environmental adaptations for vehicles, improved traffic management, business and industry transport practices, and mobility management, that is, reducing needs for private vehicle trips in the first place.

The city then set specific goals, implementing actions, timetables, and indicators to measure progress within each of these six target areas. For example, mobility management actions include initiating carpools, running bike-to-work campaigns, and providing consultations to businesses about ways to make their transport practices more environmentally friendly. Another action was to improve the safety for children's walk-to-school routes to reduce the necessity for parents to drive them to school.

Another city strategy is re-examining conventional public works policies for road improvements, since it became clear to the city that transportation "improvements" such as bypasses, road straightening, and road widening tilts people's trip choice toward driving and away from available public transit or bicycling. Eskilstuna can choose to invest resources into increasing the availability and desirability of public transit and other mobility alternatives to driving a privately owned car.

Eskilstuna's investigation revealed the importance of maintaining local stores and markets in residential neighborhoods to reduce trip generation. If householders are able to obtain food and convenience items by taking a short walk, they can reduce car trips by 200 to 1200 percent, studies found.

The city also found that car trips of less than three miles accounted for few of the total miles driven in the city; however, these short trips produced proportionately more emissions than longer trips. According to study findings, this was because catalytic converters that reduce car emissions operate less effectively when they are cold. This finding signaled to the city that its efforts to shift short trips from cars to bicycles would bring relatively high environmental gains in reduced emissions and improved air quality. Hence, the city has undertaken a systematic effort to encourage bicycling that includes expanding the present 60-mile network of bike trails, improving bicycle-riding safety, and designing traffic flows in the city center to give bicycles priority over vehicle traffic.

In efforts to improve public transportation, Eskilstuna is redesigning transit routes to increase their frequency and create more stops on those routes. Complementing these public transit improvements are corresponding restrictions on car traffic to help tilt trip decisions toward alternatives to driving a privately owned car. Eskilstuna is also working with neighboring municipalities to improve regional public transit opportunities, for example, creating additional train stops within the region and marketing efforts to increase regional transit ridership.

At the same time, Eskilstuna is working to adapt its municipal fleet of fossil-fueled buses, trucks, and cars to run on more environmentally friendly fuels such as ethanol or blended fuel mixtures. The city has begun to investigate biogas generation — gas created from organic waste — as a possible fuel source for city vehicles. Driver education courses will include eco-driving techniques that reduce fuel consumption, discussed in the next section.

To reduce truck trips, the city is helping private businesses find ways to increase truck load capacity, coordinate trips among different distributors, create more flexible pick-up and drop-off schedules, and arrange more convenient storage and terminal locations. To avoid empty truck return trips after deliveries, the city is discussing with businesses the possibility for "green returns"; after delivering their goods, trucks then pick up and return materials for recycling. To cut down on municipal delivery trips, Eskilstuna is working to improve coordination in its own public purchasing. The city is also helping businesses explore ways to decrease employee trips, using its own municipal employee trip reduction incentive program as a model.

COORDINATING GROUP

To make sure this broadbased program is implemented, Eskilstuna has organized a coordinating group of both policy-makers and implementers. These include elected officials and representatives from municipal departments, such as building, traffic, public works, environmental, and planning. The transportation project is a long-term one, setting specific emissions reduction targets in five-year increments to 2025. By then, the city aims to reduce carbon dioxide emissions 75 percent below its level in 2001.

SYSTEMS APPROACH

Eskilstuna's multilateral approach to changing its transportation system recognizes how trip choice is intertwined with availability of feasible, convenient, and affordable alternatives to driving a private, fossil-fueled vehicle. Eskilstuna is demonstrating how looking at transportation and mobility from a holistic systems perspective can create a more sustainable transportation policy.[4]

Luleå: working to reduce the dominance of the car

ABOUT LULEÅ

Luleå (Leuh'-leh-aw) is a city of 70,000 people in northern Sweden, just south of the Arctic Circle on the coast of the Baltic Sea. Among other features, Luleå is distinguished by a remarkable geographic condition. The city's land is rising about one

Figure 6.1: Bikes, not cars, predominate in this central area of Luleå.
Credit: Municipality of Luleå.

yard (one meter) every hundred years due to the reduced weight on the land after glacial melting. This phenomenon is increasing the city's land area by about one-half a square mile per year. Fifty years ago, the city's harbor was in the center of town. One hundred years ago, the harbor was even further up the river.

The car has slowly but surely been taking precedence over other transportation choices in Luleå despite its compact city center. To combat this trend, the city began a three-year project to persuade citizens to shift to buses, bikes, or walking, setting a goal to reduce car traffic by 10 percent. This translated into each city resident taking two fewer car journeys per week. The city's team for this project includes the city planning department, public works department, and the municipal bus company. Rather than using advertising or leafleting to educate citizens, the team is using a personal approach, talking directly with citizens, workers, and car and bike users. City team members offer practical advice and training, mostly at workplaces — a good way to reach car drivers. The city believes in a "carrot approach," providing incentives that encourage people to drive less and use alternative modes more often.

SURVEYING THE SITUATION

The city carried out a survey of car drivers, asking them to list the reasons they used their car. Forty-one percent said they used their cars for practical reasons, for example, picking up a child from a friend's house or an after-school activity. About 10 percent said they used their cars because there was no bus route available between their starting point and their destination. And, 48 percent of respondents said they drive their cars for reasons of personal value, for example, simply because it "feels good."

Luleå carefully studied car trip generation and alternative transportation use. During the fall of 2000, the city surveyed 60,000 residents, learning they make a total 100,000 trips per day. On average, each inhabitant made about 52 one-way trips on local buses per year. For short trips of less than three miles, 58 percent of surveyed citizens used cars, 25 percent used bikes, 9 percent walked, and 7 percent used the bus. There was not much difference between summer and winter travel patterns. In the winter, 10 percent of the travelers used bicycles, but otherwise the breakdown was the same as for summer travel. About 55 percent of respondents believed buses should have priority over cars, even though this would mean more inconvenience for car drivers. This was an interesting result, since the majority of the respondents drove cars themselves. The city also discovered that nearly one-half the cars in Luleå are more than 20 years old. In general, Swedish cars are used for 15 to 20 years, according to the city's transportation coordinator.

IMPROVING THE ALTERNATIVES

The city has a car-sharing system with several cars that municipal employees can book for taking work trips. It can be reserved at the main switchboard in city hall, so people don't have to take their own car to work. At the same time, Luleå is working to improve its infrastructure network of car alternatives. As of 2001, the city had 220 miles (about 350 kilometers) of vehicular roads and 60 miles of hiking and walking lanes, most of which were constructed 20 years earlier. The city is improving its public bus system, for example, by designing better information systems on bus schedules, giving buses priority at intersections, and improving and increasing bus stops. The city pays one-half the cost of the bus system; the rest is paid by rider bus fares. The city is developing plans for a bus exchange center featuring sheltered bus stops and waiting areas. The city considered developing a park-and-ride area, but decided this was not a good option for Luleå because of the city's low, spread-out population density. The city also has been considering closing its main central city street to car traffic and is planning a public referendum on this issue.

WORKING WITH REALITY

In Luleå, 80 percent of all households own a car, and 80 percent of residents who drive are able to use a car on any day they wish. Every working day, around 70,000 cars carrying 80,000 to 90,000 people, averaging 1.3 persons per car, enter the city. Buses carry in another 9,000 people. About 9,000 bikers and pedestrians also enter the city center to work. Luleå accepts the reality that cars will keep coming into the city center. Realizing its transit vision is not as radical as those of other communities aiming for a car-free city center, Luleå's goal is not to ban the car from the city, but rather to integrate other solutions to reduce the dominance of the car over other transportation choices. [5]

Luleå and Övertorneå sponsor eco-driving

Luleå and Övertorneå are working to educate beginning and experienced drivers about driving techniques that can save gas, hence reducing fossil fuel use and emissions. According to a Luleå official, eco-driving techniques can save between 10 and 20 percent of the fuel energy that is consumed using conventional driving habits. One eco-driving technique involves shifting quickly to a high gear after starting up the car, so that less energy is consumed in propelling the car. Slowing down when approaching a speed limit also saves gas. Eco-driving teachers explain how keeping the correct amount of air in the tires cuts down on fuel consumption. Other eco-driving techniques include reducing idling time, using the momentum of the car instead of gas on road inclines, driving at optimum speeds, and keeping unnecessary weight out of the vehicle. Planning vehicle trips ahead of time can avoid unnecessary diversions. As one program coordinator quips, eco-driving is how old men have always driven cars. In Luleå's eco-driving education program, students drive a specified route without instruction, and the energy they consume is measured. Then, students re-drive the same route while energy consumption is measured. The cost of Luleå's eco-driving program is about US$125 per person.

Figure 6.2: Only bikes can park in the parking lot in front of Övertorneå's town hall.

Övertorneå runs its eco-driving program as part of the driving curriculum for all new drivers in high schools. The municipality pays for ten driving lessons that include eco-driving techniques, a program that costs the municipality US$18,000 a year. The town also is working with the trucking association and the local business sector that generates heavy traffic. According to a town official, truck eco-driving can reduce emissions by 20 to 30 percent. Övertorneå has a three-day eco-driving educational course for business employees. The course cost per person is US$125. Town officials estimate that, through these two efforts, over 70 percent of the drivers in Övertorneå have received eco-driving education and claim this is unparalleled among Swedish municipalities.[6]

Cutting down on gas-powered cars in Stockholm

Stockholm has joined eight other European cities to lease alternative-fueled cars for city workers. The cars have high-visibility stickers that make the case for using alternative fuels, since the city's goal is to encourage drivers to switch to these cars. The first step was for the municipal government itself to make the switch, providing a good example for others. These nine cities have made agreements with gas stations to provide alternative fuels such as electricity, ethanol, or biogas. One objective was to create a consumer market large enough to motivate car companies to produce alternatively fueled cars. For example, this initiative guaranteed the Ford Motor Company a market for 5,000 alternatively fueled cars, if they would produce these.

Figure 6.3: Many bike lanes in Stockholm run along the edge of the sidewalk instead of the street.

Also in Stockholm, many groups of 12 to 14 households own or rent a car together. Different groups have different organizational structures and mileage costs. In most cases, carpool members pay a monthly fee and mileage costs. Some cooperatives use a rental corporation that works in partnership with a gas company. The rental corporation offers different sizes of cars and vans and purchases the most environmentally friendly cars. The municipal government has also purchased such cars for carpool use among its department and agency employees. Only 20 percent of Stockholm households own cars, according to the city's sustainable development coordinator. There are very few places to keep a car, and public transportation is excellent, coupled with projects such as carpool cooperatives.[7]

Conversion of municipal fleets

As part of their efforts to reduce fossil fuel use, many municipalities have converted their public vehicle fleets from gasoline and diesel to alternative fuels such as ethanol, canola (rapeseed) oil, and other biofuels. The fleets include both buses within public transit systems and municipal cars, vans, and trucks that are used by employees in carrying out their duties. For example, the city of Umeå now has over 30 buses running on ethanol — more than two-thirds of its entire bus fleet. Umeå's goal is to have 100 percent of its fleet running on biofuel by 2003.

Stockholm has replaced 300 of its 2,000-vehicle fleet with alternatively fueled cars and plans to convert 700 more in the next two years. Since 1998, municipal departments needing new vehicles purchase only alternatively fueled cars, trucks, or vans. Almost all the 250 inner-city buses in Stockholm now run on ethanol fuel instead of diesel. The city has begun to replace its fossil-fueled garbage trucks with ones that run on biogas — gas manufactured from organic waste from restaurants and commercial kitchens, as well as from sewage. The city has built a biogas production plant next to one of its sewage treatment plants that is producing the biogas equivalent of 180,000 gallons of gasoline. Using the gases generated from sewage and garbage reduces emissions from these sources and provides an alternative to fossil fuel use for vehicles — a win-win solution. Two more biogas plants that will produce several million gallons of biogas for the city are in the works.[8]

As of summer 2001, Övertorneå's municipal fleet contained 12 ethanol-fueled cars, and the town planned to lease more for its elder home care staff. An ethanol gas station has opened in town. By the close of 2001, Övertorneå reached its goal of converting all public buses and municipal vehicles from fossil fuels to alternative fuels. The town made ridership on public transport free, increasing ridership by 700 percent in the first six months following this decision.

North American examples

Municipal fleets

In North America, too, cities and towns are using more alternatively fueled buses and cars in municipal fleets. Almost 50 cities in 19 U.S. states were using electric buses as of 1996.[9] Denver, San Francisco, and Monterey County have passed ordinances to reduce greenhouse gas emissions through increased use of alternatively fueled vehicles. Canadian cities also are investigating alternatives to fossil-fueled buses and cars. In Quebec City, an eco-bus project is testing various alternatively fueled vehicles for efficiency, performance, and emissions reduction.[10]

Car rides

To make it easier to get about in the city without the necessity of owning a car, Cambridge, Massachusetts, and neighboring Somerville provide free parking spots for a local car-sharing enterprise called ZipCar. For an initial membership fee, people can rent a car by the hour on short notice to run errands, attend meetings, or for other small trips. Cars are placed around the city in convenient places within a short walk of most neighborhoods. As another example, the New York State Power Authority has teamed up with the Ford Motor Company to make electric cars available to commuters at eight metropolitan New York commuter rail stations.

Land use regulations

Cambridge is also including zoning regulations in a package of transportation approaches, to reduce car trips in the city. City zoning ordinances mandate that new non-residential development must include a plan to reduce traffic that must receive city approval before the development can proceed. Developers can propose steps such as mini-buses between public transportation and the building, encouragement of carpooling among employees, and free or subsidized public transportation passes. The city also encourages its own employees to use transport other than cars by providing subsidized transit passes, bicycles for work-related trips, and an education program about the importance of, and options for, alternative modes of travel. Other cities such as Toronto, Canada, have passed ordinances cutting down on truck or bus idling, a significant contributor to emissions and poor air quality. According to estimates, three percent of Ontario's fuel is wasted through idling engines.[11]

Public transit & transit-oriented development

In 1996, the city of Dallas, Texas, installed a 23-mile electric-powered rapid transit system connecting its outer fringes with the heart of its downtown. In the first two weeks following the rapid transit opening, its daily ridership exceeded all projections. By the end of the next fiscal year, total city public transit ridership had increased by 40 percent from the previous year and has since continued to climb steadily. Shortly after the opening of Dallas's rapid transit, its downtown center experienced its largest burst of development and business growth in 20 years. Residential development, virtually unknown to the downtown, boomed. The city and its transit authority actively participate in encouraging mixed-use high-density development adjacent to transit stops — what has come to be known as transit-oriented development. Between the opening of the rapid transit in 1996 and the end of 2002, over 10,000 housing units had been built in the city's downtown core, primarily in high-density clusters near transit stops. Dallas's new rapid transit, coupled with the development of new living, working, shopping, and cultural opportunities in its downtown core, has made it possible for tens of thousands of Dallas commuters, citizens, and visitors to get into, around, and out of the city's downtown without driving a car.[12]

CHAPTER 7

Ecological Housing

What use is a house if you haven't got a tolerable planet to put it on?

— Henry David Thoreau[1]

Un-ecological housing: A snapshot

The average-sized single-family home in the United States creates between two and five tons of solid waste through its construction and twice as much greenhouse gases per year as the average car.[2] Construction of buildings consumes one-quarter of all wood harvested. Every year, throughout the world, three billion tons of raw materials are used annually to construct buildings.[3] Buildings consume one-third of all the energy and two-thirds of all electricity used in the United States.[4] Buildings use 40 percent of the world's materials and energy. Almost one-third of newly built or rehabilitated buildings expose their occupants to sick building syndrome.[5] Every hour of the day, 45.6 acres of farmland in the U.S. is converted to development.[6] In 1950, the average size new home built in the U.S. was 983 square feet (about 91 square meters). By 2000, it had grown to 2,265 square feet (about 210 square meters), and contained two stories, two-and-one-half bathrooms, a two-or-more car garage, a fireplace, and central air conditioning.[7]

Combined with these building trends, a suburban pattern of residential development spread out from U.S. urban centers like wildfire after World War II. This pattern basically consists of subdivisions of single-family homes on lots of one to several acres. Each has its own driveway and usually a one- or two-car garage. Much has been written about this pattern of development

If a household chose to live in a multi-unit housing complex rather than a single-family home and drove a compact energy-efficient car instead of a standard-sized one, it could reduce its ecological footprint by a factor of three.[8]

that has become, among other things, the poster child for sprawl development that, although decried by planners for decades, is now widely seen as a threat to open space preservation, agriculture, and quality of life.

On the positive side, ecological building, whose design and construction moves toward the sustainability objectives listed at right, is spreading steadily throughout Europe and North America. Ecological, or green, building uses forms of renewable energy for heat and power, instead of fossil fuel. (In this chapter, "green," "ecological," and "sustainable" are intended to mean the same — moving toward the four system conditions of the Natural Step framework.) Ecological building uses materials, recycled where possible, which contain few or no toxic substances and constructs compact developments to save open space and reduce car use. It makes use of existing buildings before building new ones and uses water, energy, materials, and space as efficiently as possible.

Coupled with ecological building practices are compact housing development designs that do a better job of fostering social cohesion and a community life. Growing numbers of households, dissatisfied with the isolation of conventional suburban life, are re-finding a sense of neighborhood, connection, and social interaction in these community-oriented developments. This chapter presents some examples from Sweden.

In the housing communities of Understenshöjden and Tuggelite, households joined forces to build homes and neighborhood life consistent with their shared values of ecological living and community. In the town of Övertorneä, the municipal government helped develop ecological housing as part of its path to becoming an eco-community. Pyramiden housing in Stockholm, described later in this chapter, reversed a

ECOLOGICAL HOUSING IS HOUSING THAT:
• Reduces wasteful dependence upon fossil fuels, heavy metals, and minerals that accumulate in nature;
• Reduces wasteful dependence on chemicals and synthetic substances that accumulate in nature;
• Reduces encroachment upon ecosystems; and
• Meets human needs fairly and efficiently.

Derived from the system conditions of the Natural Step framework

Figure 7.1: As is customary in cohousing and ecological housing design, Understenshöjden's homes are grouped around paths and common spaces rather than driveways. Cars are parked at the edge of the property.

Figure 7.2:
Understenshöjden's com-
munity building will soon
include an expanded
kitchen and dining room
for community meals.

pattern of vandalism and tenant transience through an eco-renovation that restored nature to a derelict urban neighborhood. The city of Falkenberg's housing agency adopted green building policies for its publicly owned affordable housing. And finally, the town of Karlstad encouraged private sector development of market-rate eco-condominiums through a life cycle assessment competition that rewarded the most ecological building proposal.

Ecology and community: Understenshöjden, Tuggelite, Övertorneå

In Sweden, ecological housing or an eco-village has a particular meaning. A Swedish ecological housing community or eco-village is known in North America and Denmark as cohousing — a form of residential development where people intentionally come to live together as a community. The idea for this community-oriented housing design originated in Denmark during the 1960s.

In U.S. cohousing and Swedish ecological housing, each household owns or rents their own independent dwelling unit and shares common space that usually includes a community kitchen, dining room, and other facilities where people can cook, eat, and work together. The physical design of these developments supports a community-oriented way of living. For example, units are grouped closely together to allow and encourage interaction among households. Decision making about housing development and management over time usually is consensual. Cohousing and ecological housing developments are found in urban, suburban, and rural settings. Understenshöjden, Tuggelite, and Ruskola Ekoby are three examples of this type of ecological housing community in Sweden.

UNDERSTENSHÖJDEN ECOLOGICAL HOUSING

Located on the outskirts of Stockholm, about a 20-minute transit ride from the city's center, is a housing community called Understenshöjden (Eun'-dehr-stehns-heuy'-dehn). Here, about 180 people of various ages and household types live in 44 households on almost eight acres of land. In 1990, these households joined to co-design, co-build, and co-live in a housing community that would reflect mutually held values of ecological building and living styles. Housing prices in the Stockholm region had risen rapidly in the 1980s, and these families wanted to stay in the area and bring up their children here. They knew they would need larger units as their families grew. They also wanted to build their homes in a way that, while providing comfortable living quarters for them, would not be resource wasteful either to build or to occupy and maintain. Their vision was to live ecologically — to live within nature's capacity to support not only their needs but also those of future generations.

Understenshöjden is one of about 30 to 40 ecological housing communities in Sweden. According to some Understenshöjden residents, Swedish ecological housing focuses more on shared ecological values than social ones, compared with Danish and U.S. cohousing where social values are more often the founding principle. For instance, ten years after they first moved in, the residents of Understenshöjden began to enlarge the small kitchen in their shared community building in order to cook and share community meals. In contrast, shared cooking and meals is a cornerstone of most United States and Danish cohousing developments.

Green features

In first designing their site and homes, the Understenshöjden group worked with a socially and ecologically minded architect. As with many, if not most, cohousing developments, the design process was a participatory one, involving all prospective households in design decisions. With the architect's help, Understenshöjden residents decided to design their future homes in groups of attached rowhouses and townhouses. Thirty-seven units would be two-story attached homes; seven would be one-story flats. The average area of each home was about 1,000 square feet. No two interior designs were the same. Since 44 homes is considered to be large for an ecological or cohousing community, dwelling units were designed in several clusters of 10 to 12 homes that created different neighborhoods, although residents initially saw this more for easier shared building, maintenance, and cleaning than for creating social neighborhoods. Townhouses and rowhouses surround open areas, allowing parents to watch children as they play and allowing residents to chat and wave to each other as they pass by. Cars are parked, not next to every home, as in a conventional residential subdivision, but in a parking area at one side of the property. This allows homes to be grouped more closely together, again encouraging more spontaneous social interaction as well as more open space. Unit clustering is a primary design feature of cohousing developments and ecological housing.

Clustering the units in groups made it possible to leave several natural wooded areas and a wildflower meadow on the property. A walking path was created along the edge of the grounds for residents of the larger neighborhood, as well as the residents of Understenshöjden, to use and enjoy.

Nowhere on the site are there any fences. The group also deliberately decided not to build playgrounds since they believed there were too many over-planned play areas in Sweden. Instead, natural areas remain, with the addition of simple playthings, such as a small boat for children to scramble in and out of and a climbing rope in the middle of a birch glade.

All buildings and homes are oriented to the south to take most advantage of the sun's warming energy. Situating the buildings with a forest at their north side helps protect them from the cold. Solar thermal panels provide hot water and heat from April through September. A community heating system using a wood pellet-fired boiler provides heat through the dark winter months. Water heated with either solar or biomass power is piped from a single boiler to all buildings. Each group of homes has its own thermal tank that stores the solar-heated water. As a backup system, Understenshöjden is connected to Stockholm's district heating system. Building materials were carefully selected, avoiding toxic substances, chemicals, and products whose production and transport involved fossil fuels. Plastic materials, that involve all these things, were eschewed. Newspaper-based cellulose insulates the buildings. Interior painting used egg-based paints. In contrast, conventional paint is made with chemicals that emit harmful volatile organic compounds (VOCs) contributing to sick building syndrome.[9]

Exterior wooden walls were protected with an iron compound as a wood preservative rather than conventional wood preservatives that contain arsenic that can leach into the soil and groundwater and into skin when

Figure 7.3: Residents from the larger community as well as Understenshöjden householders can enjoy this walking path in an area of the site that was left wild.

touched. Gravel was used on the access road and parking area instead of concrete and asphalt whose production is heavy on fossil fuels. Gravel is also a porous surface, allowing rain to sink into the earth and replenish groundwater. In the entire development of Understenshöjden, no product or material derived from fossil fuels was ever used.

Understenshöjden residents wanted to be self-sufficient in energy use and waste disposal on their site. All households separate recyclable solid waste and materials. Food scraps and garden weeds are composted on the property. All homes have urine-separating toilets that do precisely what their name suggests. Urine is piped to an underground tank and collected periodically by a truck for use in agriculture research. Elsewhere, farmers pick up the urine that is diluted with water and used for fertilizer. Urine is basically a mixture of nitrogen and phosphorus — two key ingredients needed for plant growth. It is sterile and one of the best fertilizers when diluted with water.[10] Understenshöjden also installed a plumbing system that would allow the reuse of gray water — water from sinks, showers, and dishwashers — for plant irrigation or toilet water, when municipal officials agree to issue the permit for this system.

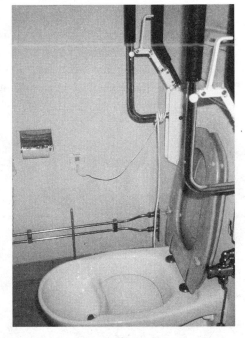

Figure 7.4: This toilet in Understenshöjden's community building allows urine to be separated, piped to a separate holding tank, and removed by a farmer to use as fertilizer.

Unit prices

Since families initially moved into Understenshöjden in 1990, only three units have turned over. The average original home price was about US$30,000, which could be reduced by another US$5,000 to 10,000 if the owners contributed sweat equity in constructing their dwelling. Recently a unit sold for US$250,000 — about nine times the original purchase price.

TUGGELITE ECOLOGICAL HOUSING

Tuggelite (Teugg'-eh-lee'-teh), in the town of Karlstad in Värmland County, was the first ecological housing community in Sweden, founded and developed in 1984 by a group of Göteborg students who were fellow antinuclear activists. As of 2001, 30 adults and 40 children live at Tuggelite.

The town of Karlstad supported the ecological housing concept and the residents' plan for development. The municipality worked with the group to identify a suitable site for the community. Although the planning and permitting process took three or four years because abutting neighbors were initially resistant, the development was finally approved and constructed.

Inspired by Tuggelite's success, Karlstad town officials have since been promoting green design.

Green features

Tuggelite's 16 one- and two-story homes are laid out in five rows that face south. This passive solar design, including large windows and greenhouse porches, contributes 10 to 15 percent of daytime dwelling heat. Air heated by the sun in the greenhouses circulates through the entire home. Carefully designed overhanging roofs provide shade from the higher overhead sun in summer without blocking light. Concrete walls provide thermal mass that absorbs solar heat during the day and releases it at night. There is an unwritten rule that no pesticides or fertilizers will be used anywhere on the property.

Figure 7.5: Sun entering south-facing greenhouse porches warms air that circulates throughout Tuggelite homes.

A centralized wood pellet-fired boiler and solar collectors provide heat and hot water for all the units. The solar collectors provide 50 percent of heat consumed. There is a backup oil burner. Electricity for most residents comes from a nearby windmill. Residents can own shares in a cooperative that owns and operates this windmill. Each share provides 1000 kilowatt hours per year.

As in Understenshöjden, some Tuggelite residents use urine-separating toilets; others use conventional ones. Some homes are recycling and reusing graywater from sinks and showers for plant irrigation.

Community life

Tuggelite's community building has a kitchen, eating area, sauna, spinning room, and a TV room. An orchestra with several resident members rehearses here weekly. During its first 12 years, Tuggelite rented its community building to the Town for a daycare center attended by children from both outside and inside the community. Meanwhile, Tuggelite residents used the center at night. Groups of families get together to eat every four or five days.

There are three or four all-day community workdays spread throughout the year. Similar to Amish barnraising, it is seen as important to work together.

The whole community also eats together on these days. If older or disabled people can't do their share of work, others will take up their share. Five alternating teams handle weekly grounds and maintenance duties.

Tuggelite community decisions are made by consensus. While this takes more time, residents of Tuggelite and other cohousing communities consider it to be a real social strength. Tuggelite's ownership structure is a hybrid of a cooperative and a condominium. For example, the association carried the bulk of the mortgage taken to construct and develop the community, while each household made payments to cover their share. Since then, the mortgage has been divided into sixteen different mortgages, one for each household to pay.

RUSKOLA EKOBY ECO-VILLAGE

The Ruskola Ekoby (Reu'-skoo-lah Ehko-bih) eco-village, in the town of Övertorneå, grew out of that town's eco-municipality journey. One of the founding purposes of Ruskola Ekoby was to attract people back to a town that had lost population to the city. This exodus of citizens had eroded Övertorneå's civic life and cohesion as a community.

Övertorneå's municipal government first bought land for the eco-village development, then subdivided this land, selling nine individual lots at reduced prices to participating households. Families were allowed to subdivide their lots one more time, if they wanted to build smaller adjacent homes for children and aging parents.

Brought together through their interest in living in an eco-

village, the nine households initially did not know each other. First, they all took part in education sessions about ecological ways to build homes, ecological ways of living, and why this is important to society. When the sessions ended, participants asked for more learning about ecological living and its relationship to global trends.

Figure 7.6: Prospective residents of the Ruskola Ekoby village designed their own ecological homes with the help of a "green" architect.

A democratic design process

Both Ruskola Ekoby's site design and building design became democratic processes. The prospective homeowners worked with a well-known Swedish "green" designer and Övertorneå's town planner, Torbjörn Lahti, to set overall goals for the eco-village and plan how these could be achieved. The designer and planner realized that buying a house is one of the biggest life decisions a household makes. They saw their job as design professionals was to offer possibilities for people to develop their own ideas — essential in any truly participatory design and planning process. The starting point for the design process, therefore, was finding out how the householders wanted to live.

In discussions among the householders, architect, and town planner, key words emerged that became guiding design principles for Ruskola Ekoby. Residents said they wanted to live in a development that was designed like an "old village," meaning a neighborhood designed according to the traditional and historical pattern of northern Swedish villages and hamlets where home life and work life were integrated and several generations of families lived in close proximity. The old village idea also stood for local democracy, coming from the thousand-year-old tradition of villagers governing themselves without feudal lords, kings, or other masters.

Self-sufficiency emerged as another guiding principle. To the greatest extent possible, households wanted to be self-sufficient in heating their homes, growing their food, and meeting other basic needs. Out of this desire came a plan to set aside common land, surrounded by the homes, where families could cultivate gardens and tend animals together. Homes were designed to be heated with wood that could be harvested in and near the site. In 1989, the first house was built. Now, nine more families with children in the local school live and work in Övertorneå.

From urban slum to urban gardens

PYRAMIDEN APARTMENTS

In a densely populated, formerly run-down and risky neighborhood of Stockholm, six seven-story former tenement buildings are noticeable for their pink exterior and lush green landscaping. As one walks through the grounds of this development, called Pyramiden (Pee-rah-mee'-dehn), one can observe butterfly gardens, a meadow garden, and rabbits hopping about in large airy cages. A compost bin stuffed with grass and garden cuttings sits next to a garden filled with brightly colored flowers. Several play areas for children and cosy sitting areas for adults are scattered throughout the site, connected by paths. Bicycles and bicycle racks are everywhere.

Several years ago, these same buildings, held by more than ten different owners, were poorly maintained and plagued with vandalism, a high apartment turnover rate, and social problems among the tenants. One by one, a city non-profit housing corporation purchased these troubled buildings and teamed up with another non-profit organization, the Swedish Society for the Protection of Nature. Together, these organizations undertook an eco-renovation of these properties, creating over 300 mixed-income, subsidized, affordable rental housing units in a restored natural setting.

Figure 7.7: Formerly run-down tenements in Stockholm now provide affordable housing and a garden atmosphere for mixed-income inner-city residents.

One of the first steps was to tear down all the fences and walls separating the properties to create open space and gardens. To involve residents in the eco-renovation, a written survey was first sent out to all tenants asking them what they wanted to see happen in the renovation. When this didn't generate much response, small groups of residents were organized to discuss problems, new ideas, and come up with suggestions and projects. More people got involved. Teenagers, who had been a big source of the vandalism problems, were hired in the summer to remove old shrubs and

Figure 7.8: A rabbit hutch on the grounds of Pyramiden provides enjoyment for adults and children alike.

put in new soil. The young people were invited to plan their own landscape. Out of this collaboration emerged, among other projects, a youth-run bicycle rebuilding and rental enterprise. Bikes are painted with rainbow colors

Figure 7.9: All the fences on the property were torn down to create gardens and sitting nooks, such as this one, for all residents to enjoy.

Figure 7.10: This knoll, in the center of the development, was restored as a natural area for indigenous plants and grasses. In the winter, children use it for a sliding hill.

and loaned free to Pyramiden residents. The teenagers also built a beautiful stone patio.

Sitting areas were developed in the gardens to encourage people to sit and get to know each other. The gardens were designed to attract birds, insects, and butterflies. A meadow garden was created for indigenous wildflowers and plants in danger of becoming extinct. In the winter, kids slide down the small hill in this meadow garden. Residents manage the compost used for the gardens.

Pyramiden has an onsite daycare center for children living inside and outside the development. There is a community recycling room from which a private company collects recyclables for resale. All residents must recycle. Residents also are involved in ongoing management decisions of the development.

Pyramiden is now a successful development property of 307 rental apartments and 36 condominiums. It has become a most desirable place to live. From rapid unit turnovers, there is now a 15-year waiting list of people wanting to move in. The average market rent for a two-bedroom apartment is US$500 per month. Some tenants receive rent subsidies. Pyramiden's experience has demonstrated to skeptics that involving residents in rental housing management is economically sound. Vandalism has been reduced, as have unit turnovers. This, of course, saves money. Pyramiden's residents now hardly ever move out.[11]

A town encourages green development

BRANDMÄSTAREN ECO-CONDOMINUMS

The town of Karlstad (Kahrl'-stahd) in Värmland County owned a one-acre piece of land in a very desirable and marketable location within its municipal boundaries. Both Karlstad and its town planner wanted to increase the supply of housing in town and also to encourage sustainable, or "green" design of new development. Led by the town planner, Karlstad's municipal government decided to issue a formal request for proposals to private developers for the most sustainable design plan to build housing on the site. The developer who submitted the winning proposal would be selected to purchase the municipal land and develop the housing. Because of the good location and marketability of the property, the town knew there would be a strong response from developers.

The town planner, who had already developed green design standards for Karlstad, designed the request for developer proposals and the competitive evaluation process that would be used to select the most ecologically sound development proposal. He chose a life cycle analysis as the methodology on which to base both the proposal criteria and the evaluation process. A life cycle analysis examines all phases of a product or material and asks questions, such as: Where did this product come from? What materials and energy were used in its fabrication? How much energy is used in its transport to the site? How much energy will be saved or expended over time by its use? When its useful life is

Figure 7.11: The Brandmästaren condominiums were developed using a life cycle analysis method to produce the most ecologically compatible design and construction approaches.

over, can it be recycled? Is it or its by-products biodegradable, and free of toxics?

The life cycle analysis method, assuming a life cycle of 100 years, was applied to four aspects of development design, beginning with the larger planning context of how well the proposal fits with the character of the neighborhood and the town. The other aspects analyzed were building design, energy system design, and other ecological features. Proposals were scored on a points system according to the analysis results for each of these planning and design components.

The town received five proposals from developers. The winning proposal, which was developed and is occupied today as the Brandmästaren (Brahnd'-meh-stahr-ehn) condominiums, consisted of 25 dwelling units contained in five buildings that are arranged around a courtyard and open space on the one-acre site. This proposal used a massive wood construction building approach where laminated layers of inexpensive wood create thick, well-insulated floors and roofs. This also resulted in a healthy indoor environment and abated noise. Bolts and nails were used instead of glue to reduce toxic chemical use and allow for eventual deconstruction and recycling of building parts. This construction method scored much higher on the town's life cycle analysis evaluation than did proposals that specified steel or concrete as primary building materials.

Other building materials were selected to create the healthiest possible indoor air quality. Insulation made with foam glass and cellulose was specified instead of chemical-based insulation. Coconut fiber was used to insulate and seal joints instead of synthetic, high-chemical-containing foam. All windows are triple-glazed to reduce energy loss.

Figure 7.12: A louvered bay window functions as a fresh air clothes-drying closet.

Natural materials were used where possible. Bathrooms were constructed of brick as a deterrent to moisture, according to the town planner. Mineral materials were used rather than organic substances that absorb moisture. Every home in every building has its own fresh air ventilation system, with fresh air piped to every room. Indoor plant terrariums further clean and purify indoor air. Kitchen larders are ventilated with cold air from the basement. This design feature builds upon the traditional cold cellar concept, keeping food cool and complementing the energy-reducing effect of high-efficiency refrigerators. Each home has an open-air louvered bay window for drying clothes. A "smart" heating system heats up when residents come home and goes down when they leave.

Earthen roofs absorb rainwater and cool and insulate the buildings. This type of roof scored well in the life cycle analysis, since the grass and sedum plantings offset the loss of onsite vegetation from building construction.

All storm water is recycled on the site. Residents use a pump in the courtyard for water to irrigate gardens and plants. Rainwater is collected in tanks and piped to this pump.

For increased security purposes, all buildings have vestibules for package deliveries, but only residents can enter the rest of the building. To encourage residents to use their cars less, bike racks are placed under a porch next to the front doors.

The Brandmästaren development was designed and sold as market-rate priced condominiums. Condominium buyers purchased these units because of their comfort, attractiveness, and building quality, not particularly because of the development's ecological features, says the town planner. The town of Karlstad succeeded in an original project objective — to demonstrate that market-rate housing can be ecological and sellable at the same time.[12]

Figure 7.13: All stormwater on the Brandmästaren site is captured and reused. Residents can draw this water from a courtyard pump to water their gardens and plants.

Greening affordable housing

FALKENBERG'S COUNCIL HOUSING

To make sure that its housing residents will live in a healthy, toxic-free environment, FaBo, the city-owned housing agency of Falkenberg, is overhauling its entire approach to building. Falkenberg's council housing, subsidized to be affordable to low- and moderate-income households, is going green.

As in the U.S. and other countries, Swedish construction methods in the 1960s and 1970s brought about a rash of sick buildings — where mildew, mold, or toxic chemicals in building materials contributed to illnesses of its occupants. (For more information about sick buildings, see Chapters 8 and 10.)

FaBo and the city realized that changing to ecological building practices would better safeguard the health of housing residents and also save the city the substantial building remediation costs to correct conditions that create unhealthy interior living space. Toward this objective,

FaBo and Falkenberg's municipal government changed building design and construction practices to aim in more ecological directions. First, the housing agency and the city undertook education and training in ecological building for all staff responsible for overseeing building quality. FaBo and the city changed building permit application procedures and materials specifications and wove environmental questions into development design review and construction specifications. Creating a healthy interior environment with a guaranteed airflow and installing systems to capture and reuse waste energy became two of the city's highest building priorities for affordable housing. These new ecological building standards were to be applicable not only to council housing but also to all publicly constructed buildings in Falkenberg.

In 2001, FaBo set two-year goals for water and energy consumption in council housing based on the 1997 levels: reduce clean water use by 15 percent; fossil fuel use by 30 percent, and energy consumption by 10 percent.[13] These goals were part of Falkenberg's citywide plan to reduce energy use and convert to renewable energy sources. Today, the FaBo municipal housing agency is certified according to the ISO 14001 internationally recognized environmental operating standards. (See Chapter 5 for more information about Falkenberg and its renewable energy initiatives and Chapters 8 and 10 for information about ISO 14001.)

North American examples

Cohousing communities are also springing up in Canada and the United States. In Canada, as of 2003, 11 cohousing developments were either forming or occupied. In the United States, 60 occupied cohousing communities and almost 90 others forming or building were located in 33 of the 50 states as of the same date. Often, municipalities have helped make possible the development of cohousing communities through such actions as removing local regulatory barriers to cohousing or helping in finding a site. For example, the Town of Amherst, Massachusetts made a parcel of town-owned land available for development, writing a request for development proposals for closely grouped residential dwellings and conservation of open space. This action brought about the development of the Pioneer Valley cohousing community.

U.S. municipalities are finding that affordable housing and green building approaches are not mutually exclusive but, rather, compatible goals. For example, in the Cass Corridor neighborhood of Detroit, a community-based development organization saved an eight-story building from demolition, converting this into 27 rental apartments for low-income households while using green building techniques. The decision to rehabilitate rather than demolish the Architects Building, financed with the help of low-income housing tax credits, prevented 800 tons of masonry and debris from being dumped in a landfill. Many construction by-products were sorted, recycled, and reused in other construction. New materials were selected for a high recycling content. The completed building has recycling chutes on every floor, allowing tenants to easily sort and recycle as many as eight separate waste streams.

As another example, Erie-Ellington Homes, developed by a community development corporation in a Boston inner-city neighborhood, provides 50 affordable rental units that reduce energy and water use by 40 percent, while costing 25 percent less to build than comparable new construction. Cities such as Austin, Texas; Denver, Colorado; and Santa Monica, California, have developed green building programs providing incentives for homeowners and builders to create homes and buildings that save water and energy, use recycled materials, and cut down on solid waste.

CHAPTER 8

Green Businesses; Green Buildings

The bottom line of green is black.
— Tedd Saunders, Co-owner, Boston Park Plaza Hotel[1]

Introduction

IT IS OFTEN THOUGHT THAT BUSINESS and industry are enemies of the environment. Many businesses and corporations, however, are leading the way toward sustainable development. Countless businesses have changed particular practices to sustainable ones in some part of their operations or products, and the number of businesses that have systematically overhauled their entire operations to move in a sustainable direction is growing steadily. Why? Because it makes good economic sense.

Elsewhere in this book, the stories of Sånga-Säby and Scandic Hotels tell how two businesses moved from near bankruptcy to leading market positions through major systematic overhauls of company operations to sustainable practices. These businesses used the Natural Step framework as their sustainability compass. The well-known example of the Interface Corporation, led by its CEO Ray Anderson, has set a zero-waste goal for its entire multinational operations and is making progress toward that goal.[2] The stories of these and other companies, such as IKEA and the Collins Pine Company, that have altered business practices using the Natural Step framework as a guide, are documented in *The Natural Step for Business* by Brian Nattrass and Mary Altomare.[3]

Communities and their municipal governments can learn from these business success stories in at least two ways. First, municipal government operations resemble business operations in many respects. The strategies for

In the sustainable society, nature is not subject to systematically increasing ...

1. concentrations of substances extracted from the Earth's crust
2. concentrations of substances produced by society
3. degradation by physical means and in the sustainable society,
4. people are not subject to conditions that systematically undermine their capacity to meet their needs.

The Natural Step system conditions for a sustainable society change and the types of sustainable practices employed are as applicable to municipalities as they are to private companies. So are the financial advantages of those changes: cost savings from reduced energy and fuel use, reduced solid waste disposal, and less hazardous material to manage.

Second, municipal governments play a significant economic development role in their communities. Municipalities influence and guide business location through land use policies and regulation. They regulate water, sewer, solid waste disposal, and, often, utilities. These types of infrastructure strongly affect business operations and location choices. Municipalities make grants and loans available to businesses through local, regional, and state economic development programs. Through these ways, municipalities have the ability to encourage, guide, and assist private business to move in desired directions.

This chapter presents examples of businesses large and small that are using green business practices, building green buildings, and local governments that help them to do so. In this chapter, green development and sustainable development are considered to be the same, defined as development that moves in the direction of the four system conditions of the Natural Step framework.

GreenZone: Big business pilots green development

In the city of Umeå in northern Sweden, a remarkable business park is home to local franchises of three multinational corporations: a Ford Motor Company sales and service dealership; a Statoil gas station, car wash, and convenience store; and a McDonald's fast-food restaurant. Nothing remarkable so far.

Figure 8.1: McDonald's green roof

Then, the visitor notices that the roofs of the buildings are green. A closer inspection reveals that grass and plants are growing on these roofs. Standing in Ford's parking lot, the visitor looks down at her feet that are resting on, not asphalt, but a grass-and-paver parking surface. Looking up at the Ford building, she notices solar panels on one side. Feeling hunger pangs coming on, the visitor pops into McDonald's and, about to order a Big Mac, sees an interesting addition to the usual

Figure 8.2: A grass-and-sedum roof on McDonald's absorbs rainwater that reduces storm water and helps to insulate the building in winter and keep it cool in the summer.

Figure 8.3: Porous parking lot pavers and grass planting also absorb rainwater, further reducing storm water and drainage requirements.

food list on the overhead menu display. A McGarden Burger? What's that? What's going on here?

What's going on is a collaboration among these corporations, together controlling 52,000 facilities throughout the world, that has developed a business park that uses 100 percent renewable energy, reuses 100 percent of its storm water onsite, and reuses or recycles 100 percent of its waste by-products. All the buildings, whose parts can be disassembled after their useful life, are made of either natural or recycled materials. The buildings are so energy-efficient that both their overall energy use and their electricity consumption are 60 percent less than those of a conventional design. Needs for fresh water use throughout the site have been cut by 70 percent.

HOW GREENZONE BEGAN

In 1997, the owner of a local Ford dealership, who also owned the land on which GreenZone now sits, got the idea to turn this land into a model eco-business park. This dealer approached the parent Ford Motor Company, who endorsed the idea enthusiastically. The Ford Motor Company and the local dealer then approached two other companies, Statoil and McDonald's, who agreed to take part in the venture. By April 2000, GreenZone was operational.

GreenZone's designers took a holistic, closed-cycle approach to the property's development. This means they followed the principle of nature's cycles where one component of the cycle serves as the "food" for the next. Because of this, natural cycles are said to be closed loops where almost everything is used and reused. Following this principle, virtually all the material and energy used to develop and operate GreenZone is either renewable or recyclable.

GREEN FEATURES

Site planners for GreenZone first carefully studied the appearance and conditions of the existing land. A vacant house on the site was moved to another location and is now a family home. Analysis of the land's structure and contours reduced excavation and landfill requirements. Grassy or plant areas displaced by construction were replaced elsewhere, for example, on the green roofs of the buildings. The designers and builders left existing pine trees that provided habitat for an endangered species of beetle. The builders transplanted an existing oak tree, rather than felling it.

Electricity for the buildings comes from a coastal windmill about 15 miles away. Statoil uses a wind-powered fan to ventilate its building. In the Ford building, skylights and light-pipes bring in daylight, reducing daytime electricity consumption by 60 to 70 percent. Motion sensors turn off lighting in rooms not in use. No air conditioning is necessary, since the grass-and-sedum roofs keep the buildings cool in summer. These roofs also absorb one-half the rainwater falling on them, thus reducing storm water management needs. The green roofs also provide habitat for birds and insects.

In winter, a geothermal pump helps heat the buildings. A heat recycling system captures surplus heat generated in each building and recirculates that heat through a connected system of underground pipes. For example, heat from cooking grills and deep fryers in McDonald's and heated water from the Statoil mini-mart refrigeration system are piped to a ground source heat pump that in turn redistributes the heat to all buildings in the business park. This system drastically reduces the amount of energy needed to create additional heat. Solar panels on the Ford building heat intake air, further reducing the need for energy.

Figure 8.4: Solar panels on the Ford building heat intake air, further reducing the need for energy.

All storm water is collected on the site. The grass-and-paver parking lot surface and gravel roads instead of asphalt ones absorb rainwater, reducing storm water runoff and maintaining the natural groundwater balance of the land. Small creeks and ponds collect unabsorbed water, channeling it to an onsite water garden that serves as a retention pond. In the gas station pumping area, plastic carpet under the paver surface keeps chemicals and oil from seeping into the ground.

Figure 8.5: This GreenZone car wash reuses 99 percent of its wash water, cleaned by a state-of-the-art filtration system.

Figure 8.6: Statoil's car wash uses onsite storm water drawn from this retention pond to wash cars.

Statoil's car wash uses the site's storm water for washing cars. A state-of-the-art filtration system cleans the water first, removing heavy metals and recapturing salt that is in turn dried and reused. The filtration system then refilters and recirculates up to 99 percent of the post-car wash water that is then reused to wash cars. The GreenZone car wash is the first in Sweden, possibly in the world, to receive an eco-label certification, according to the eco-park's managing director.

GreenZone uses three wastewater systems: one for showers and sink water, one for toilets, and one for water containing contaminants from cars. Vacuum toilets resembling airplane toilets only use 1¼ quarts (1.65 liters) of water and are connected to outside tanks. Sewage is converted to purified fertilizer and used for farming.

Building construction design allows for eventual deconstruction. All building parts are screwed or bolted together so these parts can be disassembled and reused. Building designers tried to choose materials with more than one function, for example, wood fiber ceilings that dampen sounds, insulate, and absorb humidity, then release this moisture when interior air is dry. All wires and cables installed in the buildings are free of halogens (chlorine and bromine) and PVC, so these wires and cables, too, can be safely reused and recycled.[4] The wood exterior sheathing for the McDonalds and Statoil buildings are not painted, since most exterior paint contains harmful volatile organic compounds,[5] but rather is treated with tar for waterproofing. The wood used in building construction comes from a nearby forest and timber company that uses sustainable forestry practices.

Instead of mechanical HVAC systems (heating, ventilating, and air conditioning), terrarium air filters clean and cool the building's interior air, add oxygen, and absorb carbon dioxide through the natural process of plant photosynthesis. Twice per hour, jets of water spray the leaves in the filter to wash contaminants into the soil where these are naturally decomposed. Fresh air enters the building through a duct buried in the ground that naturally cools the air in summer and heats it in winter. Then, the air circulates naturally through the building as a result of the temperature differential. Roof aspirators ventilate the roof structure, avoiding risk of moisture damage.

Statoil's gas station sells three types of fuels that are alternatives to petroleum-based gasoline and diesel. Statoil's mini-mart convenience store is experimenting with bulk sales and plastic packaging systems that can cut packaging waste by 90 percent. The mini-mart's food refrigeration system uses antifreeze for cooling instead of chlorofluorocarbons (CFCs).[6] Heat from the refrigerators is recaptured and piped to the other buildings. The company has almost eliminated store use of products containing PVC. This mini-mart also uses a terrarium air filter

Figure 8.7 & 8.8:
Terrarium air filters in the Ford and McDonald's buildings clean and cool interior building air.

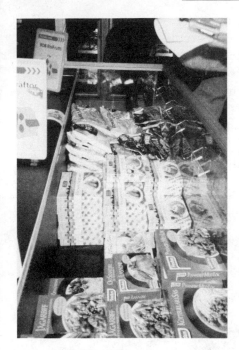

Figure 8.9: The Statoil convenience store uses antifreeze in its refrigeration system instead of ozone-depleting CFCs.

instead of an HVAC system. The store sells fresh organic vegetables and other organic and environmentally labeled products.

The McDonald's restaurant also uses a terrarium air filtration system to clean and cool interior air. Clearly marked disposal slots show customers where to recycle their various food containers. As mentioned, the menu board offers the McGarden Burger, a veggie alternative to meat burgers. Frying oil is recycled, cleaned, and reused to make cosmetics.

In the Ford car service building, a "liquid bar" recycles waste oil and fluids. The service center orders oil and antifreeze in tanks with tubes that pipe these substances directly into the car engine. Tubes also suck waste oil and fluids out of the engine so workers don't ever see or touch these substances. The service center is seeking ways to reuse the oil after cleaning, for example, as oil for lawn mowers or industrial engines. Vegetable oil, as opposed to petroleum-based oil, lubricates the hydraulic car lifts. Shelving for car parts is made of recycled wood instead of metal. Car servicing is generally considered to be a significant contributor to environmental problems. This service center is showing how it is possible to service cars within a value framework that respects nature.

Contrary to conventional practice in preparing used cars for resale, the Ford service center decided not to wash used car engines. After studying the alternatives, the service center determined that dirty engines were preferable to creating a disposal problem of chemical and oil-contaminated wastewater. This measure, since it eliminates the disposal problem of contaminated wash water, also saves money.

Figure 8.10: The GreenZone McDonald's offers a vegetarian alternative to Big Macs — the McGarden Burger.

As part of its shift toward sustainable practices, the Ford service center design assures a healthy, pleasant work environment for employees. State-of-the-art air ventilation, lighting, and electrical and magnetic field management systems were designed to create the healthiest possible employee working conditions. Tests reveal that Ford's workplace magnetic field levels are at least five times lower than the recommended minimum thresholds, according to the manager.

The service center has adopted several innovative management approaches. For example, the company has eliminated service representatives who serve as middlemen between customers and mechanics. Instead, the mechanics take care of everything. Customers walk into the auto workshop and discuss their car needs directly with the mechanics. Each customer gets the same mechanic every time.

To make sure that the design of the GreenZone business park and the shift to sustainable business practices brought about systematic, across-the-board changes, Ford, Statoil, and McDonald's used the four Natural Step system conditions for sustainability as a guiding framework. The GreenZone architects and company staff applied this framework to all aspects of site design, building design, business operations, and management practices. In doing so, the architects and companies used a whole-systems approach, rather than a one-by-one, single-issue approach to change, for example, installing energy-efficient appliances one year, and recycling more waste by-products the next year.

The three GreenZone businesses provide ongoing environmental education and Natural Step training for their employees to make sure sustainable practices are continuing. This also gives employees the opportunity to continually offer new ideas for additional improvements.

MARKET ADVANTAGE

Since occupying its new facility in GreenZone, Ford has experienced how sustainable practices create financial as well as environmental benefits. During the first year of operation in GreenZone, the dealership's car sales shot up 150 percent from its previous yearly average, and its service business revenues increased by 100 percent. In 2002, 100 percent of Ford cars

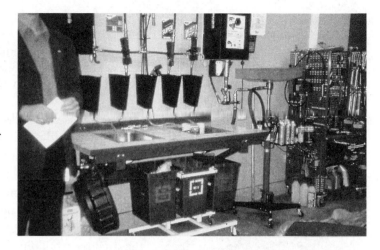

Figure 8.11: A "liquid bar" removes waste oils and fluids from cars for recycling, so workers do not need to handle or even see these substances.

Figure 8.12: Vegetable oil instead of petroleum-based oil lubricates the hydraulic car lifts.

Figure 8.13: A Natural Step system conditions poster hanging in the hall of the Ford dealership is a reminder for making sustainable practices part of everyday business.

sold were flexi-fuel cars that use either conventional or alternative fuels. Before GreenZone, Ford occupied the nineth or tenth market position in its regional market area. Now, Ford is first in its size category. Ford's GreenZone facility was the first car dealer to receive the environmental ISO 14001 certification.[7]

"THIS IS NOT ENVIRONMENTAL PHILANTHROPY, IT IS SOUND BUSINESS"

Following upon GreenZone's success, McDonald's and Statoil are discussing collaborations in similar eco-ventures internationally. The Ford Motor Company is actively pursuing green projects in both car design and building design. For example, Ford's new Rouge assembly plant in Dearborn, Michigan, contains state-of-the-art green building features, including a 500,000-square-foot green roof, solar panels, and fuel cells. Describing the Rouge plant, Bill Ford Jr., Chairman of the Board, said, "This is not environmental philanthropy; it is sound business, which, for the first time, balances the business needs of auto manufacturing with ecological and social concerns in the redesign of a brownfield site."[8]

GREENZONE AND THE CITY OF UMEÅ

The city of Umeå worked closely with GreenZone's designers and the three companies in the development of the eco-business park. Since the park treats and recycles all its own storm water and wastewater, it is not hooked into either the city's sewer system or storm water system. City planning staff had to review and issue permits for GreenZone's innovative wastewater and storm water systems. Umeå city planners and designers see GreenZone as a testing ground and learning opportunity for sustainable building and site planning practices. For example, city staffers now want to encourage grass-and-sedum roofs in future Umeå development projects. GreenZone also is providing an ongoing database of experience with various eco-practices and eco-materials for the project participants, including the city.

GreenZone is attracting national and world attention as a demonstration of sustainable development in action. Over half-a-million people visit the park every year, including Sweden's Minister of the Environment and the European Union's Environment Commissioner.

The three companies and designers of GreenZone are showing how site planning, non-residential building development, and business operations in the automobile and convenience food sectors can preserve and protect nature's resources without compromising function and comfort. They also are showing how sustainable business practices and financial gain can go hand in hand.[9]

Sånga-Säby: Green development is good for business

Sånga-Säby (Song'-ah Seh'-bih), a hotel and conference center 45 minutes outside of Stockholm, needed to expand its guest facilities to serve a growing clientele attracted to its healthy, ecologically oriented accommodations and dining. A new CEO, Mats Fack (Mahtts Fahck), who had led the company back from the brink of financial disaster using sustainability objectives as a guide, decided that the design and construction of the annex would also follow these sustainability objectives. The objectives were the four system conditions of the Natural Step.

Mats Fack and Sånga-Säby's board of directors set a goal to build the new annex as ecologically as possible and wrote both this goal and requirements to implement it into the building's construction specifications. As one example, the construction contract required the builder to forfeit US$12,000 for every tree he cut down.

GREEN FEATURES

The building's designers located and constructed the building to achieve maximum solar exposure. Solar power heats the buildings from March through October. During the rest of the year, geothermal pumps partially heat the building, supplemented by hydroelectricity to boost the temperature from the geothermal level to room temperature. The designers placed heating pipes under the floor, reducing heat and power needs by two degrees.

Grass-and-sedum roofs also help cool the rooms in summer, eliminating the need for air conditioning. In winter, these roofs provide insulation. Walls are further insulated with recycled glass fiber. All building materials were bought from ISO 14001 environmentally certified companies.[10]

Figure 8.14: Sånga-Säby's new annex was built with the least possible disturbance to the existing site and vegetation. A clause in the construction contract required the builder to forfeit US$12,000 for every tree he cut down.

Mats Fack and the Sånga-Säby board of directors set another goal for the annex construction: to make guest rooms that were luxurious as well as healthy. They picked furniture that was labeled acceptable by the Swedish Association of Persons with Allergies. They did not buy IKEA furniture even though some IKEA products are environmentally labeled. IKEA beds last for 3 years; Sånga-Säby's beds will last for 20 years, according to Mats Fack. These beds are made from all-natural materials; hence they contain no chemicals. Mattresses are stuffed with horsehair carefully washed to remove allergens. Instead of having a polyurethane finish, the wooden floors are oiled once or twice a year, and floor scratches are removed with sandpaper.

EDUCATING THE SUPPLIERS

Mats Fack also used the construction of the Sånga-Säby annex to teach the building and supply companies "how to make hotels in the 21st century." Often, contractors and suppliers said it would be impossible to provide Sånga-Säby with products that met the hotel's high standards of sustainability. Also, suppliers often were not aware of the toxic substances used in their product preparation. When Sånga-Säby demanded in its building proposal request that eco-labeled wood be used in building the annex, nine responding construction companies said they didn't know what this product was. These companies then went to their lumber suppliers and discovered these suppliers didn't know what the specification meant either. Finally, one contractor returned after doing some research and agreed to provide wood from certified forests, but at a US$10,000 higher price. Sånga-Säby agreed. The considerable publicity in the building industry

Figure 8.15: Mats Fack, Sånga-Säby's CEO, points out the chemical-free and allergen-free features of a guest room in the new annex.

about this process began to establish provision of eco-labeled wood as a competitive factor for suppliers, according to Mats Fack. Forestry companies began to see that they needed eco-certification in order to meet a growing demand for this product.

Prior to ordering leather furniture for the common sitting areas, Mats Fack asked the furniture company whether the leather was tanned with chromium — the conventional tanning agent that is toxic — or with vegetable oil. The furniture supplier did not know. Mats Fack said, find out. When it turned out chromium was indeed used as the tanning agent, Mats Fack called the furniture supplier's CEO and said that the leather must be prepared with vegetable oil instead of chromium. The head of the furniture company said this would be much more expensive. Mats Fack proposed that Sånga-Säby would pay a somewhat higher price for the leather furniture, pointing out that, in producing non-toxic, vegetable oil-tanned leather furniture, the furniture supplier would have a product on the market that no other firm offers. The deal was cut.

MARKET ADVANTAGE OF GOING GREEN

Sånga-Säby's ecologically sound purchasing and building decisions for the annex construction, as well as changes to more sustainable hotel practices, did cost more — about 20 percent higher than the costs of conventional construction and supplies. Given the dire financial straits of the company when Mats Fack first became the CEO, it is not surprising that some people in the company initially were skeptical about this investment. Today, however, Sånga-Säby is one of the most profitable and successful hotel and conference centers in Sweden. Many organizations that formerly scheduled conferences and retreats elsewhere have switched their locations to Sånga-Säby. The healthy, chemical-free, allergen-free guest rooms have attracted the attention of the growing sector of Swedish society with allergies — about 20 percent of Sweden's population, according to some estimates. Organizations such as the Swedish Association of Persons with Allergies now gather primarily at Sånga-Säby. High occupancy rates, increased room charges, and lower maintenance and operating costs have more than offset the higher initial costs of buying and building ecologically. Sånga-Säby demonstrates how green development is good for business.[11] For more about Sånga-Säby's transformation to sustainable practices, see Chapter 16.

Figure 8.16: Sånga-Säby insisted that its furniture supplier use leather tanned with vegetable oil instead of the customary (and toxic) tanning agent chromium.

Small businesses do well by doing green

It's not just big businesses that can do well by doing green. Small businesses are springing up to fill eco-niches — market opportunities created by the growing customer base demanding products and services that are benign to the environment and healthy for people. Some businesses, such as the Bölebyn Tannery, have been doing this from the start. This section describes three different types of small businesses in northern Sweden that are doing well by doing green.

THE BÖLEBYNS GARVERI TANNERY: TANNING LEATHER THE NATURAL WAY

Figure 8.17: The Bölebyns Garveri Tannery tans leather the natural way through a process more than 5,000 years old.

In northern Sweden, in the town of Piteå (Pee'-the-aw), a three-generation family business tans leather using a process more than 5,000 years old. Using a combination of spruce bark and water, the Bölebyn Garveri (Beuh'-leh-been Garr-veh-ree') company tans cow and ox hides, then fashions attractive bags, shoes, and other products from this leather. These products are as healthy to wear as they are beautiful. In old times, people with skin diseases would come by the tannery and their skin would improve, according to Inger Sandlund, who, together with her husband Jan, owns the Bölebyns Garveri business. Jan is also the granddaughter of Bölebyn's founder. The bark-and-water process was the traditional method used by craftspeople to tan leather until 1920, when chemicals arrived on the scene. As Inger Sandlund says, the old-fashioned way is turning out to be the ecological way.

"A conventional leather shoe is a monstrous hybrid."
— William McDonough & Michael Braungart[12]

Currently, almost all the leather in the world is tanned with chromium. Many tannery workers get sick, says Inger Sandlund. For example, she says, in some countries, workers put their feet in chromium tanning vats during the tanning process, and in Italy, tanneries near Florence have destroyed drinking water to a depth of 150 feet. Every time someone throws out shoes, they throw out chromium.[13]

How a natural tanning process works

The Bölebyns tannery purchases cow and ox hides for less than US$1 apiece from local farmers. First, tannery workers salt the hides to preserve them. When 25 hides are salted, these are placed with water in a large, slowly revolving drum for one month to remove hair and other material. Next, the hides soak in vats of water and bark for four months. Workers stir the vats every day. Tannic acid in the bark is the tanning agent. After two months of soaking, when all the bark's tannic acid is gone, fresh bark replaces the old, and the used bark goes to the compost bin.

Next, hides hang in another vat of water and bark, where they take on the bark's color. Then hides are nailed onto stretching racks for a month.

The tannery uses a rotation schedule as hides go through the tanning process, so there are hides always ready for leather craftspeople to make shoes, bags, and other goods. The tannery needs to use only about 55 pounds of spruce bark every year. Although workers periodically top off vats with water, the vat water hasn't been changed since 1918. This entire operation takes place in a workroom area less than 1,000 square feet.

Jan and Inger Sundland took over the business in 1987 and now work with two employees. When Inger's grandfather founded the tannery in 1900, the business used the leather only to make shoes. Now, Bölebyns Garveri makes briefcases and 200 other leather products. Briefcases carry a fifteen-year guarantee.

Figure 8.18: Hides and water revolve in this drum for one month to remove hair.

Figure 8.19: Bölebyn's beautiful and healthy leather products appeal to a growing clientele who prefer chemical-free, breathable leather next to their skin.

Healthy for people; healthy for business

The bark-and-water process can tan between 150 to 170 hides per year. A modern factory using chemicals can tan several hundred thousand hides per year, since chromium tans hides in only 24 hours. While the ecological tanning process is unlikely to become a mass production process, there is growing customer demand for higher quality leather products that are free of

Figure 8.20: A local worker assembles heat pumps that reduce home heating requirements at the NaturVärme company.
Figure 8.21: Besides vistas of green farmland, Värmland County features a growing regional green business economy.

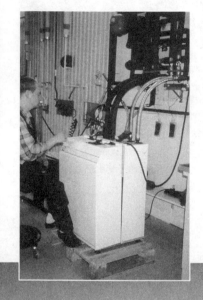

toxins and that breathe. Naturally tanned leather shoes cost about US$40 to $50 more than conventional, chemically tanned leather shoes, but these shoes can last for 20 years, says Inger Sandlund. Two other tanneries in Sweden tan leather with vegetable oil.

With a leather goods boutique now flourishing in a fashionable section of Stockholm, Bölebyns Garveri shows that an old-fashioned way of doing business and an ecological way of doing business can also be a profitable way of doing business.[14]

NATURVÄRME: GREEN HOME HEATING IS GOOD BUSINESS

In the small village of Junosuando (Yeu-nuh-suh-ahn'doh) in the town of Pajala, a local citizen won the Swedish lottery. While some winners might have pocketed their earnings and headed for a South Sea island, this citizen, who was also the village school's gym teacher, quit his job and invested those earnings in starting a local eco-enterprise. This business, called NaturVärme, builds and sells home heat pumps that use geothermal heat to reduce home energy requirements. A home heat pump system costs about US$7,000. According to NaturVärme's owner, a heat pump installed in a 2,100-square-foot home can pay for itself in three or four years.

NaturVärme now sells its heat pumps to customers in Norway and Finland as well as Sweden. The company runs an education center to train local youth, prospective assembly workers, and salespeople. The company also plans to expand this facility as an energy education center. Here, local residents and business people can view different types of renewable energy technology such as solar panels and subfloor heating design, also reducing home energy needs.

NaturVärme now employs 12 local workers. In a village of 450 people, this is a big boost to the local economy. The NaturVärme company is one of many eco-enterprises that blossomed during the eco-revitalization journeys of villages in Pajala and Kalix. For more about Pajala and Kalix village eco-revitalization, see Chapter 9.

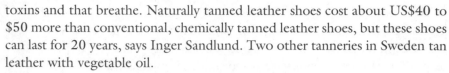

Environmental Action Värmland: A county boosts regional green business

About 150 miles west of Stockholm, a county government is helping businesses and municipalities to go green. Värmland (Vehrm'lahnd) County, home to Alfred Nobel, founder of the Nobel Prize, has set a goal to become a sustainable county. Its slogan is "Sustainable development through the market."

One County sustainable development initiative is called GreenMarket. Through GreenMarket, the County helps businesses and organizations in three ways: developing, buying, and selling environmentally friendly products, making buildings and operations more energy-efficient, and educating businesses about the global importance, as well as benefits, of sustainable business practices.

Värmland County also provides targeted business assistance in material technology, marketing, environmental management, patents, database searches, and eco-design of new or existing products. The County helps companies understand and apply life cycle analyses to product design. This in turn helps qualify company products for environmental certification and labeling, providing a greater market advantage. For more information about life cycle analysis, see Chapter 7.

To inform municipalities about available environmentally friendly products, and to help develop markets for those products, the County has developed a green purchasing manual for all municipalities within its jurisdiction. The County put together a green product development program for small businesses, inviting these enterprises to participate in a training and technical assistance program. The first phase of this program was an orientation session about sustainable business for the new millenium. Next, working as facilitators, county staffers helped these companies envision future sustainable possibilities for their business. Next, the County provided funding, through a combination of grants, enabling businesses to hire technical consultants to evaluate specific ideas generated in the brainstorming sessions. Through this program's assistance, the first seventeen participating businesses were able to significantly reduce their energy and materials use that in turn reduced costs. Participating businesses in the county program included a linen manufacturer, a pen and marker manufacturer, a heat pump company, a hardwood processing company, a battery regeneration business, and an electric sign manufacturer.

Värmland County teamed up with the University of Lund to help spur entirely new green product development. A basic premise was to design

"If environmental work is to catch on, it must be profitable." — Fredrik Jonsson, Environmental Action, Värmland County

Figure 8.22: The town of Degerfors has assisted this paint store and other eco-businesses by renovating vacant mill buildings and leasing space at affordable rates.

Figure 8.23: This paint store sells interior paints derived from eggs instead of petroleum, responding to the growing market of consumers demanding healthy, chemical-free living and work environments.

products from a problem-solving starting point. County and University project leaders realized that many inventors have ideas for new products, but they often are not clear what problem their invention is trying to solve. In this program, project facilitators identified some problems, then presented these to three groups of inventors. Over the next three weeks, the inventors generated almost 1,000 product ideas to solve those problems. Next, the program examined ways to connect problems with people eager to solve those problems. The County and University organized forums that brought organizations with problems — companies, manufacturers, policy-makers — together with inventors eager to find solutions.

As one result of the county's GreenMarket initiative, regional market sales of high-efficiency, environmentally friendly appliances shot up 25 percent in three months and have since increased steadily.

Värmland County also sponsors eco-product competitions. The most eco-friendly product wins orders from companies who band together for joint purchasing, issuing a single product specification. In another effort, the County worked with a group of businesses that use insulation in their operations, helping these enterprises write up specifications for environmentally benign insulation, then prepare advertisements and a request for proposals to supply the most eco-friendly product. The County ran a similar competition for solar heating systems that involved demonstrating and testing different household solar energy systems. The best-running system was then marketed as a well-tested and demonstrated home heating product.

Environmental Action Värmland is a partnership among the Värmland County Council, the County Administrative Board, the regional Chamber of Commerce, the Swedish Association of Local Authorities, and a private company called ALMI. This County initiative receives funding from the municipality association and the European Union.[15]

One Värmland County business that has found an eco-niche is the paint store, shown in Figures 8.22 and 8.23, located in the city of Degerfors. This enterprise has developed a line of interior house paints derived from eggs instead of petroleum. These paints, emitting no VOCs (volatile organic compounds), are healthier than conventional petroleum-based paint that does emit these toxic off-gases.[16] The market for egg-based paint is growing steadily, as consumers come to understand the importance of alternatives to VOC-emitting paint products. The paint store occupies space in a former mill building acquired and renovated by the city of Degerfors as part of the town's economic development program.

For more about the town of Degerfors, see Chapter 5.

Figure 8.24: This traditional method of fence construction is one of many historical building techniques being preserved by the Center for Building Preservation in Eksjö.

Figure 8.25: This building demonstrates the traditional Swedish building method of corner timber construction.

"A timeless way of building" [17]

In the municipality of Eksjö (Eh'k-sheu), in the Highland region of southern Sweden, a non-profit organization is working to safeguard the knowledge of traditional Swedish building techniques. Eksjö helped to found the Center for Building Preservation in 1995 to show how to better care for historic buildings, and to make sure that traditional Swedish building practices, formerly passed down from generation to generation, are not lost to future generations.

The Center offers training programs in historic wooden building techniques, such as the corner timber construction method. Most of the Swedish artisans who understand and use this building technique are now in their 80s. Through preserving and reteaching this building technique, the Center helps assure that young artisans will understand and carry on this construction approach that creates particularly strong, stable, and lasting building frames. The Center's courses also combine modern building techniques with historic building and construction approaches.

The Center's training for architecture students and craftspeople combines theory and practice. Carpenters with 30 years' experience study and work alongside high school girls and boys. A learning objective is to see, rather than memorize, building techniques. Students learn how to balance traditional building methods with modern needs, combining the new and the old to achieve the best of both.

A Center slogan is: "Looking for the forgotten past in the development of the future." Building design and construction in Sweden has deteriorated, says the Center's director. He believes historic preservation can be a source for the rebirth and development of quality and ecological practices in contemporary building. He describes a new trend of intimate architecture where new buildings are influenced by the culture of the old. He gives an example of how the historical way was a sustainable way: Swedish homebuilders in times past would plant trees so that their children would have enough wood to build their houses when they were ready to start families.

The Center also works with recent immigrants to Sweden who bring knowledge and skills in traditional building design and construction techniques from their own countries. The Center also works with builders in other countries. For example, a Center course on corner timber construction will take place in Russia, where upkeep and restoration of historic houses has been neglected for many years. Russian people are proud of their heritage even though it has been neglected, says the Center's director. To solve this problem, he observes, one must combine appropriate modernization techniques with the traditional approach. The Center will teach Russian builders how to merge appropriate modernizing methods with historic techniques such as corner timbering.

Eksjö's Center for Building Preservation works cooperatively with the Royal Stockholm School of Architecture and the Chalmers National Technical School in Göteborg to teach courses in traditional building, design, and preservation techniques. One such course involved architecture students in an exercise where they designed and constructed interior spaces for eating, sleeping, and bathing, using natural building materials, all within a giant box of about 300 square feet.

The Center itself is situated in a historic Palladian-style house and farm formerly owned by an 18th-century Eksjö mayor. Visitors and students can study exhibits of historic wallpaper and view and purchase items at the Center's historic building materials shop.[18] For more about Eksjö and its sustainable development work, see Chapter 12.

"Looking for the forgotten past in the development of the future."
— The Center for Building Preservation, Eksjö

North American examples

Businesses large and small throughout North America also are switching to ecological practices and green building development. Ford's new Rouge assembly plant in Dearborn, Michigan, mentioned earlier, will feature an ecological roof of 500,000 square feet that will absorb several inches of rainfall and cut down on a corresponding amount of storm water. Storm water will be reduced further through using porous paving for parking lot surfaces. A conventionally designed storm water system for the site would cost US$48 million to develop, according to Rouge's architect, Bill McDonough. Instead, he describes a plant-based storm water system costing US$13 million that will save the company US$35 million in development costs. Solar panels and fuel cells will reduce the Rouge plant's fossil fuel energy use. Plants will help shade and cool the building, further cutting down on energy needs for air conditioning. Ford has taken steps to reduce hazardous substances in its car production process, eliminating chromium from car paint and removing mercury switches and PCB transformers. Ford also has begun a waste reduction initiative that has cut in half the waste stream of at least one of its plants three years after the program start. At Ford's St. Thomas assembly plant in Ontario, the company has replaced disposable packaging with returnable containers, has increased metal scrap recovery, and has installed recycling stations along the assembly line.[19]

As another example, Guilford of Maine and its parent company, Interface, Inc., have systematically overhauled production and buildings in ecological directions. Guilford, the largest producer of interior office fabrics in North America, has switched the fuel source of its entire Maine plant heating system from oil to wood chips. The wood chips come from a nearby tongue depressor manufacturing company, which otherwise would send hundreds of tons of wood by-products to the municipal landfill. Interface, which used the Natural Step system conditions to guide its transition to sustainable practices, has declared its intent to become a zero-waste producer. As one of the largest carpet manufacturers in the world, Interface's goal is to lease carpets, not sell them, to its customers. Interface will replace worn-out carpets, and recycle and reuse the worn-out material.[20]

Small U.S. businesses also are switching to ecological practices. For example, a tiny dry-cleaning business in Arlington, Massachussetts, offers its customers an alternative to the conventional dry-cleaning method using perchloroethylene, a known carcinogen. Utopia Cleaners, assisted through the Massachusetts Toxics Reduction Institute, cleans clothes effectively through a natural enzyme-based wet dry-cleaning method using no hazardous substances.

Municipalities and states across North America also are encouraging businesses and developers, as well as their own public buildings, to adopt green building practices. New York, Pennsylvania, and California have adopted incentive programs such as tax credits for green building, or green building requirements for all new state buildings and facilities. New York City has developed green high performance building guidelines for all new capital construction in the city. Scottsdale, Arizona, encourages green building through a package of strategies that include fast-track permit review for green design proposals, green building certification by independent inspections, and promotion of green builders and designers. Scottsdale also uses a systematic approach to encouraging development of green building standards through applying a life cycle analysis approach to construction, energy, and resource use in the city. Arlington County, Virginia, offers density incentives for green buildings that are certified to standards developed by the U.S. Green Building Council.[21]

CHAPTER 9

Journeys to Self-sufficiency: Community Eco-economic Development

> *In a sustainable society, human needs are met fairly and efficiently, and basic needs are met first before provision of luxuries.*
>
> — Based upon System Condition #4 of the Natural Step framework

Why is self-sufficiency important?

Self-sufficiency is critical for a community to be sustainable, be it a small village, medium-sized town, large city, or a region. The ability to meet community needs for food, water, affordable housing, jobs and means of livelihood, goods and services, energy, and mobility is essential for the survival and well-being of a community over time.

Consider what can happen when a community is not able to provide for itself in one or more of these areas. For example, what happens when a community is not able to provide its own water? Water then must be brought in from away, and probably needs to be paid for. The community then becomes dependent upon both the water provider and the delivery system, rendering itself vulnerable to the needs and wishes of the water provider, to the safety and working condition of the delivery system, and to the cost-setting policies of the provider. The degree to which a community cannot provide for itself, and where its households cannot meet basic needs is the degree to which that community is vulnerable to "hitting the walls of the funnel," described in Part I. If a crisis were to occur in the supply of essential services or goods from away — food, energy, or water, for example — the households, businesses, and institutions of that community would quickly also find themselves in a crisis. If this seems like a farfetched notion to those of us living in the bountiful United States, all we need do is recall the events and effects of the California energy crisis of 2001.

The same principle holds true in a local economy of jobs, businesses, commerce, and income generation. When people are not able to find jobs or a means of supporting themselves in their own town or city, several things can happen. People may either move away to other places to find work, leaving behind a smaller work force, diminished purchasing power, and reduced tax base and population base. Residents may commute to jobs outside of the city or town, contributing to, among other things, traffic congestion and sprawl. People may remain in the community but, unable to find work, they then may not be able to provide food or shelter for their households.

A less drastic but subtler version of this syndrome can be observed when businesses from away locate in the community. To be sure, jobs are provided, wages are paid, business revenues are generated, but where are these going? Many times the jobs go not necessarily to people already living in the community but to people from outside, either brought in by the business when it locates there, or else filled by commuters from away. It cannot be guaranteed, therefore, that wages paid will be spent in the local community. When the business headquarters are located away, then the revenues generated locally also may leave the community. More business revenue generated locally flows back to corporate headquarters, while less revenue recirculates in the community, supporting other activities in the local economy. The vulnerability of a community to this situation becomes most evident when one or more large companies dominate the local business scene. What happens if and when one such company picks up and leaves for a perceived better location? The unemployed people left behind, the loss of revenue for other businesses, the chunk cut out of the local tax base, and the spiraling financial losses from these effects all too often sadly testify to the vulnerability of communities dependent upon a few large businesses.

This is not to suggest that communities are, or should be, islands of economic and social isolation, completely separate from their surrounding region or neighboring cities or towns. Such a scenario is neither realistic nor desirable. It does suggest that when communities can better provide for their own essential needs such as food, water, affordable shelter, energy, means of livelihood, mobility, and key goods and services, they will reduce their vulnerability to crises of others over which they have little or no control.

Another important dimension of a sustainable community is expressed in the sustainability objective listed at the beginning of this chapter. This is the dimension of fairness and justice for everyone. A local society cannot be sustainable if the basic human rights or means to fulfill basic human needs are denied to certain members of that society. This has functional as well as ethical implications. Precluding certain community members from the means and rights to fulfill basic human needs will compromise that community's ability to preserve the environment and the stability of its social structure. The world situation since September 11, 2001, is a global testimonial to this principle. The riots in United States cities following the assassination of Dr. Martin Luther King in April 1968 were a local testimonial.

In learning about the successful journeys to self-sufficiency of the Kalix and Kangos villages in northern Sweden, we can see how a community might support or begin its own journey to sustainability. Next, the journey of the Sámi people in northern Sweden shows how an indigenous minority is working to preserve their basic human rights, economic rights, and their culture, and how some municipalities are offering their support.

Joining together: The villages of Kalix

ABOUT KALIX AND ITS VILLAGES

Nestled in the northern region of Sweden just below the Arctic Circle, far from centers of jobs and commerce, are 18 small villages within the municipality of Kalix (Kah'-lix). Only 350 people altogether live in these eighteen villages. While 18,000 residents live within the municipal boundaries of Kalix, most live in, or near, the town's downtown center, about 15 miles from the 18 villages.

Kalix's jurisdiction covers a geographic area just under 700 square miles, roughly equivalent to that of metropolitan Stockholm. Famous for its slow-growing pinewood forests, considered to be one of Sweden's finest raw materials, it is not surprising that wood processing and wood technology are important industries in Kalix. The town also is a center for electronic, mechanical, and communications businesses, most of which are located in, or near, the downtown center.

While downtown Kalix experienced economic prosperity during the 1970s and 1980s, the town's outlying villages and hamlets were losing population, as young people moved into downtown and other urban centers in search of higher-paying work. Remaining village residents had trouble finding work or means to put food on the table for their families. The one local store was in danger of closing. School population was dwindling. The municipal government was considering closing the villages' only school. The future for the villages seemed bleak.

FIRST STEP OF THE JOURNEY

In the late 1990s, a revitalization effort brought together inhabitants from all 18 villages to find ways that would strengthen economic and social self-sufficiency in ways that were also ecologically sound. As a first step, a flier was sent out to all inhabitants, calling for a community meeting to discuss the situation and what alternatives might be possible. At this meeting it became clear that, if all the villages banded together, they would be able to accomplish more. Not long after this meeting, inhabitants of the villages formed an association called Övre Bygd (Oeh'vreh Bigd). The association raised funds to hire one employee, who was also a village resident.

THE RESULTS

A group of villagers joined to save the general store, which by that time had closed. Small groups formed to investigate alternatives, then got back together to discuss these ideas. The decision was made to raise funds and apply for a small government grant for the Övre Bygd village association to purchase and run the store as a cooperative venture.

The store now is the social, economic, and public information center for all 18 villages. It is the shopping center, fuel center, and telecommunications center where villagers can come to use a computer, the Internet, and a fax machine at any time. People can come to drink coffee, buy a pizza at the store, heat it up in the microwave oven, eat in the store's social area, and read the newspapers. Rotating books are available from the Kalix library. Övre Bygd hires village residents to work in the store. A balance is sought between paying people to work for the store and finding volunteers. Too many paid employees can discourage needed volunteers, says the Övre Bygd chairman, adding that it also is challenging to have 18 different villages with 18 different opinions.

Figure 9.1: The Kalix village association chairman points out the villages of Kalix on a painting at the general store.

A village initiative to provide services to elder residents also developed. A group of villagers started a cooperative service to make it possible for elder residents to continue living at home. When elder citizens remain in the community, the villages benefit economically from their continued presence.

Services for elder citizens include grasscutting and food purchasing. The village cooperative contracted with the Kalix municipal government to provide elder services instead of through the municipality. The cooperative bills the municipality for services rendered. (In Sweden, municipalities are responsible for eldercare provision). Existing villagers are hired to provide the elder services. Elders can call up the store for food and supplies; service workers will deliver it. If the elders live more than half a mile from the store, they pay a small fee.

Figure 9.2: This general store, run by the Kalix village association, is the economic, social, and cultural center for 18 rural villages.

Another casualty of the dwindling population of the villages was a threatened loss of village recycling pickup by the municipality's recycling contractor. The recycling contractor said it was not cost-effective to keep the villages on its pickup route because they often found village recycling bins to be empty. This meant that residents of all 18 villages would have to individually drive their cans, bottles, glass, and paper to the downtown center of Kalix 15 miles away, a waste of time and fuel. A group of villagers in the association got together to discuss what could be done. They made a cost-effective proposal to the recycling contractor: the village association would place a central recycling center at the store on behalf of all 18 villages and call the company for pickup when the recycling bins were full. The village cooperative does not get paid for recyclables, but neither does it have to pay for disposal costs.

As villagers came to understand better the relationship of local actions to global trends and what sustainability meant, they become more and more interested in taking action in this direction. For example, it became clear to recycling organizers that it was not enough just to tell residents where to place the glass, metal, and paper. It did help to explain how much damage humans have done to the earth in just a few seconds of its existence and why recycling is important to reversing this damage. As residents came to see this, village recycling rates shot up.

Understanding the relationship of local actions to global trends got local residents to take action themselves.

To create more paid work throughout the villages, the village association bought and rehabilitated an old railroad station, planning to rent space to a company that will create five or six local jobs — a significant economic impact in a community of 350 people. The association is also investigating long-distance work opportunities through telecommuting.[1]

THE ECO-CHAPEL OF SIKNÄS VILLAGE

In the southern region of Kalix, the 175 inhabitants of Siknäs (Seek'-nehs) village got together to discuss alternative futures. During this discussion, attention focused on the village chapel that had become rundown, with no apparent resources to restore it. Villagers decided to make the chapel's renovation part of their futures project. As a first step, they approached the parent church, a local sports organization, and the Siknäs Framtid (Seek'-nehs Frahmm-teed) — the Future of Siknäs association. To raise funds, villagers contacted former residents, asking for their support to rehabilitate the chapel. Next, they organized an employment training program, obtaining county government funding to hire and instruct carpenters in techniques for ecological building. They chose recycled materials for building rehabilitation where possible. Siknäs village residents contributed over 5,000 hours of volunteer labor to help restore the chapel, completing an estimated US$200,000 renovation project for about US$125,000.

Figure 9.3: Kalix villagers are renovating this former railroad station to rent to a new company that will create new jobs for villagers.

On January 1, 2000, 110 people attended a three-course celebration dinner to celebrate the chapel's reopening. By late summer 2001, the villagers had reduced the outstanding debt on the project to about US$13,000.

Kangos village eco-revitalization: "Cooperation pays"

ABOUT KANGOS

The small village of Kangos, 140 households with 330 inhabitants, is located within the municipality of Pajala in northeast Sweden, about 100 miles north of the Arctic Circle. The reader learned about Kangos's low-tech solar energy project in Chapter 5. Here is the rest of the story.

Pajala is a two-hour plane trip north from Stockholm, located close to the border of Sweden and Finland. It is a multilingual community, where Swedish, Finnish, and Sámi are spoken. The region, once famous for its iron industry that has long since past, now is known for its beautiful rivers, forests, and mountains that attract tourists, fishermen, and hunters. Winter visitors come to Pajala to participate in its Northern Lights festival, and summer visitors take part in its Salmon Festival and Grayling Day, featured as the world's longest fishing contest. Autumn brings more visitors for arts and cultural festivities.

Like the Kalix villages, Kangos village is far from the main population and job centers of its municipality — about a 40-mile drive. As in the Kalix villages, the future of the Kangos village appeared bleak for its residents. Young people were leaving for urban center life and jobs. People left behind could not find work. School enrollment was declining. As in Kalix, local authorities were threatening to close the village school and the local post office.

"Who decides our future?"

THE FIRST STEPS

At the same time, however, villagers had become involved in local discussion groups to learn about sustainable development and how the village might move in this direction. Inspired by the 1992 Rio Summit, two Kangos villagers began these group get-togethers that continued throughout the 1990s. Discussions focused on ways to reduce use of resources, increase recycling, and convert to renewable energy sources. Groups began to work cooperatively with local businesses toward these objectives and also toward a regional goal of greater county economic and social self-sufficiency. "Who decides our future?" became a rallying cry. In the late 1990s, these efforts blossomed into a full-scale initiative to chart a new course for the village's future. The village of Kangos became part of an alternative futures project, assisted by a university, a sustainability process leader, Torbjörn Lahti, and funding from the European Union. Kangos's goal for participating in this project was

Figure 9.4: Kangos villagers now run this village school, almost closed by local authorities because of declining enrollment.

nothing short of becoming the first ecologically, economically, and socially sustainable village in Europe.

THE OUTCOMES

Today, Kangos is a thriving village where an astonishing 40 to 50 enterprises have developed within its tiny 140-household community. About 60 children attend its local school in grades 1 to 9. In the village is a local general store, daycare center, assisted living housing, a nursing home, a folklore museum, and a church. A new road to the village from the nearby Junosuando village promises to bring more commerce and opportunities. Kangos residents put together a village sustainable development plan that lists 2,000 goals and objectives. The motto of this plan is "Cooperation pays." County officials took notice of what was going on in the tiny village of Kangos, in 2001 choosing it as the Village of the Year in Norbotten County.

Over the last ten years, villagers have developed a remarkable series of projects to implement their sustainable development plan, bringing the village closer to its goal of ecological, economic, and social sustainability. Here are a few of those projects.

> **Developing a multi-generational all-activity house:** Village residents volunteered 17,000 hours of labor to develop this house, opened in 1994, that includes an assisted living facility and activities for children and youths. The elders turn out to observe and take part in the young people's events and games. The young people get to know and appreciate the village elders. To fund the construction, the village borrowed over US$800,000. The project was completed US$125,000 under budget.
> **Creating a cultural and ecological school:** When public officials threatened to close Kangos's only school, villagers rallied to save it. They were able to reorganize the school and to design and manage the curriculum, teacher hiring, and administration, while still obtaining public funding. In 1993, the new school opened. Classes now incorporate ecological learning and practices. The school has become the village's cultural center for plays and performances. Villagers are also in charge of maintaining the school building. In 2000, when the school's roof needed replacement at an estimated cost of US$40,000, village residents chipped in and helped install it. This brought down the cost to US$25,000. For more about Kangos's ecological school and curriculum, see Chapter 10.
> **Developing jobs and employment training:** Kangos now operates an employment training center, training workers for the heat pump and

solar energy industries. A plan is to turn a local hotel/recreation center into an energy demonstration center to show homeowners, schools, and companies how to heat and obtain power while reducing fossil fuel use.

Developing animal husbandry: Around 1999, some Kangos villagers decided to raise animals cooperatively as a means toward greater village self-sufficiency. This idea blossomed from the plant cultivation work underway by village children. Keeping animals was seen as a natural continuation of the children's activities. A survey was sent out to all village residents to find out how many would participate in a sheep cooperative. Ten families said yes. In the fall of 2000, the village cooperative purchased 12 ewes. By the summer of 2001, this flock had grown to 30 sheep. One family takes care of the animals in the winter. The remaining families care for them during the summer. The children card the wool and make warm innersoles to sell, learning about business enterprise in the process. Another purpose of the project was to reintroduce children to animals, teaching them about life cycles and respect for animals. The cooperative uses and breeds a type of sheep that is on the brink of extinction, helping to preserve this species. Another benefit: the sheep also keep the landscape as open fields. This project made it clear to Kangos, the county government, and other villages that local enterprise development and greater community self-sufficiency could really happen.

"Cooperation pays."

Supporting the fishing industry: Kangos villagers have always seen fishing as a major component of local food production. The village has developed a long-term ecological fish management plan, inventorying certain lakes in order to seed fish for tourists according to the ecology of the lakes. The Kangos Lax (Salmon) Festival takes place every July.

Reducing waste; increasing recycling: In late spring of 2001, villagers began a project to reduce household waste and find new ways to recycle. These villagers connected with groups in Finland, Norway, and Scotland that were working on similar efforts. Villagers formed groups to train local recycling experts and explore ways to safely compost human waste and recycle sewage.

Recapturing the post office: Officials had threatened to close Kangos's post office, saying it was no longer cost-effective to operate the facility. Villagers approached the officials and worked out an arrangement where mailboxes and postal services would be offered at the local general store. Postal officials agreed, and Kangos was able to retain mail service for its 140 households.

Figure 9.5: Sámi people live in these wooden tepees during the summer months when they herd their reindeer to summer feeding grounds.

Figure 9.6: Sámi women cook a meal of reindeer meat and flatbread over fires inside a tepee.

Preserving self-sufficiency and identity: Journey of the Sámi people

North of the Arctic Circle, a group of 11 Sámi (Sah'my) families of about 100 people tend and herd their reindeer in their summer camp at Suksivaara (Seuk'sih-vah'-rah) in the municipality of Pajala. These families, called the Muonio Sámi (Mooh-oh'-nioh Sah'my) community, live and cook meals inside cloth, skin, or wooden tepees while their reindeer forage for herbs and certain hardy grasses. This natural diet is critical to the health of the reindeer and the quality of their meat, say the Sámi, who avoid using prepared feed for their herds unless absolutely necessary. In the winter, Sámi herd their reindeer to a forest region some distance away. In winter, reindeer are more easily able to dig for lichens through the softer snow under forest trees than in the hard-packed, ice-covered tundra snow. The ability to move reindeer from summer to winter feeding grounds is critical to reindeer survival, and hence to the Sámi way of life. Reindeer meat is the main staple of their diet, and their clothes, shoes, and boots are made from reindeer hides. Families run reindeer-related businesses, such as a slaughterhouse, a leather-working business, artisan crafts using reindeer horns, and a horn export business to Japanese and other Far East customers who grind the horns into potions.

The Sámi, the indigenous people of northern Sweden, Norway, Finland, and Russia, are said to be the last indigenous people of Western Europe. Since prehistoric times they have inhabited the northern regions of these countries, called Lappland by Swedes and Westerners, and called Sápmi (Sahpp'my) by the Sámi people. Altogether, about 62,000 Sámi still inhabit these lands. Almost three-fourths of the 20,000 Sámi in Sweden live in the north. Rock paintings, burial pits, and reindeer trapping hollows chronicle Sámi culture and reindeer-centered life back to 6,000 years ago.[3] The Sámi have their own language, also called Sámi, that stems from an entirely different language group than the languages of the countries in which they reside. From the late 1800s to the 1950s, Swedish schools forbade teaching or speaking the Sámi language, requiring Sámi children to speak only Swedish. Because of this, the survival of the Sámi's language, as well as much of their traditional culture, is in jeopardy.

Figure 9.7: Reindeer, now semi-domesticated, are the center of Sámi economic, social, and cultural life.

Sámi reindeer husbandry has always been an environmentally friendly and sustainable practice. Unlike cattle, reindeer do not eat everything in sight, but forage in the forest and tundra, eating particular lichens, plants, and grasses, but not others. Reindeer and the Sámi people are a part of the northern taiga ecosystem, also known as the boreal forest region, stretching from Russia across Finland, Sweden, Norway, and formerly to the Scottish Highlands.

Sámi reindeer husbandry, woven into their social and economic lives, is struggling with two competing resources. First, one of Sweden's major industries, timber, has a strong foothold in the north country. This industry, which does not always practice sustainable forest stewardship, often clearcuts sections that alter the forest ecosystem for decades. Plants and lichens, formerly a part of the forest floor, are the main staple of the reindeer diet and take up to 70 to 100 years to regrow. Lichen, for example, grows 1 to 1.5 millimeters a year (less than one-tenth of an inch). While large timber companies and the state forest association are willing to allow Sámi to herd and graze reindeer in their forests, opposition to this historical practice has been increasing among small private landowners, who combined, now own about 50 percent of Sweden's forests.[4] Both national and local governments are forced to manage competing interests — supporting the timber industry, which is a major

Figure 9.8: Sámi construct traditional log fences, such as these, to contain reindeer herds at harvest time.

economic contributor, while protecting the ecology of forests that makes it possible for the Sámi to continue to herd and husband their reindeer.

Second is the predator issue. Both the Swedish national government and the European Union have policies protecting animals, including bear, wolves, eagles, wolverines, and lynx as threatened or endangered species. These creatures are all predators of the reindeer. The Sámi disagree with these policies, believing that these animals are not in danger of extinction and that more should be killed to protect the reindeer herds. Sámi herders realize a market price of about US$300 for the meat of each reindeer. When a predator kills a reindeer, the government pays the Sámi about US$40 in compensation. In the country as a whole, there are around 230,000 reindeer. While the government estimates that about ten percent of the winter reindeer population are killed every year, the Sámi believe the number killed by predators is closer to 30,000. Traffic and trains kill another 2,000 to 3,000 reindeer annually. During the last decade, the reindeer population of northern Sweden has steadily decreased.[5] The Sámi don't want to eliminate predators, but they see a need for a better balance between protecting the predator animals and reindeer husbandry as a way of life.

Municipalities such as Jokkmokk (Yokk'-mokk) and Gällivare (Yell'-ih-vah-reh) are working with Sámi people both to promote Sámi crafts, reindeer-based industries, and to find cooperative ways to protect land while assuring that Sámi reindeer herding and trading can continue. Jokkmokk supports a three-day winter market festival. Sámi contributions are central to this market that highlights their culture, tradition, art, handicraft, and music. The festival also features Sámi reindeer racing, reindeer taxis, and reindeer culinary delicacies. In 1974, about 10,000 visitors attended the Jokkmokk festival. Today, visitor attendance has swelled to 30,000 people.

The towns of Jokkmokk and Gällivare are participating in a United Nations initiative that seeks to preserve the ecology and the culture of the northern region of Sweden called Laponia. The Sámi culture with its thousand-year-old traditions is central to this initiative. Reindeer herding, the living economy of this region, demonstrates that it is possible to have long-term economic activity even in ecologically sensitive areas. The towns, together with the Sámi, are exploring ecotourism possibilities that respect both nature and Sámi traditions, while increasing national and international awareness of the their culture and traditions through education.

The municipality of Härjedalen (Her'-yeh-dah'-lehn) is using preparation of its general (master) plan to develop a sustainable approach to the interrelated issues of tourism, reindeer economy, agriculture, forestry, and protection of the natural landscape. Working with Sámi people and other interests in the region, Härjedalen is exploring ways to improve snow scooter trails, establish noise-free areas, control erosion, and develop job opportunities in tourism, reindeer economy, and agriculture and forestry. Härjedalen and other municipalities are using their master planning process as a means to stimulate discussion among the various, and often competing, interests in Sweden's mountain region, part of a regional initiative called FjällAgenda (Fyell'-Ah-ghen'-dah), or Mountain Agenda. In this initiative, municipal officials, Sámi people, representatives of forest and agriculture industries, hunters, and private landowners are working together to find mutually supportive ways to increase ecological awareness and development of the local economy.

Journeys to eco-economic self-sufficiency: What we can learn

REDISCOVERING LOCAL CAPACITY

The first lesson we can learn from the experiences of the Kangos and Kalix villages, as well as that of Övertorneå, is that it is possible for a local community depressed in economy, populace, and in spirit, to revitalize — and to accomplish this in an environmentally compatible way. These communities' citizens were able to shift their attitudes from hopelessness to an understanding that they had the capacity to shape a different future. Once empowered, community inhabitants proceeded to accomplish this.

IDENTIFYING AND BUILDING ON EXISTING ASSETS

Another lesson is to start a journey to self-sufficiency through discovering the existing resources, assets, skills, and conditions of the local community. Next steps build upon these assets. In the case of Kangos and Kalix villagers, starting points were the surrounding forests, regional hunting and fishing traditions, an empty school building, a closed general store, a terminating recycling service, and elder citizen needs for help. All of these and more provided opportunities for building new business enterprises, work opportunities, and local income generation.

PRODUCING LOCALLY

Increasing the capacity to produce food locally was another key step in these journeys, reducing inhabitants' income-generating needs to purchase food and rendering them less dependent upon food sources from away, over which they had little control. The interweaving of the Sámi and reindeer shows how a people have been able maintain self-sufficiency over thousands of years despite a harsh climate, where the reindeer's primacy as a food source to Sámi life has been central to that self-sufficiency. Diminishing the reindeer as a food source is jeopardizing the self-sufficiency of the Sámi life and culture. While it may not be realistic for a community, particularly an urban one, to produce 100 percent of its food supply, even urban communities can take steps to increase the possibilities for local food production and, hence, reduced vulnerability.

FINDING "ECO-NICHES"

Experiences of these villages and the Sámi reindeer industry demonstrate the economic potential of ecological approaches — for example, developing "eco-niches."[6] Eco-enterprises thrive on sustainable use of local resources, providing jobs and means of livelihood, while not exceeding the renewing capacity of those local resources. Enterprises that use by-products of other businesses as raw materials in their own processes are another type of eco-niche. This acts as a "closing of an ecological loop," mirroring the efficiency of nature's cycles, where one creature or its waste is another creature's food.

MEETING NEEDS FAIRLY AS WELL AS EFFICIENTLY

Finally, the struggles of the Sámi, and the efforts of those trying to help, demonstrate the necessity to consider the needs of all in shaping a path to greater sustainability.

North American examples

In North America as well, disadvantaged communities are restoring local economies and local pride through ecological approaches to community revitalization. Here are two examples.

Washington County, Maine

In one of New England's poorest counties, nine communities around Cobscook Bay, with a combined population of 6,800, have joined to restore polluted clam flats and a shattered regional economy that depended heavily upon those shellfish beds for their livelihoods and local income. Until recently, the soft-shell clam industry, a traditional and major sector of the Cobscook Bay regional economy, had virtually disappeared because of the Bay's poor water quality and shellfish overharvesting. Shellfishers were no longer able to provide for their families. Young people, facing the prospect of a bleak economic future, were leaving the Cobscook Bay towns to find better opportunities elsewhere. In 1991, the last remaining fish smoke-house, a source of regional employment that used a traditional smoking process over one hundred years old, closed its doors.

In the early 1990s, a boat-building student from the region attended a meeting to discuss an idea to restore clams as an economic resource and indi-cator of water quality. This student's idea led to a Cobscook Bay clam restoration project and regional community-based sustainable development initiative that, by 1996, had brought about the restoration and reopening of 2,000 acres of clam flats. In the first three months of 1997, clam diggers harvested US$30,000 of soft-shell clams in Cobscook Bay. Other commu-nity-based economic development efforts include a regional farmers market, a marketing network and directory of the many self-employed people in the region, a water taxi to link Cobscook Bay communities otherwise separated by a 40-mile drive, and the restoration of the smokehouse as a museum and cultural center. Two towns have rehabilitated their waterfronts and devel-oped a new marina.

Key to this regional renaissance was community participation, says the local sustainable development coordinator. People from all phases of com-munity life — teachers, town officials, retirees, students, conservationists — took part in the efforts, made the major decisions, and hence took owner-ship of the emerging initiative. The effort was successful because the com-munity supported the effort, and because the effort reflects the values of the community, she adds.[7]

Georgia Basin, British Colombia

The Tsliel-Waututh First Nation, Aboriginals who have inhabited the Georgia Basin of British Columbia for over 10,000 years, is restoring its economy and culture through a series of ecologically oriented community-based enterprises. They are one of several First Nations in Canada, driven almost to the point of extinction, who are rebuilding shattered economies and cultural identity through ecological enterprise development and forest stewardship. A non-profit Canadian organization called EcoTrust is helping out. The Tsliel-Waututh are developing an ecotourism business and explor-ing the sustainability potential for operating a Dungeness crab harvesting license. They also have developed several hundred housing units and a driv-ing range. With EcoTrust's help, they acquired over 800 acres of forestland for sustainable forestry and are developing a certification program for sus-tainably harvested wood.[8]

CHAPTER 10

Ecological Schools; Ecological Education

Just as the twig is bent, the tree's inclin'd.
— Alexander Pope, *Moral Essays I*

Introduction

ABOUT LEARNING

As it is so often said, children are our future. If we want the future to be different from the present, then we need to engage the children early in imagining, and in bringing about, the desired future. This does not mean putting children to work in solving the problems that we adults have created, but rather showing them early on a different way of doing things and a different way of looking at the world. It means helping children experience, from an early age, their place in the natural world, and showing how people can live their lives in harmony with that world, rather than damaging it. It means helping children to see and understand the cycles of nature and to learn ways that we can eat, use material things, and natural things like water or energy in ways that mirror those cycles. It means showing children early that there are better ways to live together, work together, and resolve differences together than in anger and conflict.

This chapter presents some examples of how schools, a non-profit education center, and even a daycare program in the Swedish eco-municipalities are accomplishing these things. These schools have created learning experiences for children that make ecological ways of being seem, as one teacher says, "nothing special," in other words, just part of the natural way of doing things.

ABOUT SCHOOL BUILDINGS

It is hard to see how children can learn a better way of being in the world when their immediate world, in the form of their school environment, is an unhealthy one. The affliction known as sick building syndrome has become, unfortunately, all too familiar to citizens and public officials around the world. Sick building syndrome has come to describe an interior building environment whose air contains some combination of dust, dirt, lead, asbestos, chemical off-gassing from interior furnishings, bacteria, mold, mildew, or radon.[1] Building occupants have suffered symptoms including flu-like conditions, asthma attacks, and breathing disorders that become ongoing conditions. Public and private buildings across North America have had to be abandoned or overhauled at costs of millions of dollars to make them again habitable for workers and students.

Many school buildings constructed or renovated since the 1970s have been a victim of this syndrome. For example, on Vashon Island near Seattle, Washington, students walked out of their school to protest building conditions after children, teachers, and administrators came down with breathing and lung disorders that forced some permanently out of work. A U.S. government survey of 10,000 public schools throughout the country found that one-half had experienced at least one unsatisfactory environmental building problem and three-fourths had spent considerable sums to remove hazardous substances such as asbestos, lead, or oil in underground tanks.[2]

At the same time, awareness and efforts to prevent sick building syndrome in the first place are growing steadily. Constructing healthy buildings has become an important focus of green design and green building techniques. This chapter describes how some of the Swedish eco-municipalities, large and small, have created healthy schools for their children. It includes examples of how some schools teach their children from an early age about cycles of nature, how one school used a school building process itself as an ecological learning opportunity for its children, and an ecological learning center for both children and businesses.

Eskilstuna: a city builds an ecological school

When visitors approach Tegelviken (Teh-'gehl-vee'-kehn), the city of Eskilstuna's non-toxic elementary school, their first impression is that it resembles most other schools in Western society. A circular driveway for school buses curves around before the main entrance of attached, solid-looking one-story buildings. Initially, the only noticeable difference is the scores of bicycles parked in bike racks near the front entrance.

Then the visitor enters the building and notices almost immediately the light, airy, spacious atmosphere. But there are few, if any, artificial lights on! Daylight streams into the lobby and halls from seemingly all directions — from large glass windows, overhead skylights. The air seems to smell fresh, too. Brightly colored flags and children's artwork adorn the hallways.

During the 1990s, the city of Eskilstuna (pop. 90,000) realized it would need to construct a new elementary school. The municipality's former elementary school building was deteriorating and not able to house projected school enrollment given the region's growing population. Two other municipalities also send their children to this Eskilstuna school. In 1995, the city began planning actively for a new school facility. City officials involved over 150 school parents in the building and curriculum planning and design. Out of this participatory process, a school plan emerged, led by ecological and user-need-based design objectives. To implement these objectives, the city's municipal council made the decision to build a completely non-toxic school that would have no harmful substances — or for that matter, any chemicals at all — in any of the materials used in the building construction.

Figure 10.1: The Tegelviken School of Eskilstuna — a non-toxic elementary school.

A NON-TOXIC SCHOOL BUILDING

The result: Eskilstuna constructed a school building with no materials that contained any chemicals. Only natural materials were used, such as wood, brick, stone, and organic-based paint. No plastic products, which, of course, are made with chemicals, were used anywhere in the building, with the exception of the chemistry lab. The building was insulated with glass fiber or stone.

Initially, parents and teachers were quite concerned about the possibility of fungus growing and circulating throughout the school ventilation system.

This is increasingly associated with sick building syndrome. One of the objectives from the planning process was to create the healthiest possible interior building environment. To accomplish this, designers created a state-of-the-art ventilation system that brings in and circulates fresh air continuously throughout the building. Air travels through a central system installed in an air space under the floors. Three sections of the school have their own air circulation system.

Natural light enters the building through overhead skylights and large well-insulated windows. There are no fans or noise, features of conventional HVAC systems. The building's heating comes from a wood pellet-fired boiler and solar panels that heat hot water.

The school's sewage system separates gray water and black water. A constructed wetland on the school property cleans gray water, that is, water from the school's kitchen and bathroom sinks; the clean water is then reused onsite for irrigation. Black water, used toilet water, is composted, purified, and used by a local farmer as fertilizer. The city received a state subsidy to install this innovative sewer system, which has since become a model for other public buildings in Sweden.

Classrooms for four- and five-year-olds and classrooms for six- and seven-year-olds open onto the same common space. The idea was for children of varying ages to mix in these common areas and to allow teachers to interact as well. All classrooms have a kitchen where pupils eat, clean their own plates, compost leftovers, and recycle. All teachers, administrators, and children eat together.

The total construction cost of the school was about US$11.2 million — between 10 and 20 percent more than the cost of a conventional design. The city made a conscious decision to build the school ecologically, despite the higher initial capital cost. City officials realized that the potential human and remedial costs of an unhealthy building could be much higher and that they would save money down the road through lower maintenance and energy costs. The school already has realized cost savings through reduced heating and building operations costs.

Despite initially higher capital costs, city officials realized that potential human and building remediation costs of an unhealthy building could be much higher.

Figure 10.2: Classrooms open onto common space so children and teachers from different classes can mix.

The Tegelviken School serves 450 pupils between 6 and 16 years old and 50 pupils in daycare between 1 and 5 years old. There are 70 teachers and school staff. The school has been tracking the health of teachers and staff since the building opened during the fall of 1999. As of 2001, there were already fewer health problems and improved health conditions among building occupants.

Tegelviken's biggest challenge is class sizes that are too big. On average, there are 30 students per classroom. Since this ecological school opened, it has become very popular, says its school principal; everyone wants to go there.

TEGELVIKEN'S ECOLOGICAL CURRICULUM

An outdoor nature education program is an essential part of the Tegelviken School's curriculum. A basic premise of this program is that "positive nature experiences will create a better environmental behavior and understanding for the future," in the words of the program coordinator. The program helps children realize that natural science cannot be separated from social science. Students develop a personal relationship to global environmental issues and get the opportunity to take responsibility for their own environment. The program's approach is also based upon the idea that "It is not half as important to know as to feel." This approach recognizes that it is not just a lack of knowledge about environmental issues that causes problems, but attitudes and values as well. The children's education balances recognition and openness about feelings with the main objective of conventional education's approach — acquisition of pure knowledge. In Tegelviken's nature education, children learn about making fires and getting wet. They learn not just about the scientific aspect of these activities but also about the happiness of experiencing what is happening in nature.

The program coordinator also works with the children simply to get them to slow down. He observes that, because life is run at such a fast pace, slowing down the children for one day alone is a good achievement. He believes that there is more to measuring the value of education than through test results and statistics. For example, he says that one way of measuring value is seeing the children's eyes light up when they learn and understand something new. While this is not an objective measure, he realizes, it may be a more important one.

Figure 10.3: When children have birthdays, they sit in this throne, while the entire school sings "Happy Birthday" to them and presents them with cakes that have just the right number of candles.

Swedish research has found that children who spend a higher percentage of time outdoors get sick less frequently, says Tegelviken's nature education teacher. Their physical abilities, mental abilities, and concentration are higher than those of children who are outdoors less often. Tegelviken's program includes lots of opportunities for children to get exercise. A Swedish study found that in 1980 one-third of Swedish adults were overweight. In 1990, this proportion of overweight adults had risen to 50 percent.

In 1969, the primary focus of Swedish educational curricula was acquisition of knowledge. By 1980, curricula reflected an understanding that natural science and social science cannot be isolated from each other and that students should be prepared for taking an active part in society. By 1990, a primary curricula objective was for students to "get an opportunity to take responsibility for, and have an active role in, their own environment, as well as a personal relationship to global environmental issues."[3] For more about Eskilstuna and its sustainable development work, see Chapter 5.

Övertorneå: A small town builds an ecological school

Far in the rural north of Sweden, a small town was concerned about its children's health and their need to understand nature and their place in it. This town and its 5,500 inhabitants had emerged from a depression in both their local economy and their community spirit to redirect the seemingly hopeless course of its future to a positive one. The town was Övertorneå, whose community eco-revitalization has been described at the beginning of this book.

When its Svanstein village school burnt down, Övertorneå was faced with the prospect of rebuilding the school. During the community's eco-municipality journey, Övertorneå's citizens and town officials came to understand better how their own actions and choices affected the systems of nature, their individual and community well-being, and the well-being of future generations. Out of this understanding emerged a rebuilding of the village school that became an ecological model throughout the region. Perhaps more impressive, the town's ecological building approach grew not from a mental framework of sustainability objectives but rather from a good sense approach to design and construction, illustrating how deep the ecological awareness has grown in the community.

Övertorneå's new ecological school, whose construction was completed toward the end of 2001, resembles Eskilstuna's Tegelviken School on a smaller scale. Both schools used natural materials to construct the buildings and school furniture. In neither building are there plastic products or plastic furniture. In Övertorneå's school, the floor cover is natural linoleum.

"Positive nature experiences will create better environmental behavior."
— Nick Helldorf, Nature Education Program Coordinator, Eskilstuna

Wood fiber ceiling panels provide heat and sound insulation. Interior paints are organic-based. No hazardous glue was used in laminating, cabinetry, or any other woodwork. As in Tegelviken, the building ventilation system continuously brings in fresh air to the classrooms and common areas. An air-to-air heat exchanger captures and reuses heat extracted from stale air before it is vented out of the building.

The Miljöförskola School: Ecological education starts early

At the Miljöförskola (Mill-yeu'-feuhr-skoo'-lah) School in Övertorneå, children at five years old begin to learn about the cycles of nature. They learn that plants grow, die, and become compost, which in turn becomes earth for more plants to grow.

Figure 10.4: A classroom in Övertorneå's new ecological school, constructed with all natural materials.

At Miljöförskola, four teachers teach 55 children in classes ranging from 6 to 20 pupils per class. The school, as well as the town it serves, has lost population due to townspeople leaving for urban jobs and city life. The school, also a daycare center, serves a rural area of Övertorneå, where some children travel by school bus from 15 miles away. The school uses ecology as a theme to integrate the various subjects children learn, such as the Swedish and English languages, music, art, and painting. Plans are underway for the children to construct a windmill on the school's property. Before the summer holidays, children plant potatoes that take only six weeks to grow in the land of the midnight sun. When children return to school in the fall, they harvest, cook, and eat the full-grown potatoes, composting the leftovers and returning the compost to the garden.

About once a week, children explore a nearby forest to see how the woods change in the different seasons of the year and to visit a small house where a fairytale character comes alive in the form of a puppet named Mulle. Mulle talks to the children about the forest, about nature, and about life. The children listen avidly to the puppet. Known and enjoyed by more than two million children in Sweden, Mulle is a fairytale character that was introduced to Swedish children over 45 years ago.

At Miljöförskola School and all the daycare centers of Övertorneå, the ecological way of doing things is seen as nothing special. Awareness of nature, and doing things that are in harmony with nature and its cycles, is simply the ordinary, natural way to be.[4]

The ecological school of Kangos Village

Tiny Kangos Village, with 330 inhabitants, rallied to save its local school when public officials threatened to close it in 1993. The reader learned about the revitalization of Kangos Village, including the rescue of its school, in Chapter 9. Similar to charter schools in the United States, the Kangos school now runs independently of the regular public school system. In Sweden, local authority permission is needed to start independent schools. Once granted, public funding cannot be denied to the school.

In a manner of speaking, all Kangos village residents now own the school, says a village official. This school has become the center of village life. The school's five or six teachers all live in the village, and parents make up the majority of the school board.

Figure 10.5: Miljöförskola school children wrote and performed a play about a wicked witch who drives a gas-guzzling car. The play's heroine persuades the witch to switch to a bike.

The school also has become the village cultural center. The entire village attends school plays, musicals, and shows, most of which have ecological themes. In one musical show about the Earth's place in the solar system, children decorated the entire gymnasium with planets and examples of planetary features such as moons, craters, and frozen lakes. Understanding the connection between humans and nature links all school courses and children's activities.

The school designed its curriculum involving outdoor learning. In winter, classes go outside to look for animal tracks. A local forest company set aside some forestland for the school. Here, each child has a designated forest area of about ten square feet where they observe and monitor what they see. Children have put up birdhouses and watch to see which birds nest.

School games introduce values such as "Take only from the Earth what you need" or "take only what the Earth can renew." Everyone in the school uses both sides of paper and then recycles it. Children and teachers compost some food scraps and feed some to the school chef's pigs. The school uses the Natural Step system conditions to help children understand what sustainability means, particularly in natural science and social science courses.

A Kangos village official thinks that Swedish school testing is geared toward urban children. If the tests were designed here, says the official, the city kids wouldn't have a chance.[5]

Tvärred: A community and its children help design an eco-school

Imagine starting a process for designing or rehabilitating a building by holding a potato-carving event. Far-out, you say? But this is precisely how architects, commissioned by the municipality of Ulricehamn (Eull-ree-seh-hahmn'), near the city of Falkenberg, started a conversation among community residents and parents about what the new, revamped Tvärred (Tvehr'-rehd) elementary school building should be like.

The architects strongly believed that a building's design should evolve out of the needs and visions of the people who are going to use that building. In the case of a school building, that meant the children, parents, and community residents as well, since the school would also function as a community center. To understand what people felt were important design features and to provide a language for expressing this, the architects held a community "potato day." Elders, young people, parents, children, all were invited to take part. People found, brought, and carved potatoes at this event, making artistic objects, designing potato paint stamps and pictures, and making potato flour. Then, people talked about what they had done and what it meant to them. Through following this dialogue, listening carefully, and waiting for everyone's contributions, the architects came to understand what people wanted and enjoyed in a building. What they learned in this event guided them through the rest of the design process.

Figure 10.6: A meeting in the Kangos school — the center of village life.

The result was a school architectural design that incorporated the aspirations of many people, old and young, in the community. For example, the architects designed windows low in the walls so children could easily see out of them. Having clean fresh air with no mechanical ventilation system noise was important to teachers, so the architects designed a passive aeration system. One older man wanted very much to have a concrete part in the school's design and building, so he visited the construction site and made a sculpture that was then built into a wall. Children felt it was important to bring their own home's organic material for composting at the school, so the recycling station was placed near the school's entrance where the children could easily use it and be proud of it. Another idea was a drop-off spot for outgrown shoes that could be sent to children in Albania.

One school project involved the children in finding out whether or not the walls of the existing school building were load-bearing. Children went to the local historical museum to find archived architectural drawings of the original school building construction. Next, children located and stacked bricks to see how they could make structures and come up with different designs.

One of the children's favorite places was the cellar of the old existing school building. The architects asked the children to describe what fascinated them about the cellar, and the learning from this exercise, coupled with the idea of recycling a building, became the basis for the entire redesign of the school. The children were eager to know why certain pipes were wide, others narrow, how they worked, and where they went. It became clear that the toilets were very important to the children, as these were the only places in the entire school where one could be alone. The children insisted that considerable design attention go to the toilets and bathroom, and they helped to remake and refurbish all the doors in the school as a way of allowing more project funds to be directed toward bathroom design.

The project budget was very tight, so, to reduce the built space required, the architects designed flexible classroom spaces that could be used for several different purposes. For example, some older children's classrooms were designed for alternative use as play spaces for younger children, or for special functions such as woodworking. To cover the cost of certain ecological building features, the designers reduced room areas where possible. A particular objective was to encourage people in different parts of the school, for example, school staff and schoolteachers, to talk to each other. Dining rooms and staff rooms were located near each other and also designed for use by community residents.

Nowhere in the school building, other than in light fixtures, is there any plastic. All natural building materials were used. Teachers and staff wanted window shades, but since the decision was made not to use fabric, the architects designed wooden shades for the windows. Roof gutters channel rainwater into a wooden chute that passes over a waterwheel to an open channel lined with big rocks. In good weather, the children use these rocks as outdoor seats and play areas.

DESIGNING THE TVÄRRED PLAYGROUND

To engage the children in designing the school playground, the architects located a large room in a former mill, placed various objects around the room, and invited the children to come in, explore the space, and arrange things differently if they wished. When the children first came into the room, they were very quiet, taking everything in. Then, they started moving in and out of nooks and crannies in the room, hiding behind objects, and started to ask questions about the architecture of the room and building and how parts of the room could be moved or changed. Next, the architects asked school officials if the existing schoolyard could be made into a laboratory for designing the playground. They asked children to describe what they liked about their yard and wanted to keep in it. The architects made a big mat for the children to draw what they wanted. One eight-year-old boy identified a big, smooth stone that was his favorite place. He said, on this stone he could sit and listen to the sky, smell the leaves and bark of the nearby birch trees, and, he also scored his first soccer goal there. In this way, all the special places of the existing schoolyard were recorded and kept on the mat.

The playground design process became integrated into school study subjects such as history and woodworking. In the woodworking class, a student built an antique-style water pump, first constructing a wooden model of it, for the playground. One day, another boy put a notice on his classroom door, saying he wanted to build a bridge. Seeing this note, his classroom teacher went straight to the woodworking teacher to organize this project. Almost immediately, there were ten other children who wanted to work on this, too. They built the bridge, then the children themselves reflected on how well the building process had gone and how to improve the bridge. Next, they built an even better bridge, this time using machined timber instead of forest logs. The architect understood the importance of the children's time to reflect upon their first endeavor and having the opportunity to improve upon it.

In the end, the children decided to build towers for the playground instead of a bridge. They built some model towers, then invited the municipality's staff planner/architect to visit and inspect these towers. This architect spent time with each of the school's thirteen classes, discussing in different ways with each age group how the towers, and buildings in general, can be built. A particularly interesting discussion about pollution and how buildings contribute to pollution developed between the architect and a group of eight-to-ten-year-old children. Both the school architect and the city architect saw this process as a great way of doing planning and design. The children developed a genuine respect for the city planner/architect and also learned in a concrete way about the challenges surrounding city planning and design. Next, the children were asked to build bigger models of the building towers. If ten parents were able to jump down from a tower without injuring themselves, said the architect, the children could receive a "permit" to build the tower.

The Tvärred school renovation merged design, community participation, and eco-education in a process that came alive for its participants — children, parents, and community residents. The democratic, eco-centered process dissolved the separation that has occurred over time among building designers, building users, and nature. The school and playground design emerged organically through the engagement of children and citizens and through the creation of a common language for building designers and building users.[6]

The Tvärred school renovation tapped into what Christopher Alexander has called "the timeless way of building":

> It is a process through which the inner order of a building or a town grows out directly from the inner nature of the people, and the animals, and the plants, and matter which is in it. It is a process which allows the life inside a person, or a family, or a town, to flourish, openly, in freedom, so vividly that it gives birth, of its own accord, to the natural order which is needed to sustain this life.[7]

Ekocentrum: Eco-education for businesses and school children

Just outside the city of Göteborg (Yeu-teh-boryh') is an unprepossessing building that looks like it could have been an elementary school. Inside, however, is an independent, non-profit educational center that teaches thousands of business employees and school children about the converging funnel of global environmental trends and practical steps individuals can take to move in a more sustainable direction.

Ekocentrum is the largest environmental education center in Scandinavia. It offers environmental education courses, presentations, and also environmental exhibits for visitors and classes alike. Groups of company employees and school classes attend half-day sessions to better understand issues such as global warming and links between the use of chemicals with species extinction and risks to human health. They also see and learn practical ways to change personal, household, and business practices to help reduce these damaging trends. Of the 15,000 visitors each year, one-quarter are schoolchildren and three-quarters are businesspeople and civil servants. Ekocentrum instructors also travel to give presentations to schools and organizations.

Figure 10.7: One of Ekocentrum's teachers gives a lesson about sustainability.

Figure 10.8: A globe and piece of cloth illustrate Sweden's ecological footprint: the amount of land needed to support the consumption and waste generation patterns of its society.[9]

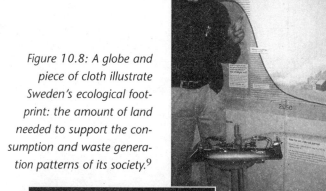

Some small companies cannot afford the cost of comprehensive training in standardized environmental management systems such as ISO 14001.[8] Ekocentrum offers such companies a shorter version, called ISO-lite training. Hundreds of small companies have sent their employees to take the ISO-lite training program. A private foundation owns and operates this education center that is also supported by contributions from businesses and exhibitors. The center receives grants and government support for the school education portion of its program. It was originally created by four non-profit organizations.

Ekocentrum uses the Natural Step framework as the basis for its education in basic science and for guiding sustainable practices. Its aim is not only to educate but to inspire people, especially given the small amount of time that participants spend in the center's programs. Ekocentrum's teaching method? Find something used in everyday life and make a story around it.

Ekocentrum has designed each of its exhibit areas around a particular theme — for example, energy and heat, water, sewage, and chemicals. Each exhibit has examples of state-of-the-art technology, donated by companies that demonstrate alternative practices that are less harmful and less polluting. For example, one exhibit contains an outboard motor that is more energy efficient and less polluting than conventional outboard motors. The exhibit tells about new gasoline available for two-stroke and four-stroke outboard engines that is presently twice as expensive as conventional gas, but releases 80 percent fewer benzene compounds into the water.[10] A solar panel charges the motor's battery that stores up to ten hours of power.

A demonstration home heating furnace, fired by wood pellets, shows how an automatic pellet feed can remove the need to continually shovel pellets into a furnace by hand. If the homeowner is away, a backup battery can run the automatic pellet feed if the power goes off. New models of washers and dryers demonstrate reduced use of energy for washing and drying clothes.

Some Ekocentrum lectures and exhibits point out the sources and harmful effects of chemicals and heavy metals that are accumulating in the environment. For example, an instructor describes how small doses of hormone-mimicking chemicals can affect small children at critical times in their growth. Other examples: 200 to 300 tons per year of acetone in Swedish wastewater comes from nail polish remover;[11] red lipstick often contains a substance called cinnobar that contains mercury, cadmium, and lead; and 30 percent of the cadmium in Stockholm's water supply comes from artists washing paint off their brushes.[12] A study of the city of Uppsala's compost found high concentrations of pesticides, including persistent, accumulating organic chemicals. An Ekocentrum instructor points out how pesticides are applied at much higher doses in the household than on farms. For example, if an insecticide soap to remove aphids doesn't work, the homeowner often moves on, as a next step, to more poisonous types of pesticides. Exhibit materials describe how anti-bacterial cleaning agents used to wash hands and countertops kill the microbes that help clean the sewage effluent in sewage treatment plants. Antibacterials in toothpaste can help bleeding gums but also can help breed resistant strains of bacteria.

Another exhibit shows how indoor plants can help purify the air. Spider plants and rubber tree plants are especially good at this job and are used in space stations for this purpose. One example in the global warming exhibit points out that a big source of greenhouse gas emissions comes from underinflated car tires that reduce gas mileage. Some tire manufacturers also fill tires with sulfur hexafluoride, a greenhouse gas, because it escapes from tires less rapidly than air.[13] The alternative energy exhibit presents examples of less polluting gasoline for gas mowers and weed whackers, as well as outboard engines. There is also race car fuel that contains less benzene.

Figure 10.9: This home heating furnace is one of many Ekocentrum exhibits that demonstrate sustainable alternatives to conventional home appliances and supplies.

Figure 10.10: These wooden pellets fire the home furnace instead of oil or gas.

Showcasing innovative products such as these can help reduce the conflict between these activities, which many people still enjoy, and protecting the environment.

Combining theory and practice, talks and demonstrations, are keys to Ekocentrum's success in helping children and adults to better understand the deteriorating global trends and what individuals and businesses can do to help. Since 1993, almost 100,000 people have learned about sustainable practices and why they are important at Ekocentrum.[14]

North American examples

School green building programs

Responding to concerns about unhealthy school buildings, some state and local governments in the U.S. are trying to help. In Massachusetts, for example, the state education department has teamed up with a state renewable energy collaborative to help and to fund local school districts design or redesign school buildings to be more energy efficient, provide healthier building environments, and hence cost less to operate.[15] In North Carolina, the regional Triangle J Council of Governments has developed guidelines for building new schools and public facilities that encourage energy efficiency, selection of building materials through life cycle analysis, heating through renewable energy sources, and recycling construction waste.[16]

Green education

In Canada, over 5,000 K-12 schools are taking part in a country-wide green schools program where school children have accomplished over half-a-million environmental projects. This program, designed and administered by a private foundation, provides instructions and materials to schools who wish to participate. Schools whose pupils achieve 100 environmental projects win a Green School banner, awarded in a special assembly, that is displayed outside the building to show that that this school is a special place. Over 200 K-12 schools have completed 1,000 environmental projects, entitling them to become Earth Schools, an even higher recognition. Environmental projects can be in any field, as long as they are actions that either "enhance the environment, communicate to others about the environment, or demonstrate wise and sustainable use of resources that make up the environment."[17]

As one example, a school class in Vegreville, Alberta, wrote their town's mayor and council to suggest ways to reduce garbage and to request a recycling center. Students in a Clayton, British Columbia, music class were given three days to write a rap song about saving the tropical rainforests or about the importance of trees. In the Seniac School in Saskatchewan, students recorded which classroom had the highest temperature setting during the recess and noon hours. Energy wasters then had to wear pig nose masks for the rest of the day.[18]

In the United States, twelve of the 50 states require that K-12 public schools include environmental education in the curriculum. Fifteen states have coordinated teacher training programs in environmental education, and ten states have developed an environmental education curriculum guide. Over one-half the states (27) have grants available for local environmental education programs.[19] Pennsylvania's teacher environmental education certification program requires teachers to be knowledgeable about ecological principles, such as influence of humans upon the environment, interdependence of organisms in ecosystems, energy flow and materials cycled within ecosystems, and response of organisms to environmental stress caused by humans.[20] California's environmental education curriculum for elementary schools, "A Child's Place in the Environment," is taught to thousands of California school children and has won a national award for excellence in both writing and implementation.[21]

Unfortunately, despite these efforts, two out of three people in the U.S. are not able to pass a 12-question environmental quiz. However, in the U.S., 95 percent of people and 96 percent of parents strongly support environmental education in schools. The researchers who discovered this also learned something else. People who understand environmental issues are more likely to see that economic development and environmental protection are not mutually exclusive, and such people are more apt to believe that it is possible for us to change our behavior to better protect the environment.[22]

CHAPTER 11

Sustainable Agriculture: Growing Healthy; Growing Locally

... there is nothing more sacred than the pact between humans and the land that gives them their food.

— Janine Benyus[1]

Unsustainable agriculture: A snapshot

Oil

In the United States today, a piece of food travels an average 1,300 miles to get onto our plate.[2] A standard loaf of white bread requires 2½ times the amount of energy contained in that loaf to produce it, package it, and get it to us.[3] University ecologist David Pimental estimates that society spends ten kilocalories (about 42 kilojoules) of hydrocarbons to produce one kilocalorie of food. By this standard, according to biologist Janine Benyus, most of us are eating the equivalent of thirteen barrels of oil a year.[4]

Chemicals

The use of pesticides in agriculture grew from almost 400 million pounds in 1964 to just over 700 million pounds in 1996. Meanwhile, the amount of crops lost to pests has increased from 31 percent during the 1950s to 37 percent by 2002.[6] Pesticides are responsible for around 25 million cases of acute occupational pesticide poisonings a year.[7] Researchers have found significant associations between deaths from cancer and agricultural chemical use in 1,500 U.S. rural counties.[8] Studies are increasingly finding links between chemical neurotoxins and organophosphates, common pesticide chemicals, and developmental and behavioral disorders in children.[9] Most of us are carrying around several hundred chemicals in our body fat that don't belong there, according to Theo Colburn, scientist and co-author of *Our Stolen Future*.[10]

Loss of farmland

Combined with all of this, agriculture is threatened with ever diminishing land available for growing food. Sprawl development is gobbling up over 400,000 acres of prime farmland every year.[11] Further, agriculture in the United States is becoming concentrated in the hands of a few "agri-businesses." Only one percent of Americans are growing the food that is eaten by all of us, and 87 percent of this food comes from 18 percent of the farms in the United States.[12] Much of this agri-business agriculture produces food in monocultures — vast fields of only one crop, which, for pests, says Janine Benyus, is like equipping a burglar with keys to every house in the neighborhood.[13]

GOOD NEWS

On the positive side, organic agriculture and the organic food business are growing rapidly worldwide. In the United Sates, the number of organic farmers is growing by about 12 percent per year.[14]

Market sales for organic foods shot up 250 percent between 1996 and 2001, according to an international organic food organization.[15] Organic food is the fastest growing segment of food sales in North America, says an organic food trade association. Organic food retail sales in the United States alone grew from US$1 billion in 1990 to US$7.8 billion in 2000 and are expected to top US$20 billion in 2005.[16] In one year, Canadian independent grocers increased shelf space for organic products by 20 percent.

HOW MUNICIPALITIES CAN INFLUENCE AGRICULTURE

Cities, towns, and local government have enormous influence over the destiny and delivery of agriculture in their communities, whether or not they choose to acknowledge or use this influence. First and foremost is in the area of land use. In the U.S. and many other countries, municipalities and county governments have the authority to designate land for agricultural use and to set development limits and standards for development on, or adjacent to, agricultural land. Second, cities and towns can influence agriculture

Figure 11.1: Stockholm city residents can stroll through fields, pick and buy organic produce, all within a 20-minute bus ride of their homes.

Figure 11.2: City children can come to Rosendal Garden to see what chickens and rabbits look like.

as an economic development activity through community economic development tools and programs. Municipalities can provide economic incentives to preferred types of businesses and to businesses that create community-desired activities, such as jobs for local residents. For example, a municipality could choose to use these types of incentives to encourage organic agriculture that uses no chemicals. Municipalities can regulate use of chemical pesticides and fertilizers through land use and public health regulations. Local governments often also control water supply, a lifeline for agriculture.

This chapter presents examples of how sustainable agriculture is flourishing in urban, suburban, and rural settings of Sweden and how a Swedish non-profit organization is promoting and supporting the organic food industry.

Rosendal Garden: An organic farm in a city center

In the heart of Stockholm, an urban organic farm sits within an easy bus ride of 700,000 people. At this farm, visitors stroll through fields of vegetables, herbs, and flowers, pick these, and pay for them at a nursery that also sells garden supplies, ceramics, and organic products. Winding paths take visitors through herb gardens, rose gardens, past chicken coops and rabbit hutches, where children watch and enjoy the antics of the animals.

An apple orchard produces traditional apples that are harvested and made into cider that is also sold on the property. What looks like a sunny greenhouse turns out to be a restaurant serving delicious lunches and tea with food harvested from the garden. On Sundays, hundreds of city residents and visitors fill the restaurant to overflowing, and carry their lunch trays out to picnic tables in the apple orchard.

When finished, visitors compost any leftover food in the bins placed conveniently near paths and place their crockery dinnerware — not paper or plastic — in collection tubs. This restaurant stays open in winter, selling coffee and sandwiches and attracting visitors to enjoy the snowy season in the garden and park.

Figure 11.3: Visitors can buy and enjoy delicious organic food grown in the fields of Rosendal Garden.

Exploring other areas of the grounds, visitors encounter a beekeeper's stand selling honey made in hives located in the gardens. In another building, the aroma of freshly baked bread entices visitors to enter. Here, they can observe bakers taking out crusty loaves of bread from a Finnish-style wood-fired oven that, visitors learn, was built by a group of international craftspeople who came to Stockholm to help construct this traditional baking furnace.

This extraordinary garden and farm, Rosendal (Roo-sehn-dahl') Garden, originally served as the royal gardens for the Swedish royalty in the 18th and 19th centuries. Later in the 19th century, the gardens became an educational center for teaching gardening. In 1961, the Swedish Horticultural Society moved its training school and offices to this garden and were its caretaker until the early 1900s. Now, a private foundation, the Friends of Rosendal Garden, maintains the garden and farm, reestablishing its tradition as a gardening and farming educational center.

Rosendal Garden is located in EcoPark, 6,700 acres described as the world's first national city park. An oak forest, said to be the largest in northern Europe, covers most of the parkland. A rare oak bark beetle survives in this forest.

Figure 11.4: A map of Stockholm's 6,700-acre EcoPark, purported to be the world's first national city park.

EMERGENCE OF ROSENDAL'S ORGANIC FARMING

Rosendal's organic gardens and related businesses themselves evolved organically. Greenhouses constructed by gardeners during the 1950s still operate today. In the early 1960s, two gardeners with experience in biodynamic gardening, a whole-systems approach to organic farming,[17] moved to Stockholm to to help restore the Rosendal Garden. They began cleaning up the grounds and planting vegetable and flower gardens. Attracted by this effort, more people came to work and garden. Volunteers began to brew coffee and bake cakes for the gardeners. Then, someone insisted upon paying for her coffee. This led to the development of a store that in turn became the present restaurant. Next, someone wanted to buy plants grown in the gardens. This led to the creation of the nursery. As word spread about the garden restoration, more people came to visit, work in the gardens, eat in the store, and shop in the nursery. The restaurant's founder wrote a book about cooking with organic produce, which brought in even more people.

The gardens attracted more and more attention. A group of landscape architects and designers participated in a design brainstorming event that developed a series of plans for different sections of Rosendal, including a rose garden, a bench sitting garden, and fields growing combinations of flowers and vegetables.

Composting and careful soil preparation is essential to the biodynamic gardening approach that is designed around self-contained cycling and recycling of nutrients within a garden or farm. At Rosendal, gardeners compost food scraps from the restaurant to make soil for the gardens and fields of vegetables. A series of six large composting boxes turn food waste, leaves, plant materials, and manure from the chickens and rabbits into rich soil. No chemicals are used. Many Stockholm residents have learned how to compost here, says a Rosendal gardener.

Figure 11.5: Food scraps from the restaurant are composted with leaves and plant material to make rich earth that is returned to the garden, one example of the onsite, cyclic biodynamic approach to agriculture and horticulture.

People don't always know why they are attracted to come to Rosendal, this gardener goes on to say. They come here to work, eat, or simply visit. There is a change in their behavior, she says, observing that in these challenging events of today, there is a need for a time and place to "wake up the senses."

THE BUSINESS SIDE OF ROSENDAL

Rosendal Garden operates as a non-profit business that uses no loans or grants. Revenues from the onsite businesses — the restaurant, nursery, bakery, beekeeping, and other garden-based enterprises — cover all staffing and operating costs. Rosendal Garden and its enterprises have inspired similar urban farming projects in other parts of Sweden, for example, in the city of Göteborg.[18]

Maskringen Agricultural Cooperative: A community-owned farm in a suburb

In the village of Gäddvik (Yehdd'-veek), a suburb of Luleå, a 25-acre farm feeds urban families while teaching visitors and students how to grow healthy, chemical-free vegetables and meat in an energy-efficient approach. A non-profit cooperative of about thirty member households owns and operates the Maskringen (Mahsk'-ring-ehn) eco-cyclic agricultural cooperative, called Kretsloppsföreningen (Kretts'-lopps-feuhr-eh'-ning-ehn) Maskringen in Swedish. Virtually all the members have full-time jobs elsewhere and work on the farm during weekends.

The farm grows vegetables, root crops, spices, flowers, and berries. A farm stand sells produce to visitors and passersby. Cooperative members also sell farm produce at regional farmers markets. Around 50 sheep graze on the remaining farmland, keeping this free of bush and shrubs for future cultivation. The farm also produces and sells meat, wool, and hides from these sheep, and grows hay on five more acres of land.

Figure 11.6: Visitors can stop by to purchase healthy, chemical-free produce at Maskringen's farm stand.

SUSTAINABLE AGRICULTURE IS A GUIDING OBJECTIVE

Sustainable food production is a guiding objective of Maskringen. The farm uses sustainable agricultural practices in its own farming and offers courses and workshops to teach others. For example, the farm worked hard to improve initially poor soil conditions, uses wind and water-powered water pumps in irrigation, and is experimenting with low-energy food production techniques. Unlike Westernized food production, whose objective is to produce the maximum agricultural yield, Maskringen's objective is to produce the optimum crop yield. Maskringen's farming approach preserves and recycles soil and plant nutrients rather than allowing these to leach into the groundwater and disperse to the sea.

Maskringen describes itself as "a community farm based upon the belief that food can and should be raised using less subsidiary energy then that used by commercial farms."[19] Cooperative members point out how conventional Western food production and processing has become a fossil-fuel dominated, energy intensive operation. While the conventional food production system has grown more efficient in terms of person-hour labor, it has become inefficient in terms of energy use.[20] The Maskringen cooperative is working with students from the nearby Luleå University of Technology to analyze the food energy return for energy invested at the farm in order to help find ways to further reduce energy use.

FOOD-ENERGY RATIO

One student's analysis found that the amount of energy obtained from eating the cooperative's vegetables was about four times more than the energy amount used to produce that food. The student compared Maskringen's food-to-energy ratio to that of the United States' food system, where, for every calorie of food produced, six calories of subsidy energy have been added in the growing stage. If distribution and packaging is included, the U.S. food system adds ten calories of subsidy energy to every calorie of food.[21]

SUSTAINABLE AGRICULTURE TECHNIQUES

To improve the soil, initially full of sediments and low in nutrients, Maskringen members worked to increase the soil's organic content, nutrients, and biological life. Cooperative members developed topsoil by mixing existing soil with compost, leaves, and manure from sheep and chickens. The farmers planted nitrogen-fixing legumes, such as beans and peas, and added raw phosphate, since the existing soil levels of this mineral were low. They used generous amounts of old hay to mulch vegetable beds. Urine is collected from urine-separating toilets and diluted with water to fertilize seedlings. (Urine, which is sterile, has a good balance of two key ingredients needed for plant growth — nitrogen and phosphorus.[22]) Through these methods, the cooperative's farmers developed a rich, living topsoil full of earthworms that dig through, drain, and fertilize that soil.

In the center of the gardens and vegetable beds, Maskringen farmers constructed a pond where a biological diversity of frogs, salamanders, dragonflies, and birds has developed. Wind-powered pumps bring water from an underground well to this pond. A water-powered pump brings more water from the nearby Luleå River into an irrigation system that distributes water and nutrients to all parts of the farm.

The Maskringen farm cooperative demonstrates how it is feasible for urban and suburban dwellers to grow and store food locally without the use of chemicals or huge amounts of energy, and how nutrients can be reused and recycled without contamination.[23]

A small family farm gets organically certified

In rural Kalix, a family is running an organic farm and dairy that was founded in the 1600s. Maria and Michael Lundbäck have been managing this farm since the mid-1980s. The couple owns 50 acres and rents another 60 aces of land used for either cultivation or pastures. The farm also includes over 600 acres of forestland where timber is harvested using selective cutting methods that keep within the forest's ability to regenerate. The harvested lumber, used primarily for window framing, contributes about 30 percent of the farm's income. Maria and Michael grow hay, grass, oats, barley, and vegetables including carrots, lettuce, cabbage, cauliflower, broccoli, squash, cucumbers, beans, onions, leeks, and peas. They sell this produce, all organically grown, to local Kalix grocers and markets.

Before the Lundbäcks arrived, the land was farmed conventionally. Among other things, this meant that previous farmers had used chemicals to control pests and fertilizers to speed plant growth. To qualify for national organic certification in Sweden, a farm must be free of chemical use — pesticides, fertilizers, or herbicides — for at least one year. Michael and Maria began the changeover to organic farming methods in 1993. Since then, the farming couple has used no chemicals to control pests. Instead, they plant a diversity of crops and flowers to reduce the chance that one pest can wipe out a whole crop, as is the risk with monoculture farms. This farm rotates crop plantings with clover, which fixes nitrogen in the soil. The clover attracts bees that also help

Figure 11.7: A traditional Swedish hay barn allows the hay to air-dry. When the hay is dry, farmers remove the rack poles to allow the hay to drop, then compact naturally. Each mobile barn load creates one ton of hay.

reduce pests. Soil is composted with cow manure, eliminating the need for artificial fertilizers.

While organic farming may not produce the same volume of produce as can industrialized farming, organic farms in Sweden can earn 50 percent more in sales revenues for certified organic produce than they can for produce that is conventionally farmed. Conventional Swedish farms receive a 30 percent government subsidy to stabilize farm income. For organically certified farms, this subsidy can be as high as 50 percent.

Maria and Michael also operate a dairy as part of a farmers' cooperative called Norrmejerier (Nohrr'-mehyeh-ree'-ehr). Their dairy consists of 12 to 15 cows, primarily Jerseys, as well as a few cows of a long-time Swedish native breed. The farm also uses four horses to plough the

Figure 11.8: Farmers Michael and Maria Lundbäck grow and sell organic vegetables, milk, and sustainably harvested timber on their organic farm and its dairy.

Figure 11.9: These cows produce organic milk, since they eat only organically grown hay and grass that is free of chemicals. Because the cows' health is robust, they need no antibiotics, nor are they given synthetic hormones to stimulate milk production.

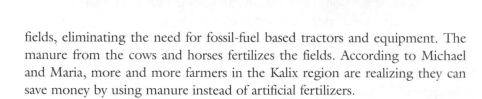

fields, eliminating the need for fossil-fuel based tractors and equipment. The manure from the cows and horses fertilizes the fields. According to Michael and Maria, more and more farmers in the Kalix region are realizing they can save money by using manure instead of artificial fertilizers.

Although their cows eat grass and hay that is free of chemicals, the Lundbäcks have not yet applied for organic certification of their dairy's milk. The reason, says Michael, is that the cooperative does not pay enough of a premium price yet for certified organic milk to make the costs of certification worth their effort. Further, there is not enough organic milk produced in the vicinity to pay for the cost of a separate truck pickup. As of 2001, however, Michael and Maria were planning to begin cheese production at the dairy.

Kostservice: An organic agriculture "eco-niche"

In the town of Övertorneå, a public organization produces 1,000 meals a day for school children, daycare centers and elders. Kostservice delivers food to two schools, eleven daycare centers, and delivers lunches and dinners to elders in their own homes seven days a week. The agency also runs a restaurant in Övertorneå's town hall annex, dubbed by one happy customer as "the best restaurant in Sweden."

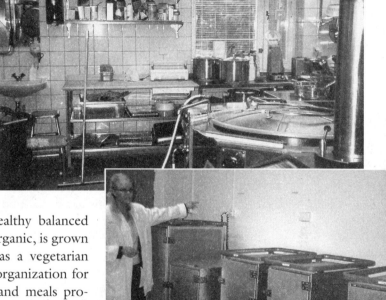

Figure 11.10: The Övertorneå food service company produces 1,000 meals every day in this kitchen.

Kostservice's mission is to provide healthy balanced meals for its clientele. Its food, primarily organic, is grown in the Övertorneå region. Each meal has a vegetarian alternative. KRAV, a Swedish non-profit organization for organic food production, certifies food and meals produced by this food service agency. At least once a week, Kostservice prepares a 100 percent KRAV-certified meal. Once a year, KRAV representatives visit to inspect the business, ensuring standards are met. The Övertorneå food service company is one of the 225 KRAV-certified restaurants and industrial kitchens in Sweden.

This food service, one of the more than 200 eco-enterprises developed during Övertorneå's eco-municipality journey, created 13 jobs for local workers and has over US$1 million in annual revenues, another example of how to do well by doing good. For more about Övertorneå's journey to become Sweden's first eco-municipality, see the Introduction.

Figure 11.11: The food service company delivers hot healthy meals to elders in their homes seven days a week, as well as providing meals for local schools and assisted living facilities.

"KRAV makes sure it's organic"
(from KRAV brochure of the same title)

KRAV is a key player in Sweden's organic food market. Run by an independent board of agriculture and environmental experts, farmers, consumers, animal welfare activists, and food industry members, KRAV develops standards for organic foods, inspects for those standards, and promotes organically certified food throughout the country. The organization inspects and certifies vegetable and meat products, farming land, commercial kitchens and restaurants, farms and dairies, and slaughterhouses for compliance with organic standards. Almost 5,000 Swedish farmers, food processors, restaurants, and retailers work with KRAV to secure and maintain organic certification. The international arm of the organization, KRAV Kontroll, works with more than 40,000 farmers and food processors around the world, primarily in underdeveloped nations. No operation is too large or too small to receive certification. For example, Michael and Maria Lundbäck described earlier, work with KRAV as their organic certifier. The Scandic Hotel chain, described in Part I, received KRAV's organic certification for all its restaurants in 2001.

Principles for organic certification

KRAV's standards are based upon four principles: a healthy environment, good animal husbandry, good health, and social responsibility. KRAV-certified agriculture uses no chemical pesticides, herbicides, or commercial fertilizer. Instead, certified organic farmers rotate their crops to control weeds and pests. Crop rotation also adds nutrients to the soil instead of depleting it through continually replanting the same crops on the same land. For fertilizer, certified farmers use animal manure primarily from their own farms.

KRAV applies the precautionary principle in its standards, meaning that the organization withholds certification of foods and substances that are not "unanimously shown to be harmless." Based upon this principle, certified products do not include any genetically modified organisms or substances. KRAV works with its associates to see that all links in the food chain — from the field to the table — meet its standards. For certification of animal farms, dairies, and slaughterhouses, their animals, including cattle, pigs, sheep, and chickens, must have indoor and outdoor free range, eat organic fodder, have spacious living and birthing quarters, and receive calm and humane treatment prior to, and during, the slaughtering process.

STANDARDS FOR SOUND, RESPONSIBLE WORKING CONDITIONS

KRAV also assures healthy and safe work conditions for farming and food-processing employees. This is particularly important for the organization's 40,000 international producers in developing countries, where hazardous chemicals and poisons proliferate in farming and food production. Farms and food producers found deficient by KRAV standards can be decertified by the organization. The organization's standards for social responsibility also stipulate that farmers and workers should receive a reasonable income and work in safe and healthy conditions.

KRAV also practices what it preaches. The organization tracks its own environmental performance, such as the amount of fossil fuels used by its traveling inspectors and how much paper is being used and recycled. KRAV and its employees continually work to improve their own environmental actions.

TRACKING THE MARKET FOR ORGANIC PRODUCTS

KRAV also tracks information about national and international trends on organic food production. Its rapidly growing clientele attest to the competitive advantage that certified organic food products and producers are gaining in the marketplace, as Michael and Maria Lundbäck point out. According to surveys of the organization's clientele of farmers and food businesses, 93 percent believe that KRAV certification has gained them a market advantage. Surveys also reveal that 93 percent of Swedish consumers recognize the organization's label as an environmental and a quality certification. As clients and consumers attest, the KRAV label can "make sure it's organic."[24]

North American examples

In the United States and Canada, organic farm cooperatives are growing fresh healthy organic produce for their members, helping these farms to survive economically and also keeping land in cultivation and away from unwanted development. These community-supported agriculture cooperatives (CSAs) sell shares to household members for US$300 to $600 per year, which entitles member households to several months of fresh organic produce, locally produced and provided weekly. The share payments provide the farmers with a secure annual income, against which they can borrow to purchase equipment and seeds. First developed in Japan, the CSA concept took root in the New England region of the United States during the 1980s. As of 2003, over 1,000 CSAs are now operating throughout North America.[25]

Community based organizations, such as the Dudley Square Neighborhood Initiative (DSNI) in Boston's Roxbury neighborhood, have turned vacant urban lots into productive, attractive farm lots where neighborhood residents, who often struggle to make ends meet, can grow their own food. In Philadelphia, Pennsylvania, the Greensgrow Farm, assisted through a community development corporation, grows greenhouse vegetables on one of the city's 30,000 abandoned lots, selling this produce directly to city restaurants. A Chicago coalition is giving homeless people job opportunities through growing greenhouse organic produce on a one-acre former brownfield site, and more organic produce at a ten-acre site in a Chicago suburb. Over 40 percent of households in the Vancouver and Toronto regions are now growing some of their own food, according to Canadian surveys.[26]

Some local and regional governments, such as Lancaster County, Pennsylvania, 60 miles from Philadelphia, have combined zoning with a package of conservation techniques to protect 25,000 acres of prime farmland. In the agricultural district, county zoning allows only one building lot of 2 acres per 25 acres of land. The State of Oregon has made farmland preservation one of its statewide planning goals and requires local comprehensive plans to address this.

CHAPTER 12

Dealing with Waste

Whatever is naturally here is all we have. Whatever humans make does not go "away."
— William McDonough and Michael Braungart[1]

From take-make-waste to eco-cycling principles

While recycling rates are improving in some parts of North America, U.S. citizens "waste or cause to be wasted nearly one million pounds of materials per person per year ... the total annual flow of waste, including wastewater, is 250 trillion pounds." This waste includes materials such as carpets, Styrofoam, discarded food, carbon from carbon dioxide, and manufacturing waste. "Less than two percent of the total waste stream is actually recycled — primarily paper, glass, plastic, aluminum, and steel. Over the course of a decade, 500 trillion pounds of American resources will have been transformed into nonproductive solids and gases," according to Paul Hawken, Amory Lovins, and Hunter Lovins in *Natural Capitalism*.[2] Added to these considerations are the increasing burdens for local governments in dealing with waste: rising costs and problems of waste disposal, closing of landfills, stricter incineration regulations, and managing disposal of hazardous substances.

What should communities do in the face of all this? Adopt mandatory recycling programs? Maybe. But recycling, in and of itself, is not enough to solve these problems. Indeed, as some point out, recycling may be "an aspirin, alleviating a rather large collective hangover ... overconsumption."[4] The observation that only one percent of North American materials ends up

If we continually convert nonrenewable resources into garbage, the prices of those resources and the costs of managing wastes will inevitably rise.
— Karl-Henrik Robèrt[3]

141

in products that are still being used six months after their sale underscores this point.[5] Ultimately, sustainable solutions lie more in the direction of designing products that are not, as Bill McDonough says, "less bad," but 100 percent good."[6] This means, among other things, designing products that are fully biodegradable or whose components can be easily broken down for reuse in industrial production.

Dealing with waste also means changing patterns of consumption. Two Canadian scientists have developed a measure called an ecological footprint, the estimated amount of land associated with a particular pattern of resource consumption and waste generation. According to these scientists, the ecological footprint of the average U.S. citizen is about 24 acres, the highest of any country in the world. The average world citizen's ecological footprint is 5.6 acres.[7]

Even if tomorrow we were to begin designing "100 percent good" products and cut our consumption habits in half, society already has created massive amounts of waste materials, much of which is hazardous and toxic, already present in the ecosphere. Then there are the products and materials currently in use that will eventually become waste. Landfills are closing. Incineration is problematic. What are we to do with the accumulating masses of nonbiodegradable materials in society? Once again, it helps to think in terms of cycles, continually reusing product materials already present before extracting and consuming virgin materials.

This chapter presents examples of how some Swedish eco-municipalities are applying eco-cycling principles to dealing with waste in different contexts and situations. In northern Sweden, the Rönnskär Smelter is recovering metals from electronic scrap and discarded computers for reuse in society. A small village in northern Sweden, Lovikka, is recycling over 90 percent of its solid waste. The town of Eksjö in southern Sweden is helping eco-teams of citizens to reduce household waste in a fun and social way. Eskilstuna and Eksjö are harnessing nature's cyclic processes by using constructed wetlands that treat city sewage.

Vulcan is hard at work in the Rönnskär Smelter

The Rönnskär (Reunn'-shehr) Smelter is located in Gallivare (Yell'-ih-vah-reh) in the Boliden (Boo'-lee-dehn) region of northern Sweden. It is Sweden's only smelting plant and one of the world's largest facilities for extracting and recycling metals, such as copper, lead, gold, and silver. Recycling precious metals is not a new practice in the Boliden region. Here, thousands of years ago, Vikings recycled gold and silver, extracting these metals from secondary raw materials.

More than 315 million computers are expected to become obsolete by the year 2004, containing an estimated 1.2 billion pounds of lead, 2 million pounds of cadmium, 400,000 pounds of mercury, and 1.2 million pounds of hexavalent chromium.
— *Kansas City Star*, May 9, 2000[8]

Today, recycled materials are the source of 20 percent of Rönnskär's smelted copper, 40 percent of smelted gold, and 80 percent of smelted zinc. Thirty percent of all the scrap metal traded in the world comes to this smelter, according to company estimates. Scrap metal arrives by train, trucks, and boats then loaded onto conveyors that bring the material directly into the plant. When there is not enough scrap metal and recycled material to process, Rönnskär uses copper concentrate and other metals extracted from nearby mines and purchased in the world market. The plant also extracts zinc clinker from recycled steel mill dust. As a smelting by-product, the plant produces "iron sand," or granulated slag. The good insulating and drainage properties of iron sand make it useful for road construction and house foundations and cut down on excavation of natural gravel, a diminishing natural resource in Sweden.

Copper and zinc ash from casting shops and the brass and bronze industries provide much of the secondary raw materials — industrial by-products to be recycled — for the plant. Rönnskär also processes telecommunications scrap, such as wire or cable, and scrap from discarded computers, monitors, and electronic gadgets. Extracted metals, once returned to their pure base state, are sold to customers throughout Europe. Rönnskär's gold, silver, copper, and lead easily meet the highgrade standards of the London Metal Exchange.

Figure 12.1: The Rönnskär Smelter recovers copper, silver, gold, and zinc from scrap material for reuse in society.

Figure 12.2: Metals are recovered from discarded computers, among other scrap material.

PROFITABILITY IS KEY

For Rönnskär to sustain its operations, profitability is key. The smelter has been operating in the black since 1985. In 2000, the facility's income exceeded its costs by 30 percent. At 34 percent of total operating costs, payroll is

Rönnskär's biggest budget line item. Materials comprise 18 percent of costs. To stay profitable, Rönnskär has had to mechanize some operations and reduce its labor force. In 1986, 2,000 employees smelted 100,000 tons of copper. In 2000, 850 employees processed 230,000 tons of copper. During 1998 to 2000, the Boliden Company, Rönnskär's owner, invested a quarter of US$ 1 billion dollars in modernizing and refurbishing the plant. As a result, Rönnskär almost doubled its copper production capacity. Thirty percent of Boliden's investment went toward improving the plant's environmental performance.

REDUCING IMPACTS

The Rönnskär Smelter also has been working to reduce its energy consumption and its emissions. Heat recovery units recapture heat from the smelting process, and a condenser turbine recaptures electricity. During 1985 to 2000, Rönnskär reduced its energy consumption by 20 percent, while its metal production increased by 11 percent. Thirty years ago, the plant emitted more than 250,000 tons of sulfur dioxide into the air per year. By 2000, annual sulfur dioxide emissions were less than 5,000 tons.

Both Rönnskär and public regulatory agencies closely scrutinize the plant's environmental performance. A state-of-the-art computer system continuously monitors emissions at the plant stacks. Air samples taken one or two miles from the site are measured for particulate matter. Sweden's national food regulatory agency analyzes samples of vegetables grown throughout the region. Sea mollusks and fish in the waters near the smelter are continually monitored and show improvement from past polluting times. Rönnskär melts 25,000 tons of electronic scrap per year without significant emissions of dioxins. These levels are well below the allowed European Union thresholds. The smelting process almost completely destroys hazardous halogen flame retardants. Over the past 20 years, Rönnskär has reduced its total emissions by 90 percent.

CONTINUING CHALLENGES

Rönnskär and the recycling industry as a whole face several challenges, according to a Rönnskär plant manager. First, he says, in many places it is still cheaper to dump solid waste at the landfill than to sort and recycle it. Swedish regulations for electronic waste still dictate that if treatment and recycling facilities are not available in the region, haulers and municipalities can obtain exemptions to dump this electronic waste at landfills. Rönnskär has the capacity to process electronic waste but does not receive sufficient volume to make this a profitable enterprise.

Second, the recycling market is unstable, says the plant manager. In 1997, Rönnskär studied the possibility of expanding its recycling operations. The facility analyzed the primary market, mining, and the secondary market, scrap metal and electronic materials. Plant analysts found that, at that time, the primary market in the developing world was considerably more stable and cost-effective than the secondary world market of recycled electronic goods. Technical problems such as energy input per output ratios that are not cost-effective present another challenge for the recycling industry that must devote time and resources to finding cost-effective solutions. Then, local authorities often dictate particular recycling methods, for example, requiring that certain products or materials must be manually dismantled. All these present considerable challenges for the recycling industry, says Rönnskär's plant manager.

PROVING IT CAN WORK

Despite these challenges, Rönnskär is demonstrating that it is feasible to recover and reuse existing metals before mining and introducing additional accumulations of virgin metals into society. To eventually be able to make products in the first place that are "100 percent good," society will need a facility like Ronnskär to extract base metals from fabricated products and purify them for return and reuse in industry. Sustainable extraction and use of metals involves efficient use of resources, profitable production, and minimal environmental impact, according to the plant manager. Rönnskär makes this possible through low costs, high metal recovery rates, recycling, and first-rate environmental care, says the Boliden Company. Vulcan, the mythological blacksmith god of fire and metalworking, is indeed hard at work in the Rönnskär smelter.[10]

In a sustainable society, nature is not subject to systematically increasing concentrations of substances extracted from the Earth's crust.
— *The Natural Step System Condition #1*[9]

Lovikka Village: Outstanding mittens, outstanding recycling

The village of Lovikka (Loo'-vick-ah), inhabited by about 120 people in the town of Pajala, has a particular distinction — it may have created the world's largest mitten. Among other accomplishments, Lovikka has been producing mittens for the Swedish military for the past 100 years. Pajala and its village of Kangos were discussed in Chapter 9.

Lovikka has another distinction. It recycles an astonishing 91 percent of its community's solid waste. The village began its own system for handling trash disposal and recycling in 1995. Through this self-designed system, Lovikka was able to reduce its total solid waste volume by 80 percent. Some estimates put the average Swedish recycling rate at 50 percent.

While Sweden's laws for producer responsibility of certain solid waste have bolstered recycling throughout the country, the system better supports urban, rather than rural, recycling efforts. Since recycling companies realize higher revenue from the greater volume of materials recycled in urban areas and less revenue from lower recycling volumes in rural areas, the companies often will not collect recyclables in small villages. To address this, villages, such as Lovikka and Kangos, and rural towns, such as Pajala, have developed strategies to combine recycled materials from several villages to make it worth the recycling companies' effort to collect.

RECYCLING COMPETITION

In the mid-1990s, the municipality of Pajala ran a competition among its 54 villages to see which village could achieve the highest recycling rate. Pajala supported the contest by providing increased recycling collection to the villages. Lovikka won this competition, achieving the highest number of product types recycled in the country — 23 different material types separated and recycled. Since then, 52 of Pajala's 54 villages have boosted their recycling rates.

Figure 12.3: Lovikka Village's town symbol.

Two strategies were essential in achieving Lovikka's 91 percent recycling rate, according to a village official. First, the village engaged all village households in first understanding the importance and relationship of recycling to global trends, then how each household could do a better job of reducing and recycling their own waste materials. Understanding how local actions such as recycling can help reduce encroachment upon nature gave added meaning and incentive to changing and improving individual actions. The village also set up a central location for collection of recyclables, next to the centrally located general store, making it easy and convenient for householders to drop them off. Next, villagers set a goal for each household to reduce the creation of household waste in the first place, then to recycle between 90 to 95 percent of the waste they did create.

In addition, Pajala and Lovikka are working on innovative approaches to manage human waste. Pajala has announced a close-the-loop contest among its 54 villages — this time to come up with eco-cyclic approaches to treating sewage.[11]

Eco-teams: Reducing household waste, and having fun doing it

The town of Eksjö (Eh'k-sheu), with 17,000 inhabitants, is one of several eco-municipalities that have helped organize citizen eco-team projects in their communities. Eco-teams are groups of about eight or ten households who band together to explore ways of living more ecologically. The idea for eco-teams comes from an international non-profit organization called Global Action Plan that works with municipalities around the world to reduce waste at the household level.

Eksjö's eco-team project idea blossomed from a well-attended community event called Lifestyle of the Future, organized as part of the town's sustainable development planning process. At that event, attendees learning about the eco-team idea helped to get this project started in Eksjö. Following that event, over 80 households got involved, meeting and working together in ten teams of eight households. Eco-teams receive information, education, and support from the municipal government.

WHAT ECO-TEAMS DO

In eco-teams, households learn ways to reduce household waste and support each other in putting these methods into practice. Buying less to begin with, choosing products with little or no packaging, composting food waste, and careful sorting and recycling of materials have made it possible for eco-team households to drastically reduce the amount of solid waste they create and discard. For example, some Eksjö eco-team members reduced their household solid waste disposal to about 44 pounds for the year. In contrast, in 2000, each U.S. citizen disposed of an average 1,642 pounds.[12]

Reducing household waste is not the only focus of eco-teams. Eco-team members learn how to shop strategically for products that are ecologically prepared and biodegradable, looking for eco-labels such as The Swan, Good Environmental Choice, and KRAV.[13] Buying more environmentally friendly products increases the market for these products, hence stimulating their production and eventually lowering their cost to the consumer. Another benefit: many companies that produce eco-certified products have also reduced unnecessary product packaging.

Eco-team members monitor their own household's energy use and help other team members find ways to reduce theirs. They advise one another, for example, about where to buy energy-efficient lamps, light bulbs, and appliances to reduce energy consumption in their homes. Eco-team members also help each other find ways to move around their communities without using gas-powered cars. Since Eksjö's downtown center is compact, it was not difficult for members to ride bikes and walk more often to do errands and shopping, instead of driving their cars.

Eksjö eco-team members encouraged each other to have more nature in their lives, for example either by growing butterfly-attracting flowers on their balconies, planting flowers and vegetables in a garden, or visiting and appreciating the lovely nature areas in their community. Eco-team members learned why local food production is important. People enjoyed, many for the first time, growing, cooking, and eating their own chemical-free fresh food.

MUNICIPAL SUPPORT FOR ECO-TEAMS

Eksjö's municipal government supports the ecological efforts of its eco-teams and citizens through a broad public outreach about how households can live in more sustainable ways and reduce stress on nature. For several years, Eksjö has used TV, radio, advertisements, and the worldwide web to spread this message. Recently, Eksjö placed a guide to sustainable actions in the local telephone book. In this guide, citizens can read about Eksjö's vision for a sustainable future, the four system conditions of the Natural Step, eco-team opportunities, and waste reduction and recycling tips. Householders can also learn from this guide how to use biomass fuel in adapted home furnaces, reduce energy costs in their household, look for eco-labeling in consumer products, and flush only appropriate materials.[14]

There is more information about Eksjö and its sustainability initiatives later in this chapter and in Chapter 16.

Sewage treatment: Plants do it better at the Ekeby Wetland

In the city of Eskilstuna, a constructed wetland is cleaning 12 million gallons of sewage a day, serving about 90 percent of Eskilstuna's 89,000 inhabitants. The Ekeby (Eh'-keh-bih) wetland, developed by Eskilstuna's municipal energy and environment department, is the largest constructed wetland in Sweden. The city's objective: to reduce discharges of nitrogen and phosphorus to the Eskilstuna River, Lake Mälaren, and the Baltic Sea.

In the early 1990s, Eskilstuna developed objectives for the quality of its rivers and water bodies as part of its overall sustainable development program. In 1993, a ten-year initiative began that eventually cut in half the levels of nitrogen and phosphorus in the Eskilstuna River. An additional city objective was to reduce fine particles in the city's drinking water, drawn from local rivers. Municipal regulations to limit agricultural runoff and industrial discharges had helped to reduce these levels, but nonpoint source pollution still remained. This type of diffuse pollution from undetermined sources was found to be the primary source of nutrients in river water. After studying various approaches, Eskilstuna officials decided upon the wetland construction method as the most suitable and effective means of sewage treatment.

HOW THE WETLAND WORKS

Nitrogen and phosphorus, elements that do not break down further, are critical and essential players and nutrients in natural systems. However, when their concentrations become too high, system overload can occur. This nutrient buildup and system overload is called eutrophication.[15]

The wetland, covering almost 100 acres of city-owned land, acts as a polishing system for the sewage effluent, since wetlands process nutrients and pollutants naturally and cyclically. Wetland bacteria transform dissolved nitrogen into airborne nitrogen. The natural sedimentation process reduces particles that become suspended in water. During the growing season, wetland plants absorb nutrients and sediments in the water for their own nourishment.

In the Ekeby wetland, an inlet channel carries the effluent through a series of three basins, then on to another series of three basins through a system of weirs and dams. The effluent takes one week to pass through the entire wetland system.

In one year, the wetland removes 70 tons of nitrogen from the water, also filtering out phosphorus and taking up bacteria. Water treated by the wetland has ten times less phosphorus and bacteria than that dictated by prevailing water quality standards. After passing through the wetland, the water meets swimming water standards.

Sludge is funneled to sedimentation tanks, where speeded-up biological

Figure 12.4: The Ekeby wetland in Eskilstuna treats 12 million gallons of sewage effluent a day. It has also become a stopover for migrating birds.

processes digest nutrients. Other processes remove heavy metals. The digested sludge becomes a composting product called bio-mull that can be used as a fertilizer. The plant is investigating ideas for recapturing and reusing more phosphorus from the sludge. The plant uses a heat pump and recovery system to recapture warmth from the sewage water. In the winter, the wetland rests.

Eskilstuna learned about the constructed wetland technology from another community where, ironically, land acquisition and permitting for construction of its wetland system have been delayed. Later, in 1995, Eskilstuna officials attended an international symposium on this technology to learn more about this innovative sewage technique.

The 100-acre Ekeby wetland has become a popular migratory bird stopover, where birders have sighted over 200 species of birds. The public prefers this type of sewage treatment solution because of its natural beauty and attractiveness for wildlife, say the Ekeby plant operators. A wetland system is also three times less expensive to operate than a conventional treatment system, they add. Building upon Ekeby's success, Eskilstuna is developing a second constructed wetland to reduce levels of phosphorus, nitrogen, and particles in the Tandla River, a tributary of the Eskilstuna River that is another city drinking water source. Besides the Ekeby wetland, Eskilstuna Energi and Environment also runs the city's district heating and cooling system, its combined heat and power (CHP) plant, electricity distribution, recycling, and telecommunications.[16] For more information about Eskilstuna and its biomass-fueled CHP plant, see Chapter 5.

Communities learn from each other: Wetland treatment and sustainable development

In the town of Eksjö, a visitor can climb a bird-watching tower, look at and listen to many birds, and observe lots of nature activity throughout 22 acres of wetland. That visitor might not even realize that she is looking at a municipal sewage treatment area, the Wetland Nifsarpsmaden (Niffs'-ahrps-mah'-dehn), constructed by Eksjö's municipal government to reduce phosphorus, nitrogen, organic material, bacteria, and metals in sewage effluent. The Wetland Nifsarpsmaden, a couple of miles from the center of Eksjö, is purifying water that flows from the Eksjö River through a lake into an estuary and then out to the Baltic Sea.

Another of Eksjö's wetland design objectives was to support biological diversity among wetland plants and animals. The visitor, if she is observant, will be able to identify many species of flowers, birds, insects, and water creatures. She might also encounter classes of school children visiting the wetland to observe and study these creatures, or local birdwatchers wielding binoculars and telescopes.

HIGHLAND COMMUNITIES COLLABORATE

The visitor would not realize, unless she was told, that this wetland is one outcome of *Höglandskommerna* (Heug'-lahnds-komm-eu'-nehr-nah), an unusual collaboration of six communities in the Highland region of Sweden. Three of these communities, including Eksjö, are members of SeKom, the national association of Swedish eco-municipalities. For several years, these communities have been working together to brainstorm ideas and implement a range of sustainable development projects. These Highland communities meet periodically and also join with other municipalities at SeKom gatherings to discuss particular implementation problems in sustainable development and share experiences and possible solutions. These communities discovered that they all were seeking better solutions for small-scale sewage treatment. They realized they could all benefit in saving time, effort, and money through exploring different treatment possibilities together rather than separately.

COLLABORATION ACROSS BOUNDARIES

Eksjö's collaborative sewage treatment efforts did not stop here. Through a 1994 twinning project sponsored by the national association of Swedish local authorities, Eksjö and seven other southern Swedish communities met with eight municipalities in northern Poland to explore how to make sustainable development happen at a local level. At this gathering, all 16 Swedish and Polish municipalities discovered they shared similar problems in public sector issues such as sewage treatment, landfills, district heating systems, and preservation of natural areas. Eksjö developed an ongoing collaborative relationship with its twin Polish community, Barlinek. Together they organized a 1997 conference in Barlinek to inform county officials in both countries about innovative small-scale sewage treatment methods. When the word spread in Poland about the coming conference, a huge public response occurred. People from all over the country wanted to attend this event. The conference received national TV, radio, and newspaper coverage. Poland's vice-minister of agriculture came to speak.

Eksjö's collaboration with Barlinek has deepened and continues to this day. Among other efforts, Eksjö has helped Barlinek obtain US$125,000 in public funding to reduce phosphorus levels in its sewage treatment works. Barlinek has developed a local sustainable development plan that has become a model for other Polish municipalities. Eksjö officials are impressed by Barlinek's commitment to a sustainable future. One conclusion of town officials in both countries: the problems are very much alike, whether you live in Poland or Sweden.[17] For more about Eksjö and its sustainable development practices, see Chapter 16.

National waste disposal: A Swedish snapshot

Both the Swedish national government and the European Union have passed solid waste disposal and recycling laws governing municipalities and authorities. Since 1993, Swedish law has required that producers of certain products, such as packaging, newspapers, cars, car tires, and batteries, be responsible for recycling of those materials. Since January 2000, regulations have prohibited dumping of combustible waste in local landfills, and as of January 2005, a national law will prohibit dumping of organic waste in landfills.

To ease the burden of these restrictions on households and communities, increasing national and international producer restrictions are emerging to help reduce waste in the first place. The Swedish government is reviewing expanded producer responsibility for waste, for example, possibly requiring electric and electronic product manufacturers to reduce toxicity in their goods. To make disposal alternatives, such as recycling, more economically attractive, the national government has taxed the amount of waste dumped at landfills since January 2000. The European Union is considering directives regulating disposal of scrapped cars, batteries, PVC, product packaging, and construction and demolition waste. The EU also is examining producer responsibility requirements.[18]

North American examples

Household recycling

The Global Action Plan (GAP) is working with municipalities in North America and beyond to organize and assist household eco-teams to find ways to use less, throw away less, and recycle more. Portland, Oregon; Seattle and Issaquah, Washington; Chattanooga, Tennessee; San Jose, California; and Kansas City, Missouri, are among the dozen U.S. cities that have worked with GAP in an effort that has changed the consumer behavior of over 30,000 citizens. Cities in 15 other countries have worked with GAP to start neighborhood eco-teams, involving over 120,000 consumers. Eco-team households send up to 50 percent less trash into the waste stream, reduce water use by 30 percent, energy use by 17 percent, and transportation fuel by 20 percent, and as a result realize household savings of up to US$400 per year.[19]

Industrial ecology

In creative approaches to sustainable practices, businesses are choosing to locate in areas where they are able to use each other's waste products as raw materials in their own operations. In a process that has come to be known as *industrial ecology*, based upon a remarkable web of by-product exchanges among facilities and businesses in Kalundborg, Denmark, eco-industrial parks have formed in Londonderry, New Hampshire; Devens, Massachusetts; and Fort Charles, Virgina. There, companies and power plants can reduce costs for raw materials and energy through using by-products and waste energy from others nearby, who in turn reduce their solid waste disposal costs for those by-products. In Canada, eco-industrial networks have sprung up in Tiverton, Ontario; Calgary, Alberta; and Dartmouth, Nova Scotia, among other localities. A national association called the Canadian Eco-Industrial Network supports these eco-industrial parks.[20]

Alternative sewage systems

Plant-based sewage treatment systems both for residential and industrial sewage are operating in Nevada, Texas, New York, New Hampshire and Massachusetts. "Living machines" or "solar aquatic systems" use plants grown hydroponically that consume nutrients and absorb many toxic substances in human and industrial sewage, resulting in an effluent that usually meets the U.S. Environmental Protection Agency's drinking water standards. These facilities, operating in the U.S. and seven other countries, are processing between 300 and 750,000 gallons per day of sewage for single-family homes to commercial institutions, such as the Ethel M. Chocolate Factory in Henderson, Nevada, and The Body Shop in Toronto, Ontario.[21] For other examples of dealing with waste, see Chapter 5 for a description of Umeå's Dåva power plant that creates heat and electricity from the city's own solid waste. Chapter 9 describes how 18 small villages pooled efforts to recycle.

CHAPTER 13

Natural Resources: Protecting Biodiversity

What you people call your natural resources our people call our relatives.

— Orien Lyons, faith keeper of the Onondaga[1]

Why are "natural resources" so important?

If the reader were to undertake a sampling of master plans, comprehensive plans, general plans, or official plans of American and Canadian municipalities, he likely would find in most of these plans a chapter devoted to "Natural Resources." Usually, such chapters would provide inventories of the various water bodies, wetlands, forests, open space areas, and wildlife habitat within the plan's area of jurisdiction. States that mandate municipal comprehensive planning or what should be in a local plan, if undertaken, almost always include "natural resources" among the topics that a plan should cover, along with land use, housing, transportation, economic development, and public facilities. Most city, town, and regional planners assume that sound comprehensive planning should address the subject of "natural resources" — the term usually used in city, town, and regional planning to describe the above features. Most localities also have a "conservation commission" charged with the responsibility of overseeing, at the least, the natural resources of water and wetlands.

But why are forests, wetlands, streams, and wild creatures important to us, not to mention in, and of, themselves? Do we, as members of our communities and larger ecosystems, really and fully understand why? Water may be the "natural resource" most widely understood in terms of its importance, at least in relation to human beings. Virtually everyone knows that water is essential to the lives of humans and other creatures; we need a sufficient quantity and quality of water to drink. It is primary to our own survival and secondary as a component of making and maintaining things we have come to believe as essential to our lives. We understand forests to be important because wood is also seen and used as an essential component in making and maintaining things we use and believe essential.

Over the last several decades, we citizens, as well as planning professionals, have come to better understand the subtle and complex roles that "natural resources" play in our lives and well-being. We understand that wetlands are a major contributor to fish breeding and flood control, for example. We know, although we often forget, that trees and vegetation produce the oxygen we breathe and absorb carbon dioxide that we exhale. Green plants are the basis of our entire food system. Many of us are aware that having open space, woodlands, babbling brooks, and singing birds nearby contributes to our quality of life. What we often forget, though, is that these aspects of nature are also our life-support system. Without enough oxygen to breathe, without enough green plants to support our food system, without enough potable water, there would be no us.

But how about the importance of other species on this planet, particularly the ones that we don't directly or indirectly eat? How about the importance of the multiplicity of those species?

These are questions about which courses have been taught, books have been written, scientific debates have raged, and activists have been jailed. The great biologist E.O. Wilson has said "... the question I am asked most frequently about the diversity of life [is]: if enough species are extinguished, will the ecosystems collapse, and will the extinction of most other species follow soon afterward? The only answer anyone can give is, possibly. By the time we find out, however, it might be too late. One planet, one experiment."[3]

Some biologists and ecologists describe biodiversity as an insurance policy that protects against loss in any one area. According to these scientists, it is possible to lose a keystone species — a species whose role is vital to the survival of other species in an ecosystem.[4] It may be easier to understand the importance of diversity in an area such as food cultivation. When a diversity of crops, as opposed to a single crop, is planted on a farm it drastically reduces the likelihood of that farm's entire produce being wiped out by a pest.

In a sustainable society, nature is not subject to systematically increasing degradation by physical means.
— *System Condition #3 of the Natural Step framework*[2]

The complexity of nature is such that we may never really know the answers to these questions until it is too late. As two scientists have pointed out:

> "[We] do not really know what we are losing when we lose species. Some ecologists have likened the loss of biodiversity to an airplane flight during which we continually pull out rivets as the plane cruises along. How many rivets can we pull out before disaster occurs?"[5]

The lack of answers to these questions, however, is not stopping efforts around the world to protect threatened or endangered species and the natural areas that foster diversity of life — forests, water bodies, wetlands, wilderness areas. What follows are two stories of how a municipality and a region in Sweden are working to protect a native species, the salmon, in their respective ecosystems.

Falkenberg protects its native salmon

The city of Falkenberg and its River Ätran are said to offer the best salmon fishing in Sweden.[6] The River Ätran, one of 23 rivers on Sweden's west coast emptying into the North Sea, wends its way through the entire community of Falkenberg.

The salmon is an important symbol for Falkenberg. Salmon fishing has been an integral part of Falkenberg life since the 1600s, when it became one of the town's prime sources of income. Sweden's largest smoked salmon industry, which uses the same recipe since it was founded in 1826, is located in Falkenberg. During the 1980s, a sign went up in town quipping that salmonfishing "pays" for the Falkenberg mayor's salary.

For many years in the mid-1900s, the indigenous species of salmon that spawned in the River Ätran declined and almost went extinct. Biologists determined that no other species of salmon in Sweden had the same genetic stock. The loss of this salmon species became an important bio-indicator to the community that something was wrong.

For decades, the quality of the River Ätran's water had been deteriorating due to industrial discharges and acid rain. Acid rain is a particular threat to salmon, as it affects the ability of their gills to function in salt water. By the late 1970s, the river had become one thousand times more acidic than the salmon could tolerate, according to a Falkenberg municipal ecologist. In 1978, the Falkenberg municipal government decided to put lime in the river to offset this acidification in order to help the salmon survive. This continues today. Now, over 4,000 salmon are migrating up the river every year to spawn.

However, another threat to the river's native salmon species materialized in the form of invaders. Many farm-raised salmon were escaping, and continue to escape, from salmon farms in Norway and Denmark. These salmon, which are bred to grow large for the market, escape to the southern Baltic Sea. The farm-raised salmon are a different strain from wild Atlantic salmon and the indigenous River Ätran salmon. These farm-raised salmon, too, were traveling up the River Ätran to spawn, and were interbreeding with the river's indigenous salmon species. The city of Falkenberg realized that, if nothing was done, the river's indigenous species could be lost forever, since its particular genetic code would be irreparably altered over generations. The city again took action.

Falkenberg launched an initiative to protect the genetic stock of its indigenous salmon species. The city hired two ecologists to physically inspect every salmon that traveled up the River Ätran to spawn, and to intercept the invaders.

To accomplish this, the ecologists set up an interception station at the lower end of a dam of a former flour mill on the river. Salmon traveling upriver are herded into a holding pool at the foot of the dam. From this pool, the ecologists transfer the salmon into a tank that is then hoisted to the upstream side of the river. During spawning season, this is carried out daily. Before throwing the salmon into the river upstream of the dam, the ecologists check to make sure that the salmon is the correct genetic type. The indigenous salmon are placed in the upstream river to continue their journey to spawn. Nonindigenous salmon end up on dinner plates, including those of households in need.

The native salmon preservation project is one result of Falkenberg's city planning objectives to preserve biodiversity throughout its community. The city's goals are to manage its lakes, rivers, streams, and publicly owned and leased lands in ways that preserve and improve their ecosystems and biodiversity. The city has made plans to set aside a major wetland as a public nature preserve and to restore eight additional wetlands. Falkenberg is

Figure 13.1: A former flour mill's dam on the River Ätran provides an opportunity to intercept salmon migrating upstream to spawn. The dam also generates hydroelectricity, enough to power the mill, its adjoining house, and over 20 nearby households.

working with other municipalities in a regional water management association, a coastal water control organization, and regional salmon and fishing management associations. The River Ätran has become an index river for salmon species monitoring in Sweden.

In other protective efforts, Falkenberg requires that all agriculture carried out in designated water protection areas must be organic agriculture. The city is also working on a conservation plan for its forests and has set aside three areas, including an old growth forest of spruce trees, for permanent protection. The city is moving toward the elimination of all pesticides and artificial fertilizers in the maintenance of its parks and green areas.

The changes in regional farming practices moving away from pesticide use, and in regional businesses finding alternatives to chemical use in their operations and production, have contributed to a vast increase in the multiplicity of wildlife found in Falkenberg, according to one of the city's ecologists. Overall, he says, the biodiversity of species found in Falkenberg today is estimated to be ten times greater than its level ten years ago. For more about Falkenberg and its sustainable development work, see Chapter 5. For more about organic agriculture practices, see Chapter 11.

Figure 13.2: One of Falkenberg's staff ecologists checks to see whether a salmon is one of the river's indigenous species.

Kalix: From sustainable practices to restorative ones

The town of Kalix is located at the mouth of the Kalix River on the coast of the Baltic Sea. (The villages of Kalix are discussed in Chapter 9.) Of the country's four major rivers, the Kalix River is one of two that have no hydroelectric plants and no dams. Hence, it is more accessible to salmon traveling upstream to spawn in its fresh waters. The Kalix River is 280 miles long. Kalix's history and culture have evolved around the Kalix River watershed, land that is drained by the river and its tributaries. Fishing, especially, has united the people that live in this watershed region.

Kalix is part of a fisheries district, populated by 18,500 people, that oversees rivers, water quality, and fishing within the region. Forestry and fishing are two of its main industries. The fisheries district is looking at sportfishing and ecotourism as future industries. During the 1980s, there were no salmon at all in the Kalix River, according to a fisheries district officer. Overfishing in the Baltic Sea, river fishing with net strung across the river to trap fish, and bulldozing the river bottom to clear channels for log flotation all depleted the populations of salmon, brown trout, and other indigenous fish species of the river.

Now, the Kalix River is the second largest producer of salmon in the Baltic region, producing 250,000 salmon per year. Its neighbor to the east, the Tournio River, which forms the boundary between Sweden and Finland, is producing 500,000 salmon per year. The average weight of a salmon caught is 17½ pounds, according to the district officer, because of the robust herring in the Baltic Sea upon which they feed. Once, every river along the Finnish coast was a salmon river. Now, every river is dammed. The other Baltic Sea countries — for example, Germany, Denmark, and Latvia — have no salmon rivers left. All have been destroyed with dams and pollution, says the fisheries district officer.

With the collapse of the salmon population in the Baltic Sea, whitefish has become a favorite. The salmon population, however, is coming back. Since 1994, the salmon population in the Kalix River has been steadily increasing.

Kalix's industries include a sawmill and a paper mill located on the Kalix River. Historically, the logging industries would float logs down the river to the sea. During the 1940s, tractors started pushing rocks out of the bottom of the river. This drastically changed the face of the river, and its ecosystems, into a canal; pools and spawning places for salmon were lost. The Kalix River has been fortunate with respect to pollutants. There is one copper mine in the region. In the last 10 to 20 years, pollution from heavy metals has been relatively low. However, the river does contain heavy metal sediments from industrial pollution that occurred in the 1950s and 1960s. The Swedish environmental protection agency decided to leave those sediments in place for fear of dispersing these toxic substances further. Kalix and other local authorities have good controls regulating the use and discharge of phosphates, says the fisheries district officer. Too much nitrogen is a problem, he adds. Several local authorities are creating wetlands to help reduce nitrogen in sewage effluent.

In 1974, the logging industry began trucking logs south, instead of floating them down the river, because it was cheaper. Since then, the town of Kalix, concerned regional agencies, and organizations have been working to find ways of restoring the river to a more natural state. The national government is spending millions to help restore the country's rivers. Among other things, it is an investment in sportsfishing. One effort underway is restoring gravel and river bottom vegetation, often by hand, to create spawning places for salmon. These and other fish need deep beds of gravel for spawning. Two years after the first loads of gravel were brought to areas of the river, many fish, including trout, that had almost become extinct returned to the river.

In order to reduce the risk of disease transmission from farmed salmon to wild salmon, it is forbidden to start a fish farm or bring in any fish from Norway into the Kalix River. Farmed fish are treated with chemicals to prevent disease but wild stock are not. Farmed fish also breed with wild salmon and weaken and change the genetic stock of the indigenous population. Almost every river in Norway has a fish farm, says the fisheries district director. Invasive fish species are a huge problem here. Studies in Scotland and Ireland show that, in mouths of rivers where there are fish farms, the wild fish get sick, he points out. Finns are still putting cultivated salmon into the Tournio River, he adds. This is affecting the genetic population of the river.[7]

SUMMARY

Falkenberg and the Kalix region understand the importance of their salmon species to their local economies and to the character of their regions. They have come to understand which human activities brought about the threatened extinction of those species — invasion of exotic species in one case and destruction of habitat and breeding grounds in the other. They are taking steps not only to halt those destructive activities but also to restore what has been destroyed before. They have moved beyond sustainable practices to restorative practices.

National efforts in Sweden

In many Swedish municipalities, according to the Falkenberg ecologists, pressure from an aware public and environmental groups has spurred on local politicians to hire ecologists to address biodiversity protection. There are also national laws requiring municipalities to attend to natural resource preservation. For example, in 1994, the Swedish parliament adopted a national preservation strategy that requires, among other things, that each locality be responsible for how its own activities and policies contribute toward preservation of biodiversity. In 1995, Sweden's national departments for environment, housing, building and planning, fisheries, agriculture, and forestry each prepared an action plan for preserving biodiversity in its own area of jurisdiction. In 1998, the European Union Commission presented a strategy for biodiversity throughout the European Union.[8] Protecting biodiversity is also one of Sweden's 15 national environmental goals, adopted in 1999.

North American examples

In both Canada and the United States, many local governments are working, often in partnerships with state, provincial, and non-profit organizations, to protect the biodiversity of critical ecosystems within their regions. In Canada, for example, a remarkable coalition has formed to protect the biodiversity of the Rideau River, flowing over 60 miles throughout Ontario. The City of Ottawa and the Regional Municipality of Ottawa-Carleton are working with 35 other public and private organizations to restore and preserve one of Ontario's most prominent rivers, brought to a biological crisis through years of pollution, over-development, and over-fishing. The Rideau River coalition is working to protect the shoreline from more development, eliminate sources of water pollution, and combat an invasive zebra mussel population.[9]

In the United States, another remarkable coalition is working to protect wetlands in the Berkshire region of western Massachusetts that are among the rarest wetlands of their type in the world. The towns of Stockbridge, Lee, and the regional planning commission have teamed up with the state highway department, turnpike authority, state environmental agencies, a university, and an international non-profit conservancy organization. These towns and agencies are working together in a systematic initiative to protect rare wetlands and bogs in the 120,000-acre Taconic region spanning Massachusetts, Connecticut, and New York. The Nature Conservancy, a key member of this coalition, has identified the Taconic wetlands as one of the highest quality calcium-rich sweetwater wetlands in the world, home to over 150 rare and endangered species, one of the highest concentrations in New England. Among the many preservation actions, the partnership is working to remove the invasive phragmite plants threatening the fragile ecosystems of these wetlands.[10]

In the end, our society will be defined not only by what we create, but by what we refuse to destroy.
— *John Sawhill, former president, The Nature Conservancy* [11]

CHAPTER 14

Sustainable Land Use and Planning

Planning for sustainability requires a systematic, integrated approach that brings together environmental, economic, and social goals and actions directed toward ... four objectives.
— American Planning Association, Policy Guide on Planning for Sustainability

If this is the chapter on planning, what have all the rest been about?

THE FOUR SUSTAINABILITY OBJECTIVES
1) Reduce dependence upon fossil fuels, extracted underground metals and minerals;
2) Reduce dependence on chemicals and other man-ufactured substances that can accumulate in nature;
3) Reduce dependence on activities that harm life-sustaining ecosystems;
4) Meet the hierarchy of human needs fairly and efficiently.
— *American Planning Association*[1]

Every chapter in this book so far has been about planning. Every topic covered in Part II — energy, housing, economic development, natural resources, agriculture, for example — is an element of what city, town, and regional planning addresses. The accomplishments of the cities and towns described in these chapters are the results of planning. The community-based, democratic processes for change toward sustainability that are discussed in the next part of this book are planning processes.

Planning addresses each of these areas and brings them together as an integrated whole. Good planning is about making sure that the policies for all these community issues are "rowing in the same direction." For skeptical readers who may think that city or town planning is superfluous, consider this: What other function or part of local government is charged with keeping track of the overall community vision and the way that policies of all parts of the municipality fit together as a whole?

All around the world, cities, towns, and regions prepare plans for guiding their future growth and development. In some places these are called master plans or comprehensive plans; in other places they are called general plans, oversight plans, or official plans. They all are the official policy documents through which local governments can systematically guide their future and assure that their policies in land use, housing, economic development, transportation, public facilities, among others, are systematically moving in the desired direction. This is why such plans are logical tools for guiding and implementing systematic community change toward sustainable development. While local governments vary drastically in the *effective* use of those plans, the comprehensive planning process remains, nevertheless, a logical vehicle for guiding and bringing about community change. The next part of this book presents suggestions and guidance for designing and executing an effective planning process to implement community sustainable development.

This chapter presents examples of two Swedish eco-municipalities that brought sustainability goals into their comprehensive planning processes tailor-made for their particular situations and circumstances. In Göteborg, with a long-standing tradition of business–government cooperation, planning combined ecological principles with strategies for competitive advantage in the marketplace. The process also honored the strong city–neighborhood governing structure of Göteborg. In Sala, which also joined comprehensive planning with planning for sustainability, the planning process became an important vehicle in carrying out the community's goal to become an eco-municipality.

Göteborg: A city and its neighborhoods plan for sustainability

About Göteborg

The city of Göteborg (Yeu-teh-boryh'), founded in 1621, was designed and laid out by German and Dutch city planners and canal builders. Located where the Göta River meets the northern Atlantic Ocean, Göteborg is Scandinavia's largest port. Traditionally, it has been a center for manufacturing and heavy industry. Nearly half a million people now live in Göteborg, many of whom were born in different countries or are transplants from other regions of Sweden.

In the late 1980s, Göteborg reorganized its municipal government to include 21 city districts governed by city district councils, whose members are appointed by the Göteborg city council and report directly to the council. The political party representation within the district councils is designed to mirror that of the Göteborg city council.

Founding goals of the city districts were to better meet citizen needs and to save money through more direct targeting and provision of services to people in need. Another objective was to broaden public involvement in city affairs. The city district councils are responsible for social, educational, and cultural affairs within their districts. They oversee libraries and provide eldercare, services to disabled people, and daycare. City districts are experimenting with various ways to strengthen civic participation, for example, by establishing debate evenings, politician phone-ins, district school boards, public health boards, and local sustainable development boards.

The city of Göteborg has taken a leadership role in environmental change. As one example, the city established the Göteborg International Environmental Prize in 1999 to help raise awareness of environmental issues both within its own city and beyond. This prize was to be given to an individual or organization making an outstanding contribution to sustainable development in the world. In 2002, the city awarded this prize to Dr. Gro Bruntland, an instrumental leader in the 1987 World Commission on the Environment and Development, whose path-breaking leadership boosted awareness and work toward sustainable development around the world. In previous years, Göteborg awarded the prize to the Forest Stewardship Council and KRAV for their efforts in sustainable forestry and organic food promotion and certification.

GÖTEBORG'S CITY PLANNING

Since the 1960s, Göteborg has experienced a series of severe environmental problems. A rapid growth rate brought a burst of sprawl development and accompanying traffic congestion. Soils became acidified, air quality standards were poor, and public health and biodiversity were declining. During the 1970s, economic problems worsened when Göteborg's shipbuilding industry went through an economic crisis. Shipyards closed down and hundreds of shipbuilders lost their jobs or were forced into early retirement. Something had to be done.

Göteborg's 1993 comprehensive plan faced these issues squarely. City leaders and city planners decided to put sustainable development at the core of plan development, bringing together environmental concerns with the city's long-standing tradition of working cooperatively with the business and industry community. "The Competitive and Sustainable City" became the catch phrase for Göteborg's envisioned future that guided the 1993 plan development.

It balanced competitive advantage and long-term sustainability. The guiding land use policies that evolved from the planning process were to:

- concentrate new development in already built-up areas of the city, while giving careful consideration to the cultural and ecological features of these areas; and
- avoid development at the fringe of the city, particularly areas not well-served by public transit.

It was important to achieve political consensus on these policies, since they were to guide both political decisions and municipal allocation of land use permits.

Göteborg's 1993 plan introduced a concept and strategy of "eco-balancing" to guide development and manage the city's resources. The eco-balancing policy called for examining the balance of carbon, water, and nitrogen and the way that new development would affect this balance. This policy included energy analyses of proposed new development.

Meanwhile, the city began the practice of requiring all municipal departments to develop environmental management plans and ways to monitor their success on an ongoing basis. Out of this policy emerged the city's environmental purchasing plan, requiring all departments to purchase environmentally benign products. Göteborg became the first city in Sweden to adopt an environmental purchasing policy. Every household and workplace in the city received an eco-handbook prepared by the city that offered practical, user-friendly advice about how to shop and conduct daily tasks in more ecological ways. The city also adopted a waste management plan that required households to recycle organic wastes, realizing that the national government was going to adopt a similar requirement. Göteborg also adopted strong traffic controls in its center core to reduce heavy, high-polluting traffic.

During the 1996 plan update, the planning process took into consideration the city's decentralization policy that had created the 21 city districts. The city's vision expanded to include "the large and small Göteborg." "Large Göteborg" was the continuation of the city as a vital regional center — the "competitive and sustainable city." "Small Göteborg" represented the many

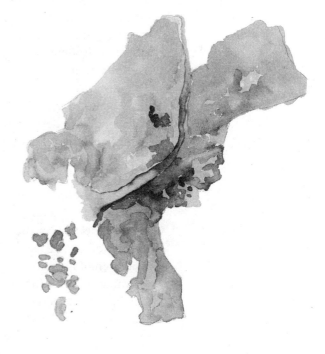

Figure 14.1: Göteborg's master plan concentrates development in existing centers, shown as dark areas in this plan map, and also concentrates development in areas well-served by public transit. Credit: Municipality of Göteborg

small neighborhoods with their own strong identities, culture, and urge for self-determination. The city district councils became important vehicles for neighborhood contributions to the plan. The 1996 plan also established the goal to better integrate social services and city planning at the district, or neighborhood, level. One such example was the Biskopsgården neighborhood.

BISKOPSGÅRDEN: NEIGHBORHOOD CHANGE THROUGH WORKING TOGETHER

Biskopsgården (Biss'-kopps-gohr'-dehn) is a Göteborg district and neighborhood of about 24,000 inhabitants, one-half of them immigrants. The neighborhood, about a 15-minute ride by public transit from Göteborg's central core, is situated quite near the shipyards, oil refineries, and other heavy industries. The neighborhood was suffering poor air quality from the oil refineries. It developed a troubled reputation, and higher-income households began an exodus. Housing was not being well-maintained, and the neighborhood became an area of high transience.

In 1993, the Biskopsgården district council, the Göteborg city planning office, and two housing agencies — one municipal, one private — teamed up to reverse these trends of neighborhood deterioration. An initial step was to build a broad network across professions, interests, and organizations to work on specific themes such as employment, physical environment, and social environment. A series of successful early actions — "picking the low-hanging fruits" — inspired neighborhood residents to get involved when they saw that real change could come out of their participation. One such early action was the painting of all the neighborhood bridges and pedestrian underpasses. Another result was a new bus line called Flexline, where neighborhood residents could call for a ride that would pick them up at their door within 15 minutes. This new bus line, for use by all, was a particular boon for elders and disabled neighborhood residents.

A long-term outcome of the neighborhood district planning process was an active neighborhood network and resident participation process that connects with the city district council organization and work. Over a period of several years, improvements in neighborhood housing conditions, employment, and more opportunities for individual residents, for example, adult education classes, changed both neighborhood and city perceptions of Biskopsgården from a trouble-ridden area to a community with promise.

BERGSJÖN: FROM PROBLEM DISTRICT TO ECO-DISTRICT

The Bergsjön (Behryh'-sheun) neighborhood, like Biskopsgården, is a 15-minute public transit ride to Göteborg's central core. Most of Bergsjön's 15,000 residents live in multifamily housing. Like Biskopsgården, half the neighborhood population comes from different countries of origin. Fifty-four different languages are spoken in Bergsjön schools. Further, these neighborhoods shared similar problems of unemployment, segregation, and population exodus. When neighborhoods experience difficulties like these, it is easy to start focusing on problems rather than on opportunities, as one Bergsjön planner says.

However, this planner and some other people in Bergsjön, including district council members, recognized the neighborhood's assets as well as its challenges. Despite its close location to the center of Göteborg, Bergsjön sits in a pleasing geography of hills, woods, and trees. Its varied ethnic population has given rise to a rich cultural life of various multicultural activities, events, associations, and clubs. Recognition of these assets helped lead the Bergsjön district council to adopt a resolution in the early 1990s to turn its neighborhood into an eco-district. Once again, similar to Biskopsgården, the Bergsjön neighborhood rallied together in a broadbased network of residents, community associations, housing companies, businesses, and district and city planning offices.

Through the eco-planning process, it became clear that an important neighborhood priority was to create meeting places — areas where neighborhood residents of all backgrounds and ages could come together and experience the feeling of community. One planning outcome was the development of a community center, built by the Göteborg municipality and run by the local Assyrian association, which also serves as a demonstration center for ecological building practices. Here, Bergsjön teachers give classes, popular among the children, about the cycles of nature. Multilingual exhibits show how solar panels, greenhouses, and woodstoves operate and how they help nature. From their experience in running this center, the Assyrian association itself has begun to adopt ecological practices in running its own organization.

In the western section of Bergsjön, another neighborhood association runs an urban farm. Here, city residents can grow and buy healthy food, bring their children to see what horses, cows, and chickens look like, and to eat or dance in the clubhouse and café. Near this farm, another meeting place called Returhuset (Reh-teuhr'-heu'set) provides activities including job training, daycare, and recycling collection. Returhuset, too, has an eco-café and garden as well as an environmental library, meeting rooms for study groups and eco-workshops, and a media group that puts out a calendar of neighborhood environmental events. Through coming together at activity centers such as these, residents feel renewed in their commitment to the neighborhood and local life, according to the district's eco-planner. Many residents also make new friends, she adds.

Not far from the urban farm and Returhuset center, Göteborg has developed a constructed wetland that not only collects stormwater but also provides a beautiful park and outdoor meeting place for community residents. Horses, cows, and sheep graze in surrounding meadows, visible from nearby apartment buildings. Horseback riders, school classes studying frogs and birds, and joggers and walkers all enjoy the network of paths and footbridges in, and around, the wetland.

Housing conditions and resident stabilization have improved as well. Tenants and management companies work cooperatively on efforts such as improving local transportation options and building appearances. Apartment buildings formerly experiencing high turnover and vacancy rates now have waiting lists of people wanting to move in. "Everyone wants to live there!" says Bergsjön's district planner.

GÖTEBORG REVERSES GREENHOUSE GAS TRENDS

Göteborg's planning and sustainable development efforts have paid off for the city as a whole in many ways. For example, in the area of energy and fossil fuel use, it has succeeded in changing its trends of increasing greenhouse gas emissions to trends of reducing emissions. The city has reduced sulfur dioxide and particulate emissions by 90 percent from its 1987 levels. Two-thirds of its district heat production comes from regained heat. The city's hookup of two-thirds of all households to its district heating system helped to reduce carbon dioxide emissions by 50 percent between 1984 and 1991.

Göteborg recognizes that planning is an ongoing process. The city is already working on its next plan update, this time concentrating on more integration of regional cooperation and attention to human needs in comprehensive planning. Göteborg's planners believe that a key contribution of planning is creation of mental readiness for change — in the words of one planner, "to think the unthinkable."[2]

Sala joins comprehensive planning with planning for sustainability

ABOUT SALA

The municipality of Sala (Sah'lah) is located about 70 miles northwest of Stockholm. More than half of Sala's 22,000 inhabitants live in the town's central core. Historically, Sala developed as a mining town in the 1600s, near a silver mine that was at one time the richest in the world. Today, Sala's main industries are farming, forestry, and small-scale business. The silver mine, which closed in 1908, has become a local tourist attraction. Sala describes its community character as "both town and country." It features a picturesque, compact town center with many well-preserved, historic buildings. Its outlying areas are predominantly farmland. Lakes form part of both its rural and urban landscapes.

Sala joined SeKom, the national association of eco-municipalities, in 1991, declaring its intent to systematically change to sustainable practices through a bottom-up, democratic approach. The entire left-to-right political spectrum of Sala's public officials agreed on this course of action. In its decision to become an eco-municipality, Sala officially committed itself to:

- changing to sustainable practices through a grassroots approach that actively engages citizens in democratic processes of change;
- fostering cooperation among the various municipal agencies, departments, companies, and other sectors of the community in adopting sustainable practices;
- interweaving social, cultural, ecological, technical, and educational aspects of sustainable development throughout municipal operations and the broader Sala community;
- guiding change to sustainable practices by vision united with action;
- using strategies of small-scale action, self-sufficiency, cooperation and decentralization;
- making clear the connection between local action and global conditions; and
- using the Natural Step sustainability framework as a compass for change.

SALA'S ECO-MUNICIPALITY PLAN: A NEW TYPE OF PLANNING

During the 1990s, Sala decided to integrate its comprehensive planning process and an initiative for sustainable development to produce a unified comprehensive and sustainable development plan — A Plan for the Sala Eco-Municipality. The guiding framework for sustainability in the combined plan is the Natural Step system conditions for a sustainable society. The plan is intended to be a long-range guide for the community's planning and development and for the municipal departments, agencies, and publicly held companies of Sala. A community-derived "Sustainable Sala" vision is the basis for the plan's goals and objectives.

In its comprehensive sustainability planning process, Sala is bringing together all city interests and increasing collaboration among the municipal departments and agencies. Another aim is to strengthen citizen influence in the planning process through increased community participation in planning before official discussions or major decisions take place. Sala's expanded citizen participation initiative, called Our Piece of the Earth, uses a variety of places and activities to bring people together to discuss the future of their community, including vision workshops, community forums, networks, workgroups, study circles, and festivals.

SALA'S PLANNING OUTCOMES

From the Sala comprehensive sustainability planning process, a variety of eco-success stories have emerged.

Changing to renewable energy

In 1992, Sala's district heating system switched its energy source from coal to a combination of biomass (wood by-products), heat recovered from industrial wastewater, and gas produced from garbage dumps. In 1999, Sala's new combined heat and power plant (CHP) went on line, producing green electricity in addition to heat for the district heating system. Sala's municipal government is now operating ten staff cars on canola (rapeseed) oil instead of petroleum-based fuel, and several local taxicabs have followed suit.

Greening business development

Sala is working with local businesses and industries to encourage ecological business practices and green product development. Together with local businesses, the municipality developed an information center for environmental product and practices, contacts, and networking called the Sala Eco-Center. It helps local businesses obtain and use biofuels instead of fossil fuels and helps collect and recycle wood ash from commercial wood-fired systems. The Eco-Center's board has representatives from the municipal government, private corporations, and local universities. Sala awards certificates to stores that adopt environmentally friendly practices. Four of the major supermarkets in the city have received this environmental recognition. Sala also runs a competition for the most environmentally sound office building.

THE GUIDING SUSTAINABILITY FRAMEWORK FOR SALA'S ECO-MUNICIPALITY PLAN:

In the sustainable society, nature is not subject to systematically increasing ...

1. concentrations of substances extracted from the Earth's crust
2. concentrations of substances produced by society
3. degradation by physical means

and, in the sustainable society,

4. people are not subject to conditions that systematically undermine their capacity to meet their needs.

The Natural Step system conditions

Recycling

Since 1991, Sala has operated a recycling center that separates and distributes 20 different types of materials. Thirty-five collecting stations separating ten types of material are located throughout the city. Sala is encouraging households to compost their organic material, rather than discard it with the trash. At present, 1,800 out of 9,700 households are taking their organic materials to the public composting center at the outskirts of Sala. The city has set a goal of increasing this number to 6,000, or 60 percent of all households in the city. Plans are underway to build a repair and resale center for discarded goods.

Preserving biodiversity

Sala is developing an ecological approach to forest management, using a municipal forest as the testing ground. The city is restoring needed pastureland and has restored a damaged wetland that was on a United Nations critical area list for global importance.

Building an ecological school

In 1997, Sala constructed Ängshagenskolan (Engs'-hah'-ghen-skoo'-lahn) an ecologically built elementary school that teaches ecological learning. The building features a sod-and-grass roof that absorbs rainwater and insulates the building. Biofueled district heating, floor heating, and a passive solar building orientation provide the building's warmth. The major brick partition wall acts as a thermal mass that absorbs the energy of the sun, then releases it over several hours. Building materials can be recycled when their useful life is over. A passive ventilation system provides fresh air, saving energy and eliminating noise at the same time. All waste is sorted and recycled, and urine-separating toilets are in the bathrooms. All classes integrate nature and the environment in the curriculum and learning methods. Special classrooms have been designed and designated for nature experiments, growing vegetables and herbs. The school grounds include ponds, vegetable gardens, apple trees, berry bushes, and compost heaps.

Teaching ecological gardening

Sala's municipal government teamed up with a high school and non-profit associations to develop Linnea's Garden, a teaching farm and garden for children and adults about four miles from Sala's downtown. Linnea, the garden's namesake, is a character in a well-known children's book. A kitchen and café draw visitors, who can also take part in ecological learning groups and activities. A dairy makes sheep cheese and yogurt for the café. The gardens demonstrate different types of ecological gardening practices and experimental cultivation of foods, such as berries. Rabbits, hens, pigs, and bees allow children the chance to see, understand, and tend animals. Children need animals in order to develop tenderness, observes a Sala planner. In workshops, children whittle bark boats, make bird nesting boxes and kites. Children also make-believe that they are in the wilderness, cooking food by campfires and learning how nature can provide.

EDUCATION, TRAINING, AND INDICATORS

During 1994–1995, 2,000 Sala employees including politicians, municipal department employees, and local publicly held companies took part in a one-day training session that introduced the concepts of sustainability and sustainable development, using the Natural Step framework as a guide. Some teachers in the Sala school system went on to take a two-day training course in the Natural Step approach. Returning to their schools, they gradually introduced these ideas to their classes. For example, teachers developed a series of games for children of different ages — "The Mission" for children from four to seven years old and "The Challenge" for children ten to twelve years old. These games, which involve cards that introduce the Natural Step system conditions in easy to understand ways, are now widely used in Sala's preschools, elementary and middle schools, and recreation centers. Ecological learning is now interwoven throughout Sala's daycare centers and schools. Most daycare staffers have taken part in a three-week ecology training session. Recycling and composting are a part of the children's everyday life.

As one means of introducing the sustainability framework to the larger community, organizers of the 1993 Sala Fair designed a large exhibit called the Eco Labyrinth. This exhibit explained the concept of sustainability and the Natural Step system conditions as a guide for sustainable action. Once introduced to these principles, the visitor would begin her journey through the labyrinth, using the framework to make environmental decisions that would bring her ever closer — if the decisions were correct ones — to the labyrinth's center. Finally at the center of the labyrinth, the visitor would be treated to a display of a "Sustainable Sala" in 2010. A publication called *The Green Dragon*, household mailings, forums, and study groups have all helped raise ecological awareness among the citizens of Sala. Ecological courses are offered to unemployed persons, who are given jobs helping to disseminate environmental learning materials throughout the community.

Over 2,000 citizens, ten percent of the population, have participated in learning seminars about eco-cyclic thinking. The city believed it was important to give as many municipal employees and citizens as possible a common basis from which to begin changing to sustainable practices.

Sala has been working with three other municipalities to develop sustainability indicators, also called environmental accounting or "nature economy." Starting with the sustainable development goals set by city officials, municipal staffers developed business ratios with different units of measurement that went beyond purely monetary ones. Progress reports using these indicators are presented each year to Sala's governing officials, agency heads, and the media. The indicators are used to measure city progress toward political goals, progress toward each of the four Natural Step system conditions, and cost-effectiveness and efficiency.

Over 100 Sala municipal employees and politicians have been trained to use the sustainability indicators of this nature economy method of analysis. The news about this analytic method is intriguing other Swedish municipalities, who also want to learn how to use the method. Sala is working on ways to get the information out to a broader audience and to use the method in its own municipality more effectively as a long-range planning tool.[3]

North American examples

In the United States, the City of Santa Monica, California, is using sustainability objectives based upon the Natural Step framework to integrate sustainable development into the city's general (comprehensive) plan.[4] The American Planning Association's policy guide to planning for sustainability offers a program for planning action guided by four sustainability objectives based upon the Natural Step framework. These are listed at the beginning of this chapter. The resort community of Whistler in British Columbia has adopted a comprehensive plan for sustainability that is guided by the system conditions of the Natural Step framework.[5]

A growing number of cities, towns, and counties in the United States are citing sustainable development as a goal in their comprehensive plans, although they may not clearly specify what sustainable development means. Even more U.S. communities have undertaken many issue-oriented or project-based sustainable development initiatives to address greenhouse gas emissions, green building, brownfields redevelopment, recycling, affordable housing, and other programs. Cities such as Chattanooga, Tennessee; Seattle, Washington; and Burlington, Vermont have publicly endorsed sustainable development as a priority and are carrying out many sustainable development initiatives. Communities such as these have helped inspire other U.S. cities and towns to follow suit. The challenge remains to find ways of integrating sustainable change systematically throughout all municipal and community practices, and to do so as soon as possible.

Planning and sustainable development in Sweden: Advantages, challenges

NATIONAL ASSISTANCE

In Sweden, municipalities are required by law to have a comprehensive plan to guide development. In the United States, some, but not all, states require a local master plan. In Sweden, a national agency helps, guides, and often funds local planning, housing, and building efforts. In the United States, a national agency assists affordable housing and community development but provides little assistance and almost no guidance for local and regional planning. Among other things, this reflects the political tradition in the United States where planning is seen as a responsibility of the state and local governments but not of the federal government.

Sweden's national government also offers considerably more assistance to local sustainable development efforts than does that of the United States. As discussed in the Introduction, Canada's national government has adopted sustainable development policies both as national guides and as directives for its own agencies and departments. As also discussed, many, if not most, Swedish municipalities have developed local sustainable development plans and have hired coordinators to help implement them.

REMAINING CHALLENGES

Despite these considerable advantages over their North American counterparts, Swedish municipalities still struggle to bring sustainable development work together with city and town planning. The dominating obstacle for integrating sustainable development at the local level in Sweden, according to the municipalities themselves, is that local governments often treat sustainable development work as a project, outside of, and in addition to, existing municipal departments and operations. Most local sustainable development coordinators are hired from outside the local government and on short-term contracts.[6] A second challenge is that many local officials still see sustainable development only as an environmental issue and hence one that should be handled by environmental protection departments instead of an over-arching authority such as the municipal council.[7]

Swedish municipalities share with their North American counterparts the challenges of encouraging more public involvement in planning, not to mention in sustainable development work. Swedish cities and towns struggle with fragmentation and specialization of responsibilities in municipal government that get in the way of municipal agencies and departments collaborating toward common goals, just as cities and towns in North America struggle with these challenges.[8]

WHAT WE CAN LEARN

The eco-municipalities and other municipalities of Sweden can teach the rest of us throughout the world not only from their successes, but also from their challenges. Swedish communities are still working, just as we must, to find effective ways to transition on an across-the-board scale to an eco-cyclic society. Their successes, described in the previous chapters, provide us with good examples to follow and the realization that these accomplishments are indeed possible to achieve. Swedish communities are struggling with project-oriented approaches to sustainable development, how to increase citizen participation in sustainable development and planning, and how to surmount departmental division and turf issues. These challenges as well as their successes can guide us to design local processes for changing to sustainable practices that effectively involve citizens and bring about systematic, across-the-board change to sustainable practices.

The next part of the book will help to do precisely this.

III
HOW COMMUNITIES CAN CHANGE

CHAPTER 15

What Gets in the Way of Change?

When most of us first hear about a new way of doing things, we want to know what it is, how it works and, of course, why it is better than the old way. So it is with sustainable development. We place our attention upon the new practice or new technology, how it works, what is different about it, how it is an improvement, and, of course, how much it costs or how much it can save.

Those of us who have worked as city and town planners with communities on land use issues are no exception. In fact, we planners have been doing this all along. We are fascinated with the tools and techniques of planning, particularly the new or "hot" ones. It is these tools and techniques that capture our attention and hold our focus: transfer of development rights, inclusionary zoning, open-space subdivisions, tax increment financing, transportation demand management, to name a few. And, of course, why not? This is the sexy part of planning, where creativity, intellect, and skill combine to craft a tool that has the potential to change land use, housing, transportation, and the character of a city, town, or region in a better, more livable direction.

But consider the history of the cluster housing land use technique in the United States. This development approach groups houses together on a given property closer than in a conventional subdivision, leaving some amount of undisturbed open land on that property. The number of houses that can be built on that property does not have to be any more than would be the case in a conventional subdivision. Sounds like a pretty sensible approach to development, right? It's a technique that could help shape development to "reduce encroachment upon nature," in line with the third objective for planning for sustainability.

The cluster housing technique is an integral part of best practices in current land use planning and smart growth approaches. It is also a land planning strategy that has been known and advocated by planners in the United States for decades. For over half-a-century, planners have been trying to convince communities to adopt zoning to encourage, if not require, this more compact, open-space-saving type of development design. Despite this 50 years of effort, the majority of suburban and rural communities in the U.S. still do not use cluster housing as a standard development practice.

Why hasn't this land use approach been more successful? Is it the planners' fault? Is it the tool's fault? Is it the communities' fault? Is it the consumers' fault?

Why do the best-laid plans often go awry?

Suppose you had a houseguest visit for several days who decided that you, your family, and future guests could use the space in your home more efficiently if its room layout was redesigned and reconfigured according to his idea. He explains to you in detail what the improved design would look like, draws pictures of the new, improved design, and calculates how much more space could be achieved without building any room additions. He shows you how the new layout, while not costing more than any other design, will add value to your home that more than covers the renovation costs. He tells you over and over again how much easier and more pleasant the new layout will be for you, your family members, and your future guests and how you will live a better life in this new environment.

You smile politely and try to change the subject, saying you have no plans to renovate at this time, but he presses on, again trying to illustrate the benefits of his approach. While his ideas may be good ones, what might you be feeling right now in the face of this persistent, unsolicited proposal?

Now, let's say you live in a condominium or village association. Your houseguest is so excited about his great home renovation idea that he next goes to the managing board of your condominium or village association, trying to persuade them to adopt it as a policy for all future home renovations in all their dwelling units. He makes the same arguments to the managing board about space efficiency, cost savings, higher quality of life. How might you be feeling about your houseguest now? How happy would you be if the managing board adopted that policy? What might your thoughts be about your guest's home renovation proposal?

Well, you might be persuaded about the idea and admire your guest's persistence and gumption. Then again, you might be experiencing something quite the opposite. You might even be trying to convince the managing board or your neighbors about how that renovation proposal is a cockamamy idea. How would you react if you were told, at this point, that your guest's proposal was the most cutting-edge idea to hit the home renovation industry in decades? Would that make up for his pressing you with his unsolicited ideas, failure to discern or even ask what your needs and wishes might be for your own home, and finally going to a higher authority in an attempt to implement his idea?

Perhaps that home renovation idea really was the most cutting-edge scheme to hit the industry in decades. If its proponent — your guest — and others like him try to get that proposal across to others in the manner he used with you, what do you think are the chances of its successful adoption and implementation in the larger homeowner community?

Regardless of the particular merits of a new idea or innovation, the way it is introduced to a potential user — be it an individual, a business, or a community — can impede, if not put a stop to it altogether. In such a situation, the merits of the innovation can become irrelevant. In our zeal to introduce sustainable practices to a city or town, or an overall approach to community planning for sustainability, can we learn from cluster housing's rocky road?

Perhaps there is another way.

"Process — as important as the product"

Over the last few decades, more and more communities in the United States and around the world are using participatory approaches to bring about community change. This means they involve citizens in the process of developing change proposals and implementation measures. These approaches, instead of limiting citizen involvement to the narrow role of reacting to others' proposals, involve a diversity of citizens early on in a partnership with planners and community officials in designing community change proposals.

These efforts reflect growing understanding that the traditional approach to public involvement in community change, more likely than not, does not work to the satisfaction of anyone — town or city officials, planners, and the public alike. The traditional approach usually involves the preparation of a planning or implementation proposal by community officials or technical professionals, or both, and the presentation of that proposal at a public hearing or forum, followed by some revisions to that proposal and a final vote by public officials.

In the example described above, the houseguest, peddling his unsolicited proposal to remodel your house, placed you in a position of having to react to a proposal you neither asked for nor had a hand in preparing. Correspondingly, in most cases the public — that is, citizens who may have either a direct or indirect interest in, or impact from, the proposal — are put in the same position. Can you recall the twinge in your gut when you realize you have been maneuvered to where your choice is essentially to either acquiesce or oppose?

Is it any wonder, then, that community change proposals in which community members have not been involved so often generate fractious, angry reactions at these public hearings? Is it any wonder that angry citizens and business people have then mobilized to stop even the most worthy of community change proposals? And, if we continue to use the conventional public involvement approach to introduce innovative sustainable practices to communities, what is the likelihood of their successful endorsement and adoption, even if they are a technically appropriate solution?

How we do things is as important as *what* we do.

CHAPTER 16

Three Change Processes That Work

Fortunately, there are change processes that work. Three strategies presented in this chapter have high success rates in adoption of change proposals. Such proposals could be business operations change to sustainable practices, sustainable development plans and projects, comprehensive plans linked to concrete action, and land use regulatory revisions. The successful adoption of change proposals within these communities and businesses had three important effects:

- Change brought about *concrete results.*
- Change occurred *systematically,* that is, it occurred throughout all or several functional areas instead of within only one area.
- Change became *institutionalized* as part of the ongoing official policies and practices of the municipal government or business corporation.

The three change strategies and the process principles are based on the experiences of:

- eco-municipalities in Sweden,
- businesses using the Natural Step strategy for change, and
- U.S. communities using the Swamp Yankee planning approach.

These successful change groups differ strikingly in location and situation. The eco-municipalities are located in Sweden. The companies that are using the Natural Step framework are based in North America, Japan, and Europe. The Swamp Yankee communities are located primarily in the United States, many in New England.

The goal of the Swedish eco-municipalities is to become sustainable communities. The goal of the Natural Step businesses is to reorient business operations and practices toward ones that are sustainable. The goal of the Swamp Yankee communities is to shape a community future that its citizens desire, using a participatory planning process as the means for that change.

Despite these differences, the change processes used by these groups reveal distinct similarities. In all cases, similar operating principles and steps are apparent despite their differences as public or private institutions, their ultimate goal, or their nationality. This suggests that these principles and steps, particularly the ones common to the processes of all three, are likely key elements for successful change.

These principles and model change processes can offer guidance to those of us interested in community change to sustainability, wherever we are. This guidance transcends differences of geography, situation, and country context. Using this guidance, communities that are rich or poor, urban or rural, located in North America, Sweden, or elsewhere, also can change to sustainable practices.

The eco-municipalities of Sweden

The design of the change process in the Swedish eco-municipalities was instrumental in their successful changes to sustainable practices. In almost all cases, municipal employees and citizens participated from the start in deciding what particular strategies toward sustainability best suited their departments, their municipality, and the wider community. In this way, the strategies for change became theirs. When the time came for implementation, the implementers were already on board since they had helped create those strategies in the first place. This democratic, bottom-up approach, combined with education, vision, and overarching goals for sustainability, helped bring about ongoing, institutionalized change throughout the countless policies, practices, and tasks of municipal government and community planning.

Some eco-municipalities have delved deeper into the process of change toward sustainability, bringing about fundamental shifts in the values, worldview, and living habits of their citizens, business people, and institutions. People in these communities now see sustainable development not just as a new problem-solving concept but also as a different way of living and working that is more deeply satisfying at both a personal and community level. These cities and towns see sustainable development as a natural way of doing

Figure 16.1: Eksjö's city center, dating back to the 1600s, features historic wooden buildings such as this church.

things that makes life better for citizens, businesses, and governments at the same time as it helps the Earth. As they learned what sustainability meant, community citizens and officials came to understand that a do-nothing course of action in the face of larger unsustainable trends was neither a feasible life choice nor an acceptable municipal course of action. This realization gave rise to the political will to change. Further, when citizens, businesses, and local governments saw that a radical change was necessary and understood that it is possible for humans to live in harmony with the cycles of nature, exciting and lucrative opportunities opened up in new ways to meet household, business, and community needs.

The journeys of the Swedish eco-municipalities toward sustainability also teach that there are no package solutions toward this goal. Each community and each actor within that community must find the particular path that fits the local terrain and situation. At the same time, there are signposts from the eco-municipalities' experiences that can help guide the journeys of other communities throughout the world. Here are some of those signposts — important elements found in almost all of their successful change processes toward sustainability. The story of Eksjö's path to become an

EKSJÖ BECOMES AN ECO-MUNICIPALITY

About Eksjö: Eksjö is a city of just under 17,000 people, located in the Highlands region of Sweden about three hours southwest of Stockholm. Eksjö is known for its historic wooden houses and town center that date back to the city's founding in 1603. It also has served as a center for military training and education since the 1600s.

Despite a picturesque setting and its renown as a historic preservation center, Eksjö struggled with population loss and increasing tax burdens on people least able to pay. Eighty percent of the increasing municipal budget was going to schools and eldercare. Younger families were leaving; the average age of the city's population was rising. Municipal councilors realized they were operating on a year-to-year basis, with no long-term guiding vision.

Beginning of Eksjö's journey: In 1986, a municipal councilman in Eksjö heard about the eco-municipality concept and thought this would be a good idea for his town to pursue. He discussed this idea for some time with his fellow councilors and eventually introduced a motion to this effect that was passed by the municipal council.

▶

eco-municipality, presented concurrently, is an example of one community's journey.

SIGNPOSTS ON THE PATH TO ECO-MUNICIPALITY

A guiding local vision leads the process

Since the first eco-municipality, Övertorneå, undertook its journey in the early 1980s, creating a unique community vision to guide the journey toward sustainability has been integral to the Swedish eco-municipality experience. In successive generations of Swedish eco-municipalities, the systems perspective and the four system conditions of the Natural Step approach to sustainability became a natural framework for their vision. Often, the general plan or the local sustainable development plan of the eco-municipality documents this framework and vision.

Using a bottom-up approach

Eco-municipalities motivate individuals at all levels and positions throughout the municipal government and community to become independent innovators and forces of change. This occurs through education and exchange of experience, avoiding top-down decrees and municipal bans.

During the next few years, a task force explored ideas for how to realize Ekjo's eco-municipality vision. Task force members investigated what other eco-municipalities in Sweden were doing, collected good examples, and determined what important principles to follow. They developed a background report and a recommended program for what the town should do next. Six years after the municipal councilman first got the idea, Eksjö officials and task force members were presenting their eco-municipality achievements at the 1992 UN World Conference on Environment and Development in Rio de Janeiro. Much of Eksjö's eco-municipality planning experience paralleled what became documented in this 1992 Rio Summit's guiding plan for local sustainable development known as Agenda 21.

Political commitments: In 1993, Eksjö's municipal council reaffirmed its commitment to becoming an eco-municipality by publicly taking responsibility in an official resolution to follow an ecological route in its operations. The council appointed a coordinating group of representatives from the various municipal departments to oversee the implementation of the eco-municipality development plan that had been prepared by the earlier task force. Later that year, the council passed an implementation program that described the proposal,

▶

Practically speaking, a bottom-up approach creates a grassroots movement throughout the villages, neighborhoods, businesses, housing complexes, and municipal agencies of a community. What is needed are enough independent and creative thinkers who dare to find their own ways and solutions. To bring this about, it is necessary to introduce the concept of sustainability to a community in a way that creates the greatest possible engagement and participation.

Achieving political consensus

From the first decision to embark on a path toward sustainability, most eco-municipalities worked hard to assure the broadest possible political anchoring of long-term goals for sustainable development. Successful eco-municipalities were able to achieve consensus on broad sustainability goals throughout the political spectrum of their elected officials.

Using a holistic and systems view

Understanding the causes of today's problems makes it easier to develop strategies for change. For example, it is necessary to see and understand the entire food production cycle in order to bring about change in a community's food sustenance ability. A holistic perspective also understands the

estimated the project costs, and allocated US$60,000 in the municipal budget to operate the program. In 1994, the council added to that program a timetable and a working method that included a commitment that all municipal employees would participate in training and education to understand an eco-cyclic way of thinking. This training, that involved 1,400 municipal employees in two six-hour sessions, took place between 1995 and 1996. Further, the municipal council adopted, as the guiding principles for its eco-municipality vision and work plan, the four system conditions of the Natural Step. In 1996, Eksjö's municipal council published and disseminated a pamphlet about these guiding principles, signed by three leading politicians, to be used by the top officials to department clerks, in decisions anywhere from developing the annual municipal budget to purchasing paper and pencils.

"Journey in the Eco-cycle" employee education program: To make the training real for municipal employees, Eksjö designed an education program that took employees on trips around the municipality to see good examples at the same time as they were hearing about eco-cyclic principles. At the beginning of the first day, employees saw a video that introduced the principles of nature, the four Natural Step system conditions for a sustainable

▶

community's dependence upon the surrounding world and clarifies what it is that local communities can control, easier in small ones where community interconnections are clearer.

Using an across-the-board approach

In order for widespread community change to occur, all parts of that community must be involved. For example, to develop more sustainable attitudes and approaches to food, it becomes necessary to bring together all local actors involved — farmers, food processing plants, retail businesses, large-scale institutional kitchens, and waste collectors. Working in cross-department networks helped elected officials and department heads understand the advantages of this approach and changed their business-as-usual separate department work routines to ones that involved staff from several departments and agencies.

Being a good example

Successful eco-municipalities are always ready to share their experience with others inside and outside municipal boundaries. Municipal governments that have changed practices to sustainable ones set a good example for businesses and households in their own communities. They have used their own

society and the reasons for them. Then, they took a bus to the municipal sewage treatment plant and a restored wetland and saw how these two facilities were operating according to the eco-cyclic principles within the four system conditions. They visited the town's landfill and recycling and compost center to see how these facilities, too, fit into the picture. The day's journey ended with a visit to the Center for Building Preservation to see how traditional ways could be coupled with modern techniques to produce comfortable, healthy, and ecological homes and buildings. Employees were treated to refreshments including ecologically grown coffee, organic bread and organic milk, while they learned why these are healthier alternatives to conventionally grown food that uses chemical pesticides and artificial fertilizers. All in all, Eksjö ran 25 of these bus trips, each with 50 to 60 employees.

Evaluation and monitoring — the second day of training: After the first day of training, which introduced the basic eco-cyclic principles and some good examples, a second training session helped employees to understand these in the context of their own workplaces — what was working well, what was working not so well, and how things could work better.

▶

action, for example, changing from gas-powered vehicles to alternatively fueled ones, as a model to inspire change in the other sectors of the community. Being a good example also demonstrates a "clean-in-front-of-your-own-door" attitude. This means starting the change process within one's own organization before telling others what they should do. This approach establishes trust for broadening the change process to businesses, households, and other sectors of the community.

Taking a global perspective

In order for local actions toward sustainable development to take root and grow, it becomes important, sooner or later, for an eco-municipality to work toward change outside its home community. By working together, as have the Swedish eco-municipalities, it may be possible to create national and international networking and lobbying systems. Taking a global perspective also means seeing the community in a global context, for example, understanding the relationship of driving fossil-fueled cars and municipal vehicles to the greenhouse effect and climate change. It can also mean an attitude of usefulness. How can our contributions help people elsewhere? What good are we doing for humanity?

During this session, employees worked to answer such questions as:

- What has already been accomplished — what good examples are in our department already?
- What is happening to waste in our department? What is, and is not, being recycled and composted?
- How can department transport functions be made more efficient?
- How much energy are we using for heat, light, and electricity needs, and can these be reduced?
- What kinds of chemicals are we using, and do we really need them?
- What eco-products can we purchase instead of conventional ones? What products can be reused? What products are we buying that really are unnecessary?
- How is the equipment in our office being used? Can we use it more efficiently to save electricity?

▶

Using outward-directed working methods

The Swedish eco-municipalities have been exchanging experiences in conferences and workshops over the last several years. These have been important in advising change processes at home. Within a community it is also important to build local internal networks among the different branches of government or within focus areas, such as the earlier example of the food cycle.

"The Compass" — the A-B-C-D of the Natural Step approach

A second strategy offers similar process principles and underscores the importance of a democratic approach to successful change. Many businesses and corporations have combined use of the Natural Step system conditions as a sustainability compass with its change methodology known as the A-B-C-D strategy. Through this approach, businesses have created across-the-board changes toward sustainable practices that have rippled through their operations in as little time as a year. These changes then became institutionalized as ongoing company practices. Businesses also used a bottom-up approach. Staff and employees worked to apply the four Natural Step system conditions to the countless policies and practices of their own departments. This approach once again demonstrates Karl-Henrik Robèrt's motto coined for

Ongoing efforts: The questions above became the framework for annual departmental reports that were presented to the elected officials and used to track progress toward the eco-municipality goals over time. Eksjö used these and questions about overall community and environmental progress to develop sustainability indicators as ongoing measures, such as:

- How many acres in agricultural use are being organically farmed?
- What percentage of total solid waste is going to the landfill?
- How many miles of per-person travel is by public transport?
- What percentage of grade 9 school students are smokers?
- What metals are present in sewage treatment sludge?
- What are nitrogen levels in sewage treatment effluent?

Eco-municipality results: Eksjö's transformation to an eco-municipality brought about countless changes in the town's practices and policies toward the direction of sustainability. Here are just a few.

▶

the Natural Step approach, "Find fundamental principles of indisputable relevance, and thereafter ask the advice of others on how to apply them." The success of these corporate changeovers to sustainable practices can be measured in — among other things — money. Eco-municipalities, such as Sundsvall and Robertsfors, described in the next two chapters, also use the A-B-C-D approach to change, calling it "the Compass."

In Part I, we described the Natural Step's framework of four system conditions for a sustainable society. This framework of four principles defines and guides the design of actions toward sustainability. The second part of the Natural Step approach — the A-B-C-D model — is a strategic process for bringing about this change. Because it is a systems approach, the method is particularly well-suited for introducing change to a complex system such as a business or a community.

The Natural Step's A-B-C-D strategy is outlined below. The accompanying story of Sånga-Säby illustrates one business that successfully used this approach to change its operations to sustainable practices.

A-B-C-D SIGNPOSTS TO SUSTAINABILITY[2]

A) Raise awareness: introduce and discuss the framework of the four system conditions. This creates a common understanding of what

Using this approach, businesses have created across-the-board change to sustainable practices that rippled through their organizations in as little time as a year.

Biomass heat: Instead of fossil fuels, Eksjö's district heating plant now runs on biomass — wood by-products — and burnable solid waste.

From gasoline to biofuels: Eksjö began renting an ethanol-fueled car as one of its municipal vehicles, which inspired several other organizations to do the same. Next, an oil company built a new gas station in town that offered ethanol and rapeseed (canola) oil fuel pumps. This all happened within nine months.

Organic farming and distribution: A project developed to expand the amount of local organic produce that was sold in local stores and to publicize this to consumers.

Sewage treatment by a constructed wetland: Eksjö is now using wetland to reduce nitrogen and phosphorus in sewage effluent. The wetland has since become a stopover point for migratory birds. Eksjö developed regional and international partnerships with other municipalities to work on wetland sewage treatment For more information, see Chapter 10.

Traditional building preservation center: Eksjö helped found an organization to preserve many traditional building and construction techniques in danger of being lost to future generations. Its center teaches builders of all ages how to combine traditional and modern

▶

sustainability means, introduces a set of shared playing rules for moving toward sustainability and helps people reach agreement and mutual trust about those rules.

B) **Scrutinize and take an inventory of present conditions.** Use the system conditions as a lens to see where you are today with respect to those four conditions. In other words, ask questions such as "In what ways are we increasing wasteful dependence upon fossil fuels, scarce metals, minerals, and chemicals in the biosphere? In what ways are present actions bringing about encroachment upon nature? What human needs are we trying to address and how efficiently and fairly are we working to meet those needs?"

C) **Brainstorm visions and solutions** to create a positive vision of the desired future where the four system conditions are met and a list of actions that will help get there. What will our organization or community look like in the sustainable society? This step can be run as a brainstorming session where there are no wrong answers, and participants apply the four system conditions to the range of operational or community issues in a future scenario. Sometimes groups can arrive at early action and investment decisions without necessarily agreeing on detailed future scenarios. This means people holding future visions that differ can

techniques to design healthy, high-quality homes and buildings. For more information, see Chapter 4: Green Business; Green Buildings.

Comprehensive plan objectives: Eksjö updated its master plan in 2001, integrating sustainability objectives as a guiding framework for the town's future planning and development.

More results: Some of Eksjö's other sustainable practices and projects included:

- adopting an environmentally friendly municipal purchasing policy,
- establishing a store called Retro that sells used goods,
- achieving an 80 percent recycling rate in its schools,
- establishing a financing program for home conversion to biomass heating, and
- encouraging families to use cloth diapers instead of disposable ones.[1]

still cooperate in the present. A key question to pose is "What early action steps are wise ones in that they open doors rather than close doors to future possibilities?"

D) **Create an action plan** based upon results in step C, and set priorities for actions through asking the following questions:

- *Does the action go in the direction of all four system conditions simultaneously?* In other words, will it serve to reduce wasteful dependence upon fossil fuels, underground metals, minerals, chemicals, and encroachment upon nature, and also meet human needs fairly and efficiently?

- *Does the action create a flexible platform for future actions, or does it create a blind alley?* For example, it may not be feasible right away to install solar panels on a new building, but if the building is built facing south, it will be possible to do so at a later date.

- *Will the action give a good return upon investment?* Does it make good business and economic sense now? To really answer this question, however, it is necessary to expand one's idea of investment beyond initial capital expenditures. Investment analysis must include social and environmental costs and benefits as well as economic ones.

THE TRANSFORMATION OF SÅNGA-SÄBY

Sånga-Säby is a hotel and conference center located about 45 minutes outside of Stockholm. In the early 1990s, the center was in bad economic straits, struggling with over US$ half-a-million deficit. Five CEOs had come and gone in five years. The board of directors gave the next CEO, Mats Fack, a deadline of three years to turn the business around from red to black. Mats Fack had met Karl-Henrik Robèrt and thought the Natural Step system conditions would be a good tool to help reshape the company economically as well as environmentally. Although the center's board of directors was opposed at first, Mats eventually persuaded them to give it a try. In many cases, a CEO and top management staff first identify their own company vision and then impose this upon the rest of the organization. Mats Fack took another approach. He arranged for about 13 days of training in the Natural Step framework for all management staff and department employees, who then together generated a vision, guided by the system conditions, for the Sånga-Säby center. It took about 18 months for staff and employees to absorb the training and integrate it into their work approach, but then things started happening.

▶

Back-casting: The A-B-C-D method is a systematic way to "back-cast from principles," a unique contribution of the Natural Step approach to bringing about change.[3] This approach places one's mind in a state of future success, defined through use of the four system conditions. Then, the planning process proceeds through deciding on what early moves will reach this goal. Systematically repeating this will increase the probability of achieving concrete, across-the-board, institutionalized change to sustainable practices. "Forecasting," the traditional methodology, takes present, often undesired, trends and projects these into the future. Then, steps are designed to accommodate a future that people don't want in the first place.

Back-casting from sustainability principles is different than back-casting from future scenarios, where problems can arise when people don't agree in the first

Figure 16.2: Sånga-Säby built a new hotel annex whose design was guided by the Natural Step system conditions for sustainability.

Employees worked within their own and other departments to learn what practices were violating the system conditions. As one example, the kitchen staff was asked to prepare a meal that met the four Natural Step system conditions. The staff conducted a life cycle assessment of the planned meal ingredients, and, when they came to the proposed shrimp cocktail appetizer, they began asking questions about the use of freon in the engines of the shrimp boats. They investigated other ingredients to make sure these did not include food products that were genetically modified.

Other staff discovered that, while the center was operating heat pumps that reduced energy needs, 30 percent of energy use still involved oil, as did the center's vehicles, tractors, and all plastic products. They discovered that virgin plastic products violate all four system conditions. The employees and management staff set goals to eliminate the use of oil and plastic products and to change to renewable energy for heat and power. In three years, they achieved those objectives. Since then, only renewable energy is used for heat and power. The center's vehicles now run on biofuels such as ethanol or rapeseed (canola) oil. A solar-powered robot lawn mower cuts the grass.

▶

place about the future scenario. Further, since human innovation and sustainable technology is constantly changing, it may be best not to lock minds into a specific idea of what a sustainable future means. As in a chess game, it helps to keep an open mind about potential scenarios as the future unfolds, while optimizing in the present moment the chances of arriving at success — be it checkmate or meeting the four system conditions of the Natural Step. **Picking the low-hanging fruit:** Related to Step D is a strategy called "picking the low-hanging fruit."[4] It means choosing some actions that can be easily and quickly achieved in the short-term. This strategy can demonstrate early success to process participants. It can energize and jump-start an action plan toward sustainable practices by providing good examples showing that change can really happen.

Swamp Yankee planning in the United States

A democratic bottom-up approach to community or organizational change, guided by a clear vision, is not confined to regions east of the Atlantic Ocean. Swamp Yankee planning has striking similarities to the successful democratic approach of the Swedish eco-municipalities and the Natural Step A-B-C-D process.[6] Originating in the New England region of the United States during the 1970s, and employed by over a hundred communities as

Employees own the process of converting use of plastic products to alternatives. They requested that items, such as plastic cups, be removed from guest rooms and replaced with glass or recyclable paper. They discovered that the center was purchasing and using about 20,000 bottles of mineral water per year. These bottles were being trucked to Sånga-Säby from southern Sweden. The staff discovered this practice broke all four system conditions. As an alternative, the staff requested that glass pitchers and recyclable paper cups be purchased and that Sånga-Säby's own excellent tap water be used instead of the bottled water. This measure, which was readily accepted by management and guests, saved the center about US$2,500 per year.

Sånga-Säby needed to build an annex to expand its guest room facilities. The decision was made to build this annex as ecologically as possible, using the Natural Step system conditions as a design guide. As one measure, the construction contract included a clause that required the builder to pay about US$12,500 for every tree he took down. The annex was built with wood from local forests and insulated with glass fiber from recycled glass. A grass-and-sedum roof keeps rooms cool in summer so that air conditioning is not required. All ▶

far afield as Anchorage, Alaska; and Recife, Brazil, Swamp Yankee planning uses a democratic, bottom-up approach to town and city planning.

The expression Swamp Yankee was created by New Englanders to capture some special characteristics found in generations of the region's down-home, regular, everyday folks who like to govern themselves. These every-day folks know their community exceedingly well. They don't like outsiders telling them what to do, but they respect wisdom, ability, and expertise. Change comes slowly to these tradition-loving people. And when change does come, it is almost always through a bottom-up, rather than a top-down, process.

These qualities are found not only in New Englanders but also in people throughout the United States and beyond. The need to shape one's own destiny is a fundamental human need. Devotion to one's own

Figure 16.3: A New England town has a Swamp Yankee festival. Credit: Philip B. Herr

building materials were bought from companies that meet the ISO 14001 internationally recognized environmental standards. According to Mats Fack, the most challenging aspect of the development project was teaching the architects a new approach to design.

These ecological decisions did result in costs higher than those of conventional solutions. For example, the general contractor informed Mats Fack that choosing sustainably certified wood products would add US$10,000 to the annex costs. Using only organic foods added 20 percent to the kitchen's budget. However, the center's occupancy rate has soared due to the added comfort and health enhancement of its improved rooms, facilities, and delicious meals. This added comfort and healthy environment also have allowed increases in room costs and guest fees. Groups and organizations have relocated their annual retreats and conferences from the most elegant hotel in Stockholm to Sånga-Säby. Through changing to sustainable practices, Sånga-Säby has gone from the brink of financial collapse to a market position as one of the top twenty hotel conference centers in the country.[5]

community, be it a birthplace or a chosen home place, with its special traditions and unique qualities is found in people everywhere. Introducing change to communities of such people, wherever they may be, requires a special approach. It needs to be based upon those fundamental values of self-determination and devotion to one's own community. To be truly effective, a change approach needs to respect and evoke that special community wisdom.

These values, and the principles that evolve from them, are at the heart of both the Swedish eco-municipality and the Swamp Yankee planning approaches to community change, even though the latter is not explicitly aimed at a sustainability goal. Important principles of Swamp Yankee planning follow, accompanied by the story of Ossipee, New Hampshire, a town that successfully used this planning approach.

SIGNPOSTS IN SWAMP YANKEE PLANNING

Begin and guide a planning process with a community-defined vision of a desired future. This sets a positive picture of the type of community its citizens and business people want it to be. Steps can then be designed to move from present-day conditions toward a future that people want. This resembles the Natural Step's back-casting and differs

---

OSSIPEE, NEW HAMPSHIRE: A SWAMP YANKEE TOWN CURBS ROADSIDE SPRAWL

Ossipee is a rural town of about 4,000 people in central eastern New Hampshire in the United States. It is a traditional New England community, featuring several small villages scattered throughout a still rural countryside. In these villages, the traditional settlement pattern still presides with buildings situated close to the street and to each other. It is possible to walk around these village centers instead of driving. Beyond these villages, much of the land is open fields and forests despite the development pressure of the 1980s and 1990s that brought rural sprawl and inappropriate development to many New England communities.

At the same time, one of New Hampshire's major north-south highway routes cuts through Ossipee. This highway, known as Route 16, brings tourists, sightseers, and skiers from the metropolitan Boston area to northeast New Hampshire's scenic White Mountains and outlet shopping centers. On an average Saturday in 1993, as many as 10,000 cars traveled along Route 16 in Ossipee. Not surprisingly, stores and businesses sprung up along this highway in a scattershot pattern. It is virtually impossible to walk from one of these stores to another. Customers wanting to shop at different stores along the highway must get back

▶

from traditional planning approaches that start with fore-casting —
data-gathering and projecting present trends into the future to estimate
what to plan for.

As an example, a conventional transportation planning project often
begins with documenting trends in traffic flows, congestion, and acci-
dents, then projects these into the future, assuming that traffic patterns
will continue in the future as they have in the past. These future projections, often viewed as inevitable, do not take into account the desires of
the community for a future it wishes. Plans and actions based on these
projections accommodate projected increases in traffic and congestion,
such as wider roads, more lanes, and additional traffic signals. Starting
instead with a community vision that identifies the desired level of
development and traffic, planners and community officials then can
back-cast to present actions that help bring about that desired level, such
as redesigned land use policies and regulations to shape and locate development in a way that reduces vehicle trip generation and use of alternative transit.

**Combine vision, planning, and action from the start and through-
out the planning process.** Start right away to find some concrete action
upon which there is wide agreement, and move forward to carry this out.

in their cars and drive from one location to another. Drivers entering and leaving the highway to and from these stores create ever-increasing safety hazards. Also, food markets,
pharmacies, and other neighborhood serving businesses were choosing to build new stores
along Route 16, rather than in the village centers where they traditionally had located. This
changing development pattern was sucking the economic life out of Ossipee's village centers, as has occurred in so many small towns in the United States.

In the late 1990s, the New Hampshire State Department of Transportation began a planning effort to help communities along Route 16 find solutions for managing land use better
along the highway. As part of that effort, citizens and town officials in Ossipee came together to figure out what they wanted to happen along the part of Route 16 within their town
borders. First, they formed a steering committee with representatives from the town permitting boards and departments that were involved with land use. Next, they organized a
community-wide visioning event to identify what land use the community thought was best
along the highway. They worked hard to make sure that citizens and businesspeople from
all interests in Ossipee — including property owners of land along the highway — were   ▶

Figure 16.4: Buildings are close to the street and to each other in the New England village settlement pattern illustrated in one of Ossipee's villages.

This resembles the Natural Step strategy of picking the low-hanging fruit. Getting started with an early action proposal that has broad community support demonstrates that planning will result in concrete change. It also can inform the planning process with reality tests for later actions.

Include the full range of community interests, values, and perspectives in a meaningful way. A plan is essentially a statement of intent — agreed to by all those whose actions it is meant to guide. If a plan is intended to guide a municipal government and its community, then their perspectives need to be involved from the beginning and throughout the process. In this way, they will come to view the plan as their own and be more likely to adopt and implement that plan.

Build connections across subject areas. Communities and regions are systems, and to change a system requires a systems approach. There is almost never one single action that will

involved in the process. At that visioning event, which included a delicious supper prepared by a local non-profit service organization, community agreement was reached on several goals. These included:

- encouraging future development along Route 16 to concentrate at three intersections in the town, and
- preserving the countryside appearance of the land along the highway in between those intersections.

The next step was to craft specific action proposals for how to accomplish those goals. Groups of citizens worked with planning and transportation professionals to come up with zoning change proposals and transportation improvements for the key intersections along Route 16 at which development was to be concentrated. The outcomes included a group of zoning proposals that overwhelmingly passed at the 2000 Town Meeting. (In the New England region of the United States, the Town Meeting is the official legislative governing

▶

solve a community or regional problem such as traffic congestion or sprawl development. There needs to be a network of interconnected actions that work together toward common objectives. For example, a systems approach to curbing sprawl might involve a combination of strategies such as pedestrian-oriented compact development zoning, open-space preservation, a transfer of development rights program, feasible transportation alternatives to privately owned cars, affordable housing incentives, inner-city education improvements, supportive public infrastructure and facilities siting decisions.

Plan in cycles, not just one linear pass. A planning cycle means going from data to goal setting, alternative framing, and alternative testing to taking implementing actions. A cycle like this can be completed in an evening, a month, or a year. A quick planning cycle that is short on data gathering but long on creative ideas can make the overall plan-making

Figure 16.5: Ossipee residents set action priorities in their initial visioning event.

body of town government. Local land use zoning regulations must be adopted by a two-thirds majority of voting residents that are present at this meeting.)

These adopted proposals included zoning revisions that allowed higher-density development at the key intersections along Route 16. This creates an incentive for development to locate at those areas, since there can be more income-producing space than there would be otherwise. Next, trip generation standards were adopted for new development in the areas along the highway in between those intersections. Ossipee became the first community in New Hampshire to adopt this type of innovative development regulation. Those standards, coupled with others, serve to discourage development that generates a lot of traffic in the more rural areas along the highway. Other zoning revisions removed regulatory disincentives to new business development in the town's village centers. This lessened the probability that new development would choose to locate out on the highway, where location and regulatory restrictions were less strict.

Because voters at Town Meeting and zoning officials in Ossipee were involved in the initial goal setting and zoning proposal, when the time came for an official vote, a successful

▶

effective by clarifying what are agreed upon community intentions. Ongoing planning continually tests viability of long-term policy goals against the experience of present implementing actions.

- **Focus on finding agreement, not on resolving disagreement.** Planning efforts are useful only if they lead to shared conclusions. It is widespread agreement about plans and actions that gives them their power, making it more likely that plans will be implemented and actions carried out. Disagreement does not need to be dwelt upon. A more effective approach is to decide upon a way to seek agreement at a future time, and move on.

- **Lead from the side.** This describes a leadership style taken by a planner, process leader, consultant, or community officials who may initiate or facilitate the planning process. It is a style that provides a structure for the planning process that in turn allows and focuses community expression of a desired future. It is a leadership style that recognizes and builds upon citizen expertise about what it is like to live and work in the community. Leading from the side also means allowing the planning agenda to evolve out of the process as opposed to imposing an agenda created by a small group, the lead agency, or a consultant.

Common threads

The successful change processes followed by many of the Swedish eco-municipalities, Swamp Yankee communities, and Natural Step businesses have much in common while they differ in situation and in geography.

Vision-led process: First, a desired vision of the outcome begins and leads all three strategies. That common vision generates energy and enthusiasm

outcome was virtually assured, because the proposals on which they were voting were theirs.

As of 2003, Ossipee is working on a compact development design for one of its three major intersections now zoned for higher-density, mixed-use development. A three-day design brainstorming event in January 2002 brought over 150 residents, businesspeople, and property owners together with design professionals to develop a plan for this area. While consensus has yet to be reached on a final intersection design and the siting of an intermodal transit center, the town, the regional planning commission, and the State Transportation Department are continuing their work to curb roadside sprawl in Ossipee.

❖

and gives purpose and meaning to the time and effort that people contribute.

Back-casting: Back-casting starts with the desired vision, defined by sustainability principles, then identifies present-day actions to move in that direction.

Picking the low-hanging fruit: Low hanging fruit are those actions that garner early agreement and that are obtainable in the short run. In a community, this can be something as basic as getting a group together to clean up and plant a visible vacant lot near the downtown center. At Sånga-Säby, switching from bottled water to tap water alone saved US$2,500 in the first year. It showed employees that their recommendations were taken seriously.

Democratic process: At the heart of all three strategies lies a commitment to a bottom-up participatory change process that engages citizens, employees, and implementers in designing the specific steps to move toward the desired vision or future. Using a democratic, participatory process is key to successful adoption and implementation of actions toward change in these three strategies.

Leading from the side: This describes a particular leadership style taken by process leaders that allows planning and action agendas to emerge from the process, rather than imposing predetermined strategies or projects. Leading from the side provides clear guidelines, such as the Natural Step system conditions and sustainability objectives, then elicits the ideas of the process participants for how to apply them.

Taking a systems approach: In all three strategies, the approach to change is a comprehensive one, aimed at bringing about change throughout the range of planning areas or departments. A conventional, less effective approach addresses issues on a one-by-one basis.

Broad involvement: In all three strategies, a wide representation of community participants take part in both identifying a positive vision and steps toward achieving that vision. Broad involvement of citizens and implementers helps assure that change will happen, since those responsible for making it happen are involved in shaping the proposals from their beginning.

Keeping it going: Planning in cycles, testing of early action proposals, ongoing education and training programs, monitoring action effectiveness with sustainability indicators, environmental management systems, all led by guiding sustainability objectives, help institutionalize change and keep adopted practices going over time.

Other examples

More and more community planning efforts in the United States are using visioning as a guiding planning tool. The State of Oregon's planning goals, required for Oregon municipalities, call for citizen participation in local planning. In the Netherlands, the national government has adopted a change strategy toward sustainability called transition management. This strategy uses back-casting to chart a course toward a vision of sustainability that guides the collaborative work toward transition goals.[7]

CHAPTER 17

Steps to Change

Introduction

The last chapter presented *principles* for a successful change process. This chapter outlines a series of practical *steps* for realizing systemic, across-the-board change to sustainable practices throughout a municipal government and its larger community. We believe that these principles and steps are applicable to all democratic communities — rich, poor, rural, urban — even if these are based upon community experiences in two wealthy industrial countries, the U.S.A and Sweden.

From our study or work with Swedish eco-municipalities, Natural Step businesses, and Swamp Yankee planning communities, we have identified a series of steps that are key to a successful change process. These steps brought about *concrete action*. They led to change that has been *institutionalized*, meaning change that has been integrated into policy and procedures that will last over time. These steps also led to *across-the-board* change, that is, change that rippled throughout the diverse policies and practices in a municipal government and its larger community. This happened within one to several years. These characteristics — change that achieves concrete results, occurs across-the-board, is institutionalized and relatively rapid — can be considered indicators of a successful change process.

In identifying what steps were key, we asked ourselves: If this step is not included, what is the likelihood of achieving any one of these four success measures? If the answer was not a strong likelihood, than we knew that step was critical.

These steps need not necessarily be chronological; they can also occur in parallel. Some steps consist of activities that may go on for several years, or, that "take a rest" for some time and can be taken up again after a year or two. Each community will need to adapt these steps to its particular situation just as the Swedish and Swamp Yankee communities did.

In the final analysis, changing to sustainable practices takes time. The intensity of activity may vary, and periodic infusions of new energy may be needed. We hope that these process development steps and the examples of success will demonstrate that it is feasible to accomplish an overall redirection to community practices that are sustainable. We offer these steps and the principles in the preceding chapter as signposts for the journey. The story of Sundsvall, presented concurrently, exemplifies some of these steps.

1. Finding the fire souls

Fire souls are community citizens who have a burning interest in sustainable development and community change. They are people who are willing and able to work hard to make their ideas come to pass. Initially, they help to open the municipal door through inducing local officials and community leaders to learn more about sustainable development and to understand its importance for the community and for the Earth.

SUNDSVALL: FROM ENVIRONMENTAL INFAMY TO ECO-MUNICIPALITY

Sundsvall (Seunds'-vahll), dating back to Viking times, is an industrial city of about 100,000 residents, located near the coast of Bothnia, the northern end of the Baltic Sea. Since the 1800s, Sundsvall has been a center for the sawmill industry, which attracted workers from all over the country to find jobs in what became the first major industrial center in Sweden. The timber industry, now producing mainly pulp and paper, is still central to the Sundsvall economy, which at the same time has expanded to become a regional center of trade and technology. Sweden's only producer of primary aluminum also is located in Sundsvall.

The city developed in a valley that is surrounded by mountains. This topography results in frequent inversions where industrial and traffic emissions do not disperse into the atmosphere, but remain at ground level, especially in cold winter weather. By the late 1980s, Sundsvall had become infamous for its polluted air — one of the worst in Sweden.

This environmental crisis led to a 1991 municipal initiative, Clean by 2000, to create a city environmental action plan. This plan included an environmental accounting system that used indicators to track annual environmental progress. Sundsvall was able to attract

▶

In most of the successful eco-municipalities, change started with about five or six enthusiastic, committed individuals such as these. They succeeded in persuading key local leaders that it made sense to participate in education sessions, for example. In some cases, such as the city of Sundsvall, a local environmental crisis galvanized fire souls in that community to persuade local officials to take action. In other communities it was opportunity, such as applying for a grant, that lit the fire.

A local network of fire souls can both help the community change process get started and, if correctly guided, become the driving force that keeps the change process going, especially in the initial phases. Networks such as these also have served as the birthplace for ideas that became the first concrete good examples of sustainable development — bolstering local understanding, enthusiasm, and belief that success was possible.

Sometimes the change process becomes too dependent on a few fire souls. This becomes evident on the day that these people, for some reason, quit the process or move away. Therefore, it is wise to adopt a paradoxical strategy that protects and involves fire souls while working to become independent of them. Individual fire souls need to not only recognize their importance but also have the good sense to step out after some time and move into a different position.

support and funding from the national government to help create this action plan.

The following year, Sundsvall began a six-year initiative called Clean Job to increase on-the-job environmental awareness throughout its municipal departments. Staff in all departments and agencies were invited, rather than required, to participate in the Clean Job initiative. Eventually, 454 employees from 200 out of 240 departments and municipal agencies volunteered to participate in Clean Job.

How Clean Job worked: The city first sponsored a two-day workshop to train municipal employees who in turn would train others within their respective departments. Workplace training involved environmental education and occasional study trips, provided at no cost to the departments or employees, to visit good examples of environmental practice. Next, employees took part in developing action plans for their own workplaces that could be implemented right away.

Clean Job results: As the Clean Job program progressed, all municipal departments experienced significantly higher environmental awareness among staff, expressing itself in visibly altered work behaviors, such as willingness to save energy, reduce resource use, and pur- ►

Sometimes, it is one or two local officials themselves who are the fire souls, such as the municipal councilman in Eksjö who introduced the initial resolution to become an eco-municipality. Fire souls who have an established working relationship and good communication with local municipal officials, not surprisingly, have an easier time getting their ear.

In some eco-municipalities, the fire souls were people viewed by local authorities as difficult and hard to work with. Involving these fire souls as well at an early stage in the change process can help channel their energy toward the common good. In this case, a job of the process leadership can be to form a bridge between these activists and the local establishment.

2. Education: Raising awareness

Education about what sustainability means and how local actions connect to global trends is key to local official endorsement, municipal staff participation, and widespread community agreement on the goal of a sustainable community. The sooner a municipality invests in a broad education initiative, the faster the community change process can proceed. Strategically, it can be important to start with education for political leaders and opinion leaders in a community.

Education fosters a shared understanding of the challenge facing humanity. It can also reveal global and local possibilities for those who

chase environmentally benign products. A teamwork attitude developed among employees, who also showed more self-reliant work habits and an increased sense of environmental responsibility for their actions. Networks developed in all formerly separately functioning municipal departments and agencies. Change also manifested in visible environmental effects throughout the community. The city that was previously known for its polluted air began to increasingly stand out as a positive example of municipal environmental behavior.

Cost-benefits of Clean Job: When staff did a final reckoning of Clean Job's costs, it became clear that all the environmental measures identified and carried out by municipal employees had resulted in large cost savings for Sundsvall's municipal government. The city's administrative cost for the Clean Job program was about US$5,600 per year. The city's savings from all the resource and waste reduction actions carried out by its workers was US$175,000 per year.

Sustainable Sundsvall by 2020: In 1994, Sundsvall's municipal government decided to create a city sustainable development program called Sundsvall's Living Environment. People from all parts of the larger community — businesses, teachers, parents, elders, youth — were

▶

choose to be on the forefront of change. The business examples in Chapter 8 demonstrate financial benefits from such foresight.

The strengths of the Natural Step framework as an education and process tool for changing to sustainable practices are its simplicity and clarity. Even elementary school children can understand the systems mistakes we make in society and the direction we should take to correct these. Almost all the eco-municipalities have used the Natural Step system conditions as the framework for educating municipal employees and as a guide to identify sustainable practices.

Basic education about sustainability and sustainable development should last at least one full day but can also occur as two or three shorter training sessions. Carefully designed training sessions can give the decisive kick to move a municipality forward. Such forward momentum is more likely when professional sustainability trainers and process leaders conduct these initial education sessions, especially those geared toward political leaders. Later, local trainers can be taught to carry out widespread education for municipal employees and community interest groups, such as businesses and farmers. These educational investments can continue over several years, if necessary, and periodically be repeated even in the organizations and agencies that took part initially.

invited to take part in this initiative. Four years later this process, involving many citizens from all interests throughout the larger community, had created a local sustainable development action plan that was adopted by the Sundsvall City Council. The plan's goal is for Sundsvall to become an ecologically, economically, and socially sustainable city by the year 2020.

Sustainable development plan: The plan identified ten different goals that together defined a sustainable Sundsvall. These goals set objectives for the local economy, health, knowledge, production, waste, transportation, energy, consumption, and rural development. At the same time, Sundsvall's top officials directed all municipal departments and agencies to develop action plans that would contribute to reaching these objectives through concrete, measurable actions. To develop a guidance system for department plan development, the city commissioned a process leader and training consultants to help train department and agency staff to become trainers within their own workplaces (the process leader was Torbjörn Lahti).

Workplace training: Workplace training was based on a guide to local sustainable development that adapted the Natural Step's A-B-C-D process strategy, known among the ▶

Sustainability education sessions sometimes benefit from linkage with current hot topics. By linking a current issue such as suburban sprawl with sustainable development, one can include a longer-term perspective while helping people understand that sustainable development also addresses current problems. A risk of this strategy, however, is that it may be challenging for participants to move beyond the hot topic to a broader perspective. Understanding the meaning of sustainable development, in particular its systems approach, also can help resolve planning and development issues that otherwise can become festering, ongoing conflicts without apparent good solutions.

3. Official endorsement of sustainability operating principles

When top officials endorse sustainability principles as a guide for their municipality, it makes clear to municipal departments, employees, and the larger community that the municipal government is serious about its commitment. In each of the eco-municipalities and businesses that accomplished broadbased change to sustainable practices, their political or organization leaders made an official commitment to an overarching sustainability framework. In Sundsvall and Eksjö, for example, the eco-municipality resolution passed by the municipal council made it clear

eco-municipalities as the Compass, for a municipal context. First, staff came together for six full days of education over an eight-month period to become trainers in their respective departments. At the end of each full day of training, participants were given homework for the next session. During the first two training days, the participants learned about the Natural Step's approach to sustainability including the systems perspective, four system conditions and the Compass strategy for change. This education phase corresponds to Step A of the Compass process.

At the third training session, participants were asked to describe what activities in their departments violated the four system conditions and what information they might need to answer this question more effectively. For example, public works department staff might need to research what type of chemicals were contained in their engine cleaning supplies and what the properties and risks associated with these chemicals were in order to learn whether the present cleaning supplies violated the second system condition. This inventory phase corresponds to Step B of the Compass strategy.

The fourth training session completed the inventory phase and began the visionary ▶

that the council meant business. Use of the Natural Step framework to define sustainability offered a common set of sustainability playing rules for each department or agency in Sundsvall and Eksjö to use in formulating its own game plan for changing to sustainable practices.

Local political leadership eventually must support the transformation process to sustainable practices in order to succeed. The question is how to gain that support. In a democracy, one can always work toward the desired political climate via the electoral process. This road, however, is often long. A speedier route is to gather allies within the existing political establishment. There is often an elected official in the political leadership, such as Eksjö's municipal councilman, who is willing to spearhead sustainable development issues. Experiences from the Swedish eco-municipalities show that keeping a change process going is easier when the initial political decisions to begin that process are consensual ones, rather than wins by majority vote. It may be wiser to wait for an official decision until enough elected officials are on board with the idea rather than to force a decision where the opposition is bulldozed.

An official endorsement of sustainability principles is the beginning of the institutionalization of municipal change. If the municipality makes an official commitment to a general concept of sustainable development, this

phase that corresponds to the Compass Step C. Here, participants were asked to evaluate how Sundsvall's existing sustainable development goals related to the four Natural Step system conditions. Participants also described how their own department roles and activities related to achieving these goals.

The fifth and sixth training sessions addressed Step D of the Compass, where participants discussed a possible action program that included goals, indicator measures, and a follow-up system. By applying the system conditions and the Compass change strategy to their own work situations and contexts, these trainers-in-training came to understand in a practical way how the Compass change strategy works. The approach to designing the Sundsvall change process became the basis for the approach to sustainable development used in the town of Robertsfors, described in the next chapter.

City departments adopt plans for sustainable practices: The six-day training for key departmental leaders eventually spurred all Sundsvall municipal departments and agencies to educate their personnel about what sustainability meant at the global level and on the job. This deeper understanding of what sustainable development meant inspired municipal ▶

is an adequate beginning. It gives individual public servants and community citizens a public mandate to move forward in any way they can. If the municipality endorses the system conditions of the Natural Step as a marker for what sustainable development means, this is an even better start, since it clarifies the concept. If the municipality allocates or seeks resources to begin a multi-year change process, the prospects of success increase still further. Experience has shown that official resource allocation can galvanize municipal change toward sustainable practices.

To help the municipality make the decision to manage the change process systematically, it may be helpful for change leaders to raise financial arguments as well as ecological and social reasons for change. There are many good examples of economic benefits, ways to economize with scarce resources, and ways to start community development processes that create new enterprises and job opportunities. Several of these are described in Chapters 8 and 9.

4. Involving the implementers

Involving municipal implementers
Although it is critical that the local governing officials of a municipality officially commit to a goal for sustainable development, this alone will not

employees to carry out operational changes in their departments in the direction of the guiding sustainability principles that Sundsvall's municipal leadership endorsed.

While it was not feasible that during a six-day training session participating staff would prepare action programs for their departments, all Sundsvall municipal departments eventually adopted their own action plans for changing to sustainable practices. Most of these departments have implemented these plans. Each year, the Sundsvall City Council reviews and discusses reports about the department plans and implementation progress.

Using crisis as an opportunity: Sundsvall's experience shows how a municipality can take hold of a perceived crisis situation and use it to motivate a broader change process toward sustainable practices. To implement these practices, the city's strategy included both carrots and sticks. Initially, the change strategy used a volunteer approach, appealing to the engagement and interest of municipal employees. As general awareness about sustainable development has increased and spread throughout its departments, the city has put into practice more forceful decisions, including the requirement that every municipal department and agency create its own action plan for changing to sustainable practices.

guarantee a successful change process. To assure that implementation of sustainable practices will occur throughout the municipal government, all departments, agencies, and organizations that are going to be responsible for implementing the changes need to be involved. This involvement takes several forms.

First, local officials need to make it clear that the adopted sustainability goals apply to all municipal departments and agencies. If this does not occur, it is unlikely that the change process will move forward or spread throughout all city activities. Some communities that went further to establish a sustainable development office and staff have found that even this action was inadequate when municipal departments were not at the same time charged to work with these offices and staff.

Second, the likelihood of successful municipal implementation is much higher when the implementers — municipal departments and agencies — become engaged in designing their own strategies and action plans to meet the sustainability objectives endorsed by the elected officials. Successful eco-municipalities, such as Sundsvall and Eksjö, and successful businesses, such as Sänga-Säby and Scandic Hotels, adopted a sustainability framework as a new set of playing rules then encouraged department staff to come up with their own specific plans to change practices in the direction of those sustainability objectives. When department staffers helped to develop concrete ideas and action plans, their creativity and enthusiasm motivated them to put these into practice and to continue them. For example, the involvement of Scandic Hotel employees in action plan design led to implementation of over 1,500 employee change proposals within one year following the company's initial endorsement and adoption of the Natural Step framework. Involving the implementers puts into action two key principles for success discussed in Chapter 16 — designing a change process that is democratic in nature and has broad involvement.

INVOLVING COMMUNITY IMPLEMENTERS

Implementers not only are municipal employees, agencies, and organizations, they are also the citizens of a community. Citizens vote for important municipal decisions; for example, New England Town Meeting decisions about land use and zoning changes. Citizens elect local officials who may or may not support change to sustainable practices. As Swamp Yankee planning communities demonstrate, citizens are more apt to vote for community change proposals such as zoning revisions, when they themselves have been involved in shaping those proposals. Citizens can be implementers of change to sustainable practices in their own household, consumer, and civic behavior patterns. Businesses, corporations, and institutions, too, can be implementers of change.

To become a sustainable community, change needs to occur not only in municipal operations but in the practices of citizens, households, and businesses throughout that community. How can we make this happen?

One route is through a comprehensive planning process that engages all interests and sectors in a community in determining a future that is sustainable. As a tool of change already used by municipalities in North America and beyond, the comprehensive plan (master plan, general plan) is a logical instrument. It is intended to guide future development, and it also cuts across issue areas, such as housing, land use, economic development, and transportation, just as does the concept of sustainable development. The city of Sala, described in Chapter 14, successfully used its comprehensive planning process as the vehicle for its eco-municipality journey.

Whether or not a municipality chooses to use a master planning process as a vehicle for engaging its larger community, all interests in that community must be involved from the beginning in a change process toward a sustainable community. It helps to first carefully identify these interests in the community. Community interests means more than stakeholders — organizations or individuals who hold a particular view, opinion, or stake in the outcome. Rather, it refers to all the situations in a community that shape how people look at community life, public affairs, and public expenditures. These people can include parents with school-age children, farmers, large landowners, elders, homeowners, renters, youth, and businesses.

Once all community interests are identified, a steering committee can recruit an individual from each interest group to invite several more people who share that interest to attend an initial community event. The purpose of this event would be to learn what sustainability means and to help identify what a sustainable future might look like for that town or city. Swamp Yankee planning communities have successfully used this participation design approach to bring about broadbased citizen participation early on in shaping the guiding vision, objectives, and early actions of a planning process aimed at a desired community future. From that point on, people can be involved in topical work groups to refine change proposals for presentation at a future public event where local officials also are present.

Another approach to involving community interests is to actively seek contact with representatives of various community organizations. The change process leadership needs to work with many groups at the same time.

People also can be invited to association meetings, tourism meetings, farmers meetings, village meetings, and so forth. This is how a particular community group can be engaged in discussion and where members can also participate in later stages of inventorying existing conditions and shaping action proposals. At some point, community priorities need to be identified for the change proposals emerging from the topic group or interest group work. One way to do this is in a public forum where all topic groups can present their findings to the larger community and to local officials, and where discussion and priority setting among representatives of all topic and interest groups can occur.[1]

Whatever the method used to involve all interests in a community, it is important to do so in the earliest possible stage of the change process. In this way, these community interests learn that the process includes them. A basic condition for sustainable development is that all people cooperate. A holistic systems perspective that everything is related and mutually influencing is also essential. The change process must involve all social sectors and all interest groups in parallel. Even if time and resources limit the ability to do this in practice, an open attitude to this possibility should be present.

5. Applying the Compass: Sustainability framework, inventory, vision, actions

a)   Introducing the sustainability framework

Before launching into a change process toward sustainability or before starting any sustainable development project, it is important that all involved share a clear understanding of what sustainability and sustainable development mean. Creating a common sustainability language allows municipal officials, staff, and community citizens to communicate about and explore possibilities for how to proceed. Agreement on new playing rules for sustainable practices clears the field for the next steps — identifying present unsustainable practices, developing a sustainable community vision, and creating an action plan to move toward that vision.

Developing a common language and playing rules occurs, not surprisingly, through education, as discussed earlier in this chapter. Part I offers the Natural Step sustainability framework as that common language and new set of playing rules that all sectors of municipal government and community life can simultaneously use as a guide to develop their own strategies for changing to sustainable practices. This is the framework that now guides the more than 60 Swedish eco-municipalities in their continuing journeys toward sustainability. The stories of

Sundsvall and Eksjö illustrate how two communities introduced this framework as the common set of playing rules for their municipal employees. The story of Robertsfors in the next chapter will offer yet another example.

b) **Inventorying present conditions**

As with development of any kind, it helps to clarify the factual situation as soon as possible. A wise process leader learns early in a change process what are the greatest challenges in the local community from a sustainability perspective. These may consist of seeing that the community depends heavily on fossil energy sources for transportation and heating, for example, or, that the community's capability for subsisting on food grown within the region is extremely limited. By getting a picture of the material and energy flows in the community, the process leader can then see where important pieces of the puzzle are missing. One strategy in the change process design can be to fill in the missing pieces — for example, developing new business opportunities for local entrepreneurs. Volunteer organizations or public grants or financing might fill other gaps.

INVENTORYING PRESENT CONDITIONS
• In what ways is our department/community systematically dependent upon fossil fuels? Upon scarce metals and minerals?
• In what ways is our department/community dependent upon persistent chemicals and other wasteful use of synthetics?
• In what ways does our department/community encroach upon nature?
• In what ways is our department/community not meeting basic needs fairly or efficiently? What are those basic needs?

Identifying a community's greatest challenges does not usually require extensive investigation. At the same time, systematic work can begin to map important material and energy flows in the local community so as to construct an accounting system for monitoring and measuring sustainable development progress over time.

Inventorying present conditions can also work as an educational tool in the change process, especially if many people get involved. Inventorying can go on for several years when the aim is to map gaps in community knowledge. A risk in an extensive inventory phase, however, is that it can bog down, or even halt, a change process. Spending too much time and effort on inventorying and measuring can sap the enthusiasm and available time of community participants and deplete resources and energy that could otherwise be channeled into development of an action plan.

Often, there are not easily available data for satisfactory sustainability accounting. Building new accounting systems to measure sustainable development progress usually takes a long time. Lack of data, however, should not block taking action. Using sustainability objectives based upon the Natural Step framework makes it possible to analyze existing conditions even when no data is available. Following these objectives coupled with the precautionary principle — First, do no harm — can highlight local unsustainable trends and conditions that require attention. This framework also can reveal ecologically sound development potential, such as for new business opportunities.

Inventorying existing conditions also includes identifying the positive aspects of community life. With "sustainability glasses" one can often detect efforts not previously recognized or valued as sustainable development. They may include organic farmers who are working against the tides of diminishing land and increasing market domination by large-scale businesses, or schools that teach and practice an ecological perspective. Other existing efforts might include community gardens cultivated in urban centers, or green buildings developed by private organizations. Making an inventory of these good examples can provide important local models in the continuing change process. All communities have good examples that deserve more attention and that can act as a positive force in community transformation.

c) Identifying a guiding vision

Attractive shared visions are driving forces in all types of change processes. Starting a change process through identifying a common vision generates energy for keeping that process moving and focused upon a common goal. A vision that is widely shared throughout a community can be implemented in many different ways. A community vision, of course, is a long-term goal. This, however, need not prevent process leaders from forming early opinions about possible sustainability objectives for the municipality. Discussions about future possibilities will likely take place in the first meetings with fire souls and elected officials.

When it comes to sustainable development, it is not enough to identify an attractive and pleasant community vision. The envisioned future must also be sustainable, that is, must be within the ecological limits posed by the first three Natural Step system conditions and meet the economic and social

IDENTIFYING A SUSTAINABLE COMMUNITY VISION
What will our community look like when we eliminate:
1. Wasteful use of fossil fuels, scarce metals and minerals?
2. Dependence upon persistent chemicals and wasteful use of synthetics?
3. Contributions to encroachment upon nature? and,
4. When we also meet human and community needs fairly and efficiently?

objectives posed by System Condition #4. Therefore, it is more effective to carry out systematic community vision building after basic education has taken place about the systems perspective and Natural Step system conditions — Step A of the Compass. Otherwise one risks creating wishful thinking that ultimately may not be sustainable — for example, future development scenarios that heavily depend on use of fossil-fuel energy for transportation or heating. It also helps to have some inventory work completed at the vision building stage to be able to offer some information about how current community conditions look in relation to sustainability as defined by the four system conditions.

Using the Compass change strategy, community participants can build visions that are attractive while also meeting the four system conditions. The challenge is to be able to paint a picture of a world that is equally attractive while using resources, such as energy and materials, more efficiently and in less quantity. To do this, it is necessary to understand what conservation strategies are available to recapture resources and economize energy use.

System Condition #4 of the Natural Step framework encourages us to ask questions about what is important in life. What do we really need for our well-being as individuals and households? What basic needs in our community are not being met? When the larger community begins to ask this type of question, it is possible to hold serious community visioning events where the end result is a more pleasant, interesting, and sustainable society than exists today.

In practice, vision building can occur in one or more workshops or community events. One approach is to start with elected officials, following different themes as starting points and allowing different interest groups to hold similar workshops. In the end, however, these visions, which may differ among the groups, must be brought together and reconciled.

Another approach is to hold a single community-wide event where citizens representing all community interests come together to define a common vision. After an introduction to the systems perspective and system conditions, interest groups can work separately and concurrently to form their own vision for how the municipality and community can meet the four system conditions and define early actions that move toward this vision. Then, groups can come back together to share their respective visions of a sustainable community. When all groups have presented their results to the wider audience, a facilitated discussion can take place, finding and seeking agreement on the common and seeking agreement on those common themes. Early actions can be posted on the walls, inviting participants to indicate their action priorities through the red-dot voting method.[1] The results of this event, if correctly designed and facilitated, can identify a broadbased community vision of a sustainable city or town and help set the overall agenda and early actions to kick off the change process toward this goal.

d) Developing an action plan

The fourth step of the Compass change strategy, preparing a municipal action plan, creates the implementing strategies for practices that can lead the way to a sustainable community — a city or town that meets the four objectives of the Natural Step framework.

Identifying implementing actions follows naturally from the inventory and vision steps of the Compass approach. The back-casting technique described in Chapter 16 is useful here, starting with the vision of the desired sustainable community, defined within the parameters of the four system conditions, then identifying specific actions to get to that desired vision. For example, a town that has set a goal of becoming 100 percent fossil-fuel free might identify an action step to replace its municipal fleet with alternatively fueled vehicles over the next five years.

Everything cannot be done at once, of course. Therefore, it is necessary to develop sustainable development implementation plans and time schedules, just as cities and towns already prepare five-year capital improvement plans or comprehensive (master) plans. This requires setting priorities and taking into account the realities of budget, staff time, and political climate. Other considerations for process leaders include discerning where local enthusiasm and energy lies and making judgments about important findings from the inventory phase.

In the case of a community-wide change process, such as for developing a sustainability master plan, it is critical to honor community priorities for action proposals. This will assure continued community support and participation in the process, including change in individual citizen and household behavior to sustainable practices. Identifying community priorities can occur through such techniques as red-dot voting at public meetings, described in endnote 1.

The credibility of a change process depends to a large degree on showing visible results as soon as possible. In the general public's view, it is not enough to talk and produce good-looking documents about planning and sustainable development. Visible results count the most. Process leaders need to take this reality into account, even when they realize that the most important longer-term results are the altered attitudes of community citizens and officials. For this reason, it is important to show concrete good examples early in the change process.

In the initial phase of a change process, it is wise not to invest energy in developing a large-scale good example. To make sure the change process keeps going, it is important that the first concrete sustainable development projects are successful ones. If too much time and energy are tied up early on in a large project, the process may well bog down before it has had time to pick up real speed. It is wiser to invest in simple projects in the early stages of the change process; for example, developing a demonstration wood pellet-fired home heating system, as opposed to investing in a large bio-gas production plant. Eventually the time will be ripe for large-scale projects.

Further, asking three questions can help set priorities among the many action proposals that will emerge in the change process. First, which proposals will move toward all four sustainability objectives at the same time? Proposals that satisfy these objectives can be fairly well assured of moving in the right direction, solving more than one problem at the same time. Second, which actions can provide a platform for future actions? For example, designing a new school building with a southern orientation allows future installation of solar panels that might not be financially feasible in the initial construction phase. Locating the building facing north would preclude this future alternative. Third, does this action provide a good return on investment? In answering this third question, it is important to think beyond the costs of initial capital investment. Investment also includes benefits such as improved public health and worker productivity, security from future cost escalations, and the value of nature's work, such as the flood protection that is provided by wetlands.

SETTING ACTION PRIORITIES BY ASKING:
1. Which actions meet all four sustainability objectives?
2. Which actions provide flexible platforms for future actions?
3. Which actions give a good return on investment?

6. Whole plan endorsement

At some point, all of the action plans developed by municipal departments, agencies, community interest groups, and citizen working groups need to come together in an integrated whole, receiving official adoption as municipal policy. Official municipal endorsement is critical for institutionalizing change proposals. In the case of a comprehensive (master or general) plan in U.S. communities, often the local planning board or commission has the authority to adopt the plan. In some states, local city councils officially adopt the master plan. To the degree that the plan is intended as a guide for the entire community, plan endorsement should come from the highest level.

Prior to official adoption, it helps to hold a public event, even if not officially required, where all the groups that have been working on particular topic or department proposals come together to discuss all the plan proposals from the full range of working groups. At such an event, community participants or department employees can learn about the proposals presented by other groups, reconcile differences, and identify community or municipal priorities. Obtaining general agreement from participants at such an event can add power to the plan by sending a message to the local officials with ultimate adoption authority that the plan is a community-backed initiative.

7. Keeping it going

Once officially adopted, plans for sustainable practices need to become part of ongoing department or municipal policy and practice. New actors who enter the scene — new employees, department heads, or elected officials — may need orientation and education about sustainable practices and their importance. A critical part of continuing both sustainable practices and the overall change process in the municipality and larger community is ongoing education, training, and efforts to raise awareness about the importance of sustainability and sustainable development.

Using the Natural Step framework as a guide, combined with sustainability indicators that measure action progress toward the system conditions, can provide both an education tool and a way to monitor progress of action plans. Sånga-Säby, Scandic Hotels, and the city of Sala are among those businesses and communities successfully using these methods. Other businesses and communities have combined use of the Natural Step framework as a sustainability guide with environmental management systems, such as ISO 14001, to keep sustainable practices on track.

> **Using existing municipal planning and regulatory tools:** To integrate new sustainable practices into existing municipal activities, it helps to establish a guidance system for reviewing and gradually revising all additional municipal planning instruments to harmonize with the adopted sustainable practices and sustainability objectives. These planning instruments include the general (master) plan, capital improvement plan, municipal budget, land use regulations, building codes, and specific policies, such as for energy, solid waste, education, eldercare, and social services. Review of existing municipal planning tools in the light of sustainability objectives can begin well before adopting a specific sustainable development guidance system. The change process also can be

integrated into reviews and updates of these municipal tools. A proposed update of the master plan, for instance, can become an excellent vehicle for establishing and integrating a municipal and community change process toward sustainable practices.

Establishing coordinating organizations: At some point in the change process it may help to establish a permanent organization to support ongoing work toward becoming a sustainable community. A local or regional technical assistance center for sustainable development that is separate from the municipal government can then assist both private and public sector sustainability practices. The source and process for financing such an organization of course will influence its design. In Sweden, these types of technical assistance centers are usually regional ones that include public and private sector members as well as non-profit advocacy organizations. Their financing has usually combined public funding and business contract fee-for-service work. A municipality that is established as a pilot model for sustainable development, such as Robertsfors, described in Chapter 18, has particularly good prospects for establishing this type of organization early in its change process, even if this organization's purview is a regional or national one.

There may also be a need for business-oriented organizations to help with efforts such as marketing and sales of ecological products or sustainable tourism development. While these are best developed within the local business community, even here a municipality can help provide start-up energy. Often, the seeds for these new organizations are found in networks established earlier in a community change process. An established network can progress naturally into a permanent organization, especially if that network includes small business enterprises with limited potential for marketing on their own. County governments can play this role as well, for example, Värmland County's environmental business program, described in Chapter 8.

Regional initiatives: Regional organizations and county governments can help create opportunities for transforming entire regions into Silicon Valleys of public and private sector sustainable development. This is where municipalities that are leaders in sustainable development can make a big contribution to others. Systematic, patient work toward sustainable practices will lead to a municipality's improved ability to sustain its local economy at the same time as strengthening its competitive edge. With ability and good fortune, that region may become an internationally known example of how sustainable development can create abundant economic potential.

Today, several regions in Sweden are systematically marketing the sustainable development knowledge and techniques that have been steadily accumulating in their businesses and organizations. These regions are leaders in the world's rapidly growing environmental business movement. This position provides them with opportunities for international business. Billions of people around the globe have problems with unsustainable development. What a market for those who have solutions! And, these leading regional initiatives began with change to sustainable practices in *municipalities*. The demand for sustainable products and sustainable techniques started in municipalities. It was in the small steps taken in household recycling and in environmental purchasing by municipalities, schools, and households that the development of these flourishing regional sustainable development models began. This movement started with individual people coming to understand it is possible to do something on a small scale to change our non-sustainable world to a sustainable one.

CHAPTER 18

Inside the Head of a Process Leader

Since August 2001, Torbjörn Lahti (Toohr'-byeurn Lah'-tih) has been leading a community-based process in the northern Swedish municipality of Robertsfors to help this town become an international model as a sustainable community. Here are his experiences and thoughts about what is important in designing, beginning, and carrying out a process for systematic change to sustainable practices throughout an entire community and its municipal government.

Introduction: The role of a process leader

While it is possible for a town or city to self-administer the type of change process being discussed here, it can go easier when an experienced process leader takes a leading from the side approach. A process leader holds the vision of the overall change process, its steps, and guiding principles. This skilled leader designs a process that enables local citizens and employees to devise sustainable development strategies and plans in a way that these become their own and, hence, more likely to be adopted and implemented.

City and town planners or persons with planning education and experience are logical process leaders for cities and towns, since these professionals are trained to understand all municipal functions and planning issues. They also understand how a municipality operates. Knowing one's target audience is important and a considerable advantage. Having a fundamental and clear grasp of the concepts of sustainability and sustainable development, especially the criteria for sustainability, also is critical. Ideally, the sustainability trainers and the process leaders will be the same in a given municipality, although this may not always be possible.

At least as important as these qualifications, however, are the abilities to create municipal and community engagement and participation and to lead a well-organized change process. There are few schools in the world today where one can learn how to become a good process leader for sustainable development. However, it is not the paper credentials that are important so much as personal characteristics such as patience, humility, openness, and absence of personal ambition for prestige.

For someone taking on a process leadership role, it is important as soon as possible to start a learning process from others with similar experience that can provide missing knowledge and insights on an ongoing basis. The less experience one has, the more important this is, of course. It is important to face one's personal challenges with a critical and non-ambitious attitude and to be open to learning from others. The stronger the network of technical assistance a process leader can build, the more she can compensate for her own knowledge and skill gaps.

If you are a process leader, it is also important to clarify what your own role is in the process and how long you plan to act as the community's change process leader. Ongoing sustainable development often fares better when fresh individuals take over this leadership after some time. For myself as process leader, it is important to work right from the start toward eventually being able to shed this role without disrupting the continuation of the process.

The challenge for a sustainable Robertsfors

In the summer of 2001, when I became the process leader for the Robertsfors initiative, I saw it equal to the challenge that I accepted as project leader during the 1980s for Övertorneå, Sweden's first eco-municipality. In Robertsfors I would have the chance to put into practice learning from twenty years of work on sustainable development in Övertorneå as well as more recently with many municipalities and businesses in Sweden and beyond.

On one hand, the conditions for a successful change process toward sustainability in Robertsfors are exceptionally favorable. It is a five-year initiative — long enough for a change process that is meaningful. I have three assistant co-workers. We are fortunate to have enough financial resources so that the process won't founder for lack of funds.[1] Robertsfors' political leaders had already signed onto and enthusiastically endorsed the municipality's decision to become a model sustainable community before I took the job. So, community officials already understood the great potential for the sustainability initiative to benefit the town's future.

Robertsfors' officials had already come to understand the importance of sustainable development several years before the beginning of the sustainable community initiative. This has made the present change process easier. Local commitment to sustainable development was also pivotal in the Environmental Forum's decision to select Robertsfors as the pilot community, as described on page 226. The town is small and easy to move around in. The social networks are strong; everybody knows everybody. The change process, therefore, will be more about influencing individuals than about influencing large anonymous organizations.

On the other hand, the challenge is to transform a municipality that is not now on the cutting edge of sustainable development into a leading, internationally known, sustainable community model within five years. If anybody knows how long this type of process takes, I do. Most of the Swedish municipalities that today are on the front-line of sustainable development have had at least 10 to 15 years of active and systematic change experience and in many respects are far ahead of Robertsfors in producing results. If we succeed in our work in Robertsfors, we will demonstrate a change process that will cut in half the time it takes for an overall, across-the-board community change to sustainable practices. This streamlined change process approach could become Robertsfors' primary contribution to sustainable community

ABOUT ROBERTSFORS

Robertsfors (Roh-behrts-fosh'), a community of 7,200 people in an area of 500 square miles, is 35 miles north of the city of Umeå. Just over 2,000 of these residents live in Robertsfors' town center. Beyond the town center is rural countryside, nine villages with between 200 and 800 inhabitants, and 20 hamlets with less than 200 people. Many residents commute to work in Umeå while others hold jobs based in Robertsfors.

Robertsfors developed as a traditional iron mill community around iron works established in the early 1800s. Although these iron works have long been abandoned, their legacy lives on in the region's metal industry, an important part of the regional economy.

Agriculture is still the most important sector of the regional economy despite the drastically reduced number of active farmers over the last decade, as elsewhere in northern

▶

change around the world. I also want to see the Robertsfors initiative helping to form the fifth generation of eco-municipality development. In this
stage, heart and brain becomes combined in a holistic perspective working
toward becoming a sustainable community. For more information about the
first four generations of eco-municipalities, see Chapter 4.

Another challenge: the town of Robertsfors is not in a crisis situation.
Experience has taught that it is often easier to begin change processes
toward sustainable development in communities that are going through
some form of major economic, social, cultural, or environmental trouble.
For example, Övertorneå, described in the Introduction, was undergoing a
depression in its local economy and community self-esteem. Sundsvall,
described in Chapter 17, experienced a severe air pollution crisis. Regardless
of whether the nature of the crisis is economic, environmental, or social, it
is easier to embrace a new way of thinking when there is a compelling reason to do so. This is more difficult when communities are relatively comfortable and have few disputes with the status quo. In crisis situations, people are more likely to be receptive to new ideas and to get involved in community affairs. While Robertsfors has lost population over the last ten years,
this exodus is no more extreme than in other northern Swedish communities; nor are any major environmental or social welfare problems apparent in
the town. By some standards, the community of Robertsfors is rather idyllic, where its inhabitants live in relative well-being without need to worry
much about their own or other people's problems. Is it at all possible, in
such an agreeable community climate, to engage officials and citizens in
work that may be more about global problems than pressing local problems?

Sweden. Milk is the principal agricultural product, further refined into the renowned
Vasterbotten cheese. Robertsfors and its neighbor Skelleftea sit at the heart of what is marketed as Sweden's Cheese Country.

Traditionally, the political orientation of the Robertsfors municipal government has
walked a steady middle-of-the-road course. As of 2003, a colorful four-party alliance leads
the local government. This alliance consists of the leftist social democrats, the environmental party, the moderate folk party, and the right-leaning conservatives. Formed in the 1998
municipal elections, it has maintained leadership in subsequent municipal elections. The
amiable working relationship among these oftentimes conflicting political interests stems in
part from a Robertsfors tradition of collaboration across party lines, and also because no one
party in town ever has had a dominant political position.

Inside the head of a process leader

As a leader, it is important to have insight about one's self and the role one plays in the change process. I am aware that I play an important role in how the model Robertsfors sustainable community initiative develops, regardless of whether I desire this importance. Initially, the initiative depends substantially on what change strategy I recommend to community officials and leaders and how I behave toward those co-workers. It is also in the beginning phase that I can save time if I know enough to behave correctly right from the start, even if the local environment is relatively unknown. For example, quickly learning what all the interests are in the community and which political and community leaders to approach first saves valuable process time.

I must also work toward gradually removing myself as leader and creating an ongoing community change process, independent of the funding that will end in four more years. When the funded work is complete, this initiative should be barely perceptible, because the motivators that propel the ongoing change process will be well-established and self-propelling.

GETTING STARTED

It is important to meet people in their reality to be able to engage them in the change process. Therefore, a sustainable community initiative needs to be seen as emerging from what is already happening in the community and

> If we succeed in our work in Robertsfors, we will demonstrate a change process that will cut in half the time it takes for an overall, across-the-board community change to sustainable practices.

HOW THE ROBERTSFORS JOURNEY BEGAN

Throughout the 1990s, Robertsfors undertook a variety of sustainable development projects that helped generate local understanding of sustainability and why it is important for communities to pursue it. While Robertsfors' officials had not joined SeKom, the national association of eco-municipalities, they referred to their town as a "becoming" eco-municipality. Hence, in 1999, when Robertsfors' officials and citizens learned of an exciting chance to become a model municipality in sustainable development, the local stage was set to grasp this opportunity.

A collaboration called the Environmental Forum, consisting of representatives from the county government, Umeå University, and several regional economic organizations, was offering regional seminars about becoming more economically self-sufficient in an ecological way. At one seminar, an idea emerged to develop a pilot municipality in sustainable practices. Seminar participants believed that such a model town could inspire others to follow suit. The Environmental Forum collaborative developed, refined, and ▶

municipality. In Robertsfors, previous community events led to the beginning of the Sustainable Robertsfors initiative. Many large and small changes are occurring in the municipal government and its community. These all are part of the ongoing overall change and transformation of society. Some of these efforts may appear to oppose each other. Some efforts may seem far from what we often define as sustainable development. It is my experience that most people become interested in sustainable development only when someone sells it to them in the best possible way. If the problems and the realities of the participants form the starting point, it is usually possible to find a way to help them see how the sustainable community initiative might improve their particular problems and situation. At the same time, it is a big step for that person to move from a generally positive inclination to becoming an active collaborator in the change process.

In the beginning, it is natural to design a change process toward sustainable development as a concrete initiative with time and resource limitations. It is important that resources be sufficient, especially for professional personnel and project leadership, for a realistic prospect of success. The experiences of Swedish cities and towns include not only successful eco-municipalities but also less successful communities where failure often was related to resource allocation that was inadequate in proportion to the project's ambitions. Unqualified personnel have been put in the position of managing sustainable development projects with scarce funding and technical assistance. The political intention may be a good one, but if the project does not

presented this idea to all municipalities in the county. The town of Robertsfors took the bait and designed a program of action that began in August of 2001.

In signing on, Robertsfors declared its intent to become a model of a community that integrates ecological, economic, and social perspectives throughout all its municipal and community activities. Robertsfors aims to be a demonstration for other Swedish municipalities and also for communities around the world. Robertsfors' sustainability initiative will develop model practices for:

- how to start and carry out a local democratic change process toward sustainability,
- how to shift a local economy toward a sustainable direction, and
- how to bring local environmental goals into harmony with broader national or global goals.

❖

have resources to employ or contract professional expertise then this good intention can fall on its face. Frustration, apathy and burnout can occur among the unfortunate project implementers who, despite having their hands tied by lack of resources, are still forced to defend the political good intentions. It is wiser to adjust the intentions and ambitions to a realistic level and view the first project as a platform to a later start-up of a comprehensive process or project when adequate resource allocation supports the initial ambitions.

ADMINISTERING THE CHANGE PROCESS

A municipal steering committee including elected officials usually should have the oversight responsibility for a municipal change process to sustainable practices instead of one department, such as an environmental agency.

There are essentially two ways to administer the change process. The first approach is to design the process as a project that is coordinated outside ordinary municipal operations and department activities. The advantage of this approach is that the project can be less likely to be perceived as competing with existing operations and instead can be viewed as providing additional technical assistance support and energy to existing operations. This organizational structure can help to avoid the pitfalls of internal politics since project personnel are outside the regular municipal department staff. On the other hand, it is important that the change process engages department staff as soon as possible and that the change process permeates throughout department activities.

A second organizational approach that can accomplish a ripple effect is to involve all department heads or their representatives in a coordinating committee that oversees concurrent change processes in all departments and involves employees in developing Compass-guided department action plans. When plans are complete, the coordinating committee and top officials can then assemble, integrate, and approve them. This approach can avoid the pitfalls of the former, wherein municipal departments can disregard the efforts of an outside sustainable development project coordinator. Whatever the organizational structure, including one that combines these two approaches, it is important that the top municipal officials make it clear to all departments and agencies that the change process is to be taken seriously.

It helps to design a change process toward sustainable practices that grows out of the municipality's own history and situation. It is also important to design a process that from the beginning is aimed at independence from direction and grant money that comes from outside the community.

The initial idea for a local sustainability initiative and the political decision endorsing this are important platforms for designing the change process. A strategy that creates and uses platforms helps assure that the change process can produce lasting results and can surmount setbacks, such as the resignation of a key leader. Platforms might include certain political decisions, master plan preparation or review, or the adoption of an environmental management system. At the same time, it is important to remember that it is not reports that change society but the many concrete actions of individual people both within and outside a municipal government. However, these people's efforts will have more lasting results when their work is supported through use of platforms that integrate sustainable policies and practices into ongoing operations.

FINDING AND INFORMING THE FIRE SOULS IN ROBERTSFORS

The first strategy that I chose in beginning work in Robertsfors was to make sure that all key municipal and community opinion leaders understood the Sustainable Robertsfors initiative and that they were positively inclined, if not necessarily active, within the initiative. The second strategy was to find the fire souls who were willing to actively contribute to, and help lead, efforts within the initiative. It was my good luck to find many fire souls in Robertsfors, several of them within the schools, daycare centers, and village community development groups.

I have learned that community engagement and motivation for changing to sustainable practices will occur only if people come to understand the nature of the unsustainable problems with which we all wrestle, and have access to a mental model for more sustainable behavior. Helping people to understand and using the Natural Step sustainability criteria as the mental model is central to my work approach for community change. If enough people participate in our community workshops about sustainability, it will be possible to engage enough people in the change process.

IDENTIFYING AND WORKING WITH THE RANGE OF COMMUNITY INTERESTS

Our goal, at least in principle, is to work with all Robertsfors community interest groups at the same time — including school and childcare teachers and administrators, municipal employees, elected officials, businesspeople, farmers, youth, and advocacy organizations. One strategy is to develop pockets of good examples of sustainable practices within all those interest areas. Those pockets can then become change agents within those interest groups.

Community engagement and motivation for changing to sustainable practices will occur only if people come to understand the nature of the unsustainable problems with which we all wrestle, and if they have access to a mental model for more sustainable behavior.

This strategy places demands on our time and our capability as process leaders to engage and motivate individuals and groups. It will be existing community citizens, leaders, municipal officials, and employees in Robertsfors that will accomplish the majority of the change process work — not leaders such as myself. In order to have these citizens and public servants work with us, the change process must be based on their life situations and take place on their terms. We are here for them, and our role as process leaders is to act as coaches and supporters, not autocratic directors.

Initially, the highest priority interest groups for contacting were the top elected officials, certain key department heads, for example, the school superintendent, and the village associations within the municipality. The Sustainable Robertsfors initiative gained good political backing from the start, but this does not mean that either elected officials or civil servants understood what this initiative entailed. Because of this, I devoted a large part of the first few months to constant meetings with local officials and different community interest groups, explaining the initiative and how it benefits the community. These types of meetings are likely to continue even though the change process is already well established within most of the target interest groups, within which pockets of people are directing efforts toward some change to sustainable practices.

It was a conscious strategy initially to reach out to Robertsfors' school and daycare teachers and staffers. These individuals are in frequent contact with residents who are parents, grandparents, employees, students, or others interested in children's everyday environment. If we succeed in engaging school and childcare staff, these individuals and institutions will help spread the word throughout all other social interest areas in the community. The village associations are important because here one can find fire souls who have a burning interest in improving their neighborhood and who can devote time to work on similar improvements.

The young people of Robertsfors are a high priority group. The Sustainable Robertsfors initiative has teamed up with Robertsfors' youth to develop a Community Youth Forum (KUF). This organization, supported by the Robertsfors municipal government, will have its own agenda and will be directed by the youth themselves.

Applying the Compass in Robertsfors

STEP A — THE EDUCATION PHASE

The sooner that systematic education of many residents can take place, the faster the community change process can occur. The basic idea is to have many people within the different social and interest groups who share the same insight — a systems view and sense of connection to the globe. This is most easily accomplished through sustainability education, even though we try to remind people of these things in other work efforts when we have the opportunity.

In Robertsfors, one outcome of high outreach priority to schools and childcare staff was one-day sustainability education workshops attended by almost all teachers during the first two months. In the following year and a half, we followed up with additional training for teachers and childcare staff. This training developed a network of representatives from all Robertsfors' schools and childcare facilities. This network meets once a month to exchange experiences and to discuss common activities related to sustainable practices. Another outcome: almost all of Robertsfors' schools and daycare facilities have started work to qualify for national certification as environmentally compatible schools and daycare facilities.

We also have held several community workshops for different Robertsfors' interest groups and citizens on themes including the sustainable community, sustainable sustenance, sustainable building, and the sustainable economy. While the subjects and interests of workshop participants have varied, everyone has learned the systems view and sustainability system conditions as the perspectives that cut across and connect interests and topics. A cautious estimate is that, so far, between five and ten percent of the adult population in Robertsfors has taken part in these education sessions.

OVERALL FRAMEWORK FOR CHANGE PROCESS DESIGN AND IMPLEMENTATION IN ROBERTSFORS

The starting point for the Robertsfors sustainable community initiative is the Compass strategy based upon the Natural Step's A-B-C-D approach, described in Chapter 16. This change process strategy is directing the entire Robertsfors initiative including all the business enterprise, organizations, associations, and schools that we hope will participate. It uses four steps to design and guide a change process to sustainable practices:

A. Defining criteria for sustainability using a systems view and the system conditions.
B. Inventorying present conditions according to the system conditions.
C. Identifying a sustainable community vision within the system conditions.
D. Developing an action program, including short and long-term strategies, that moves from unwanted present conditions to the envisioned ones.

❖

During 2003, the plan is to double or triple this proportion of people participating in sustainability education through a 16-hour training session for the school and daycare network, expanding this to include about 150 staff. A similar training session is planned for all elected officials and municipal employees. At the same time, citizen sustainable development discussion groups will begin throughout the community, using a reading guide that I wrote and have used in other communities to stimulate learning about local sustainability. This guide is based on the four system conditions and the Compass change strategy of the Natural Step. It expands upon questions of economic and psychosocial sustainability and analyses of human needs — not only basic physical needs, but deeper ones as well. We use this material in all our basic education. The questions posed in this sustainable development guide permeate the approach to developing the eventual action programs in Robertsfors, at least as I see it at present.

STEP B — ROBERTSFORS' INVENTORY PHASE

We have also started a basic inventory of existing conditions in Robertsfors, parallel to community education and network building. The purposes are to obtain a clear community picture and to establish in what ways the municipality is not sustainable today, from the perspective of the Natural Step sustainability criteria. Where are the problems and the threats? Another objective, as described in the last chapter, is to identify good examples of existing community sustainable practices and particular ones that might offer possibilities for new or expanded projects. These good examples also stimulate community motivation and engagement. If we only see the negative side of community affairs, we fall prey to frustration and despair about the future that is latent in many attitudes. Instead, we want to highlight good examples already underway to demonstrate it is feasible to become a model municipality in sustainable development, even if we are aware of the challenge this involves.

I believe it is possible to find good examples of sustainable development in every municipality. Good examples mean activities demonstrating some aspect of sustainable development good enough to showcase and to serve as models in the continued change process. This is why we directed some inventorying efforts toward finding good examples in Robertsfors. Also, frequently behind those good examples there is a driving force — fire souls who can become activists in the ongoing community change process. With "sustainability glasses" it is often easy to see them. With "non-sustainability glasses" or "home familiarity blindness" it may be difficult for some community members to detect either these individuals or existing good examples of sustainable development. Therefore, it wasn't surprising to me, for example, that the number of organic farmers in Robertsfors turned out to be 12, instead of 3 or 4 as a town staff person guessed. To learn, however, that 25 percent of all tilled fields in Robertsfors are organically farmed was a positive surprise. To learn further that almost every school and daycare facility in the town is working somewhat systematically on issues that demonstrate aspects of sustainable development exceeded my wildest expectations.

I had heard about the work of the village associations in Robertsfors before I started my job, but, upon hearing the detailed descriptions of their work, I was even more impressed. We found a strong base of sustainable development practices in these villages; all this in a community that was not known for sustainable development! By showcasing these good examples, especially to foreign visitors to Robertsfors, we also have highlighted these examples for Robertsfors residents and officials. This strengthens and encourages many of the positive efforts already under way.

The credibility of the change process is based heavily upon visibility — people's ability to see that something is happening. Visions and plans are important, but if we only talk, people will lose patience early on. Therefore, we encourage people in all community interests to find new, concrete projects to develop as part of the Sustainable Robertsfors initiative. For example, in the Robertsfors village of Åkullsjön (Auh'-kuell-sheun'), residents collaborated to clear up old grazing land for new calves during the first summer after the initiative started up. This project also served as training for village youth to learn how to clear forest and forge iron for fences and gates. In another effort, the village school developed an earth cellar for vegetable storage during the winter. From the perspective of the Sustainable Robertsfors initiative, these village projects serve also as forms of education that demonstrate how sustainable development can be on the ground, not just an abstract concept. Each of the town's villages has been encouraged to look for more projects to carry out as part of Sustainable Robertsfors.

While inventory work is occurring most intensively during the first year and a half of the initiative, it should be ongoing. An important premise of inventorying is to fill the gaps in community knowledge. A continually learning society will always need updated information and feedback to deepen community wisdom. This is one cornerstone of a psychosocially sustainable society.

Inventorying in Robertsfors so far has identified several important themes that are starting points for strategies to increase the community's self-sufficiency — not dissimilar to the self-sufficiency strategies described in Chapter 9.

If we only see the negative side of community affairs, we fall prey to frustration and despair about the future that is latent in many attitudes. Instead, we want to highlight good examples already underway to demonstrate it is feasible to become a model municipality in sustainable development.

These themes include waste, energy, food production, housing and building, hospitality and tourism, forestry, and transportation. During the spring of 2003 we systematically reported our inventory work to inform the next phase of the change process.

STEP C — MY ROLE AS PROCESS LEADER IN ROBERTSFORS VISION-BUILDING

The importance of the vision as a driving force in change processes is well known. This creates energy and motivation bringing the strength to make tough decisions and changes later in the process. If a vision is to have the desired effect, all community interests including as many community residents as possible, need to create, share, and accept that vision through political consensus. The vision should be clear and easy to understand. In the vision-building phase, step C of the Compass strategy, residents from all community interests paint a picture of their desired future community within the framework of the sustainability criteria — the four system conditions.

As process leader, early in the Robertsfors work I knew where the change process should lead to and how the municipality could develop in a sustainable direction over the long term. These early insights are important for effective process leadership, especially in the beginning months. Choosing not to set direction for the change process until a bottom-up community vision is in place would jeopardize important guiding impetus needed at the beginning of a change process. This does not mean that I call off democratic leadership. One of my responsibilities as a professional process leader is to use my judgment in guiding the change process in the direction I think is necessary. For example, my co-workers and I make initial decisions about what questions and themes are to be treated in all the meetings, educational programs, and workshops that we organize. The discussions following these events guide the continued design of the change process.

Leadership style: There are considerable demands on our ability as process leaders to listen and be flexible. We continually adjust the change process design according to the ideas of the participants. At the same time, however, we need the ability to introduce new questions and themes that we believe are important to the change process, even if nobody in town has yet thought of these ideas. From many years of experience in sustainable development, I have acquired several aces up my sleeve that can help at different phases of the change process. For example, I might suggest strategies, such as a local trade and bartering system or an interest-free financing program, to spur economic growth. The challenge is to be sensitive about when to produce these aces. If I am uncertain, I need to test these cautiously and be willing to put them aside if the timing isn't right or use them if they are appropriate and well-received.

As process leader I walk continuously on a tightrope, balancing when to guide and when to be guided. The more experience I have in a particular community and the clearer I am about the goal for the change process, the easier it is to guide. However, the risk is that my vision could turn into authoritarian guidance, where participants become dependent on me as the leader. One way to avoid this is to guide through asking the right questions, encouraging community residents to find solutions themselves. I can also act as technical assistance coordinator by connecting identified development problems and needs with appropriate professionals in our technical assistance network. I often refer such questions to others even when I do have the knowledge to design a technical solution. In this way, I am able to avoid falling into the role of the person with answers to all questions and with whom everyone must be in contact in order for the change process to move forward.

Thus, the change process goals that I envision for Robertsfors are important and have helped to guide the initiative so far. Also, many exciting visionary discussions have occurred in the sustainability workshops and training sessions. I see these discussions as a warm-up for the actual vision-building phase of the change process. In this phase, we systematically and broadly involve as many participating residents as possible in starting the discussion about the future sustainable Robertsfors.

Holding vision workshops: An initial visioning workshop for the elected officials of Robertsfors' municipal administrative board took place in the spring of 2003. A few months later, a larger future workshop occurred, involving all community interest groups and all others who wanted to participate. These community workshops were the kick-off events for a continued vision phase. Our plan is to hold vision workshops for each of the specific themes included in our proposed self-sufficiency strategy — food, housing and building, and waste, for example. Each Robertsfors village will be invited to hold future workshops. In the workshops, participants will develop shared visions of a desired future that is also sustainable according to the Natural Step system conditions. The results of all workshops will then form an overall vision document that will guide the revision of Robertsfors' general (master) plan toward the sustainability objectives.

STEP D — SHAPING AND IMPLEMENTING ROBERTSFORS' ACTION PROGRAM

In this phase, municipal and community participants develop action plans that move toward the Sustainable Robertsfors vision. While there needs to be a clear vision before a large-scale municipal and community program launches into action, this need not deter community activists from starting sustainable development projects before the large-scale ones are ready.

Early actions: Already in Robertsfors, sustainability education has visibly influenced municipal policies and practices. The Sustainable Robertsfors initiative is well-established within the full political spectrum of the town's elected officials. The municipal government has decided that all municipal projects and activities will be designed within the four sustainability criteria and under the umbrella of Sustainable Robertsfors. For example, the municipality already has replaced all petroleum gas-fueled service cars with flexible-fueled vehicles that can use either ethanol or gasoline. The municipal government will use the sustainability criteria to guide all capital investments and municipal purchasing.

Schools and daycare facilities already involved in environmental certification processes are using the Natural Step sustainability criteria to rework their action plans. Nineteen businesses will work cooperatively to develop action programs for environmental certification. Village associations will be revising their revitalization plans to aim in more sustainable directions.

The municipal government of Robertsfors intends to develop an operations guidance system for sustainable development that will be directly connected both to the town's long-term general (master) plan and also to short-term municipal budget preparation and review. The platform, an earlier municipal financial planning tool used for budgeting needs, is the basis for developing the new sustainable development guidance system.

Economic strategy: Business and town interest groups will help shape a sustainable economic plan as part of the Sustainable Robertsfors initiative. This economic plan will address the themes identified so far in the change process — waste, energy, food production, housing and building, hospitality and tourism, forestry, and transportation. These themes are part of what we call the "near economy" (*när-ringar* in Swedish) that has several meanings. "Economy" means enterprise that supports life; near economy means local life-supporting enterprise. Working groups for each sector of the near economy should include all interests within that sector — producers, consumers, distributors, and stakeholders. For example, the near economy of the food production sector in Robertsfors includes farmers, food processing industries such as dairies and slaughterhouses, grocery stores, institutional kitchens, consumer groups, sewage treatment workers, and organic recycling managers.

Participants developing these near economy action plans also will use the Compass change strategy as a process guide, working in roundtable discussions. Each theme-based action plan will contain a vision for that theme, for example, an energy plan vision for freedom from fossil fuel dependency, coupled with strategies and implementing actions to move toward that vision. These action plans will be combined to form the basis for Robertsfors' general (master) plan and its sustainable management plan of implementing actions and measures.

The seeds for some of these near economy strategies already have been planted in previous workshops. Those early workshops were designed to be action oriented, where participants were able to discuss both short- and long-term strategies and action. For example, the Åkullsjön village's natural grazing field project developed as a direct outcome of the food production workshop. Plans to rehabilitate and better manage historic buildings and to develop a "feel-well village" emerged from the sustainable building workshop. The feel-well village plan will create several ecologically designed homes in an existing village. One goal is to shape a community life that slows down the tempo of everyday living and where all inhabitants can meet basic and deeper human needs, such as connection to community and nature. Interested potential residents and developers are being invited to jointly participate in the planning process for this village housing.

Expanding democracy and community participation in Robertsfors

Democracy is a key word in the Sustainable Robertsfors initiative. It encompasses all activity in the broadest sense — how to enable people to better participate in community life, for example. In a community change process to sustainable practices, democracy involves reshaping the dynamics that create community social norms so they occur more democratically. Today in Robertsfors, we do not yet have a precise vision or a thought-out strategy for how to do this. As one experiment, we are testing ways to make community meetings more exciting and to elicit greater public engagement. We are examining good examples in other communities that also are working to improve democratic practices, such as ways to expand resident participation in the political process, decentralize municipal functions, and delegate more municipal responsibilities. Little by little, we will discover democratic and participatory approaches for increased local involvement and public decision making that suit the Robertsfors municipal government and its residents.

Using technical expertise in the change process

I organized a network of technical assistance professionals to be on-call for the Sustainable Robertsfors initiative. This network consists of several leading Swedish experts in sustainability within their respective fields. They include the ecological architect and designer of the GreenZone eco-business park described in Chapter 8, a food systems ecologist, sustainability accounting experts, a consulting firm in democratic processes, business enterprise specialists, and Karl-Henrik Robèrt, founder of the Natural Step. These collaborative partners already have made valuable contributions to Robertsfors.

I do not expect the Sustainable Robertsfors initiative to come up with sustainability innovations in all theme areas. Rather, it makes sense to use existing knowledge and experience of sustainable practices learned elsewhere. The uniqueness of Robertsfors' contribution as a model sustainable community will lie in its systems approach that brings together all the separate innovative sustainable development practices and policies and joins these with the ability to use the right practice at the right time.

Building networks

Building different forms of networks is central to a successful change process. This involves networks not only within the community but also external at several levels, including:

- regional networks with nearby municipalities or regional organizations,
- national networks with other municipalities and organizations throughout the country, and
- international networks, preferably directly connected to municipalities in other countries but also with collaborating international organizations.

The larger and broader the network, the greater the prospects for absorbing important and useful knowledge and experience from where one least expects to find it, for example, from municipalities with seemingly completely different conditions from those of the home community.

External networks, meaning those beyond the boundaries of the municipality, are important in both the initial and later phases of a community change process toward sustainable practices. In the initial phase, there is nothing to lose and everything to gain by learning from other communities who are further down the road toward sustainability. In later phases, a community can collaborate with other like-minded municipalities to influence national and international action toward sustainable development. This has been one function of SeKom, the national association of eco-municipalities in Sweden. During the mid-phases of a community change process, however, the need for external relationships can seem less urgent, especially when an intensive implementation phase requires all available energy. Eco-municipalities have chosen to be less active in the SeKom network at times but often later become more involved. A good piece of advice is never to completely lose the external contacts, since it is more difficult to rebuild them once lost. Correspondingly, it is important to keep the external world informed about the change process to sustainable practices in one's own municipality. The world needs good examples.

Importance of a global perspective

My ambition is that we in Robertsfors continually look out at the rest of the world, especially to other municipalities that are working in the same sustainability direction. There already have been contacts between Robertsfors and municipalities in Estonia, Russia, the U.S.A., Spain, Germany, Mexico, and Japan. During the first year of the Sustainable Robertsfors initiative, visitors arrived from Japan, Estonia, the U.S.A., Mexico, and Italy. Representatives of six indigenous peoples from Guatemala, Mexico, the U.S.A., and Canada also visited Robertsfors as part of a world journey to build alliances with cultures and other local populations working seriously toward sustainable development. We in modern society have a lot to learn from the philosophies and ways of thinking in indigenous cultures.

In the final analysis, a sustainable community will see its own work in a global perspective. In the bigger picture, sustainable development needs to involve all humanity transforming toward a sustainable direction. We live in an ever more globalized world where we must come to see humanity itself as an entity. If we can develop a network of municipalities in many countries, it will be more likely that the sustainable community model constructed in Robertsfors can be used around the world. Correspondingly, we in Robertsfors have much to learn from other people in other cultures.

Epilogue

The stories of the Swedish eco-municipalities, their accomplishments, and their examples of successful change processes demonstrate that it is possible for communities of any size and, we maintain, anywhere in the world, to change on an across-the-board basis to sustainable practices. No one is saying it is easy. But it is possible to change, and these communities point the way for how the rest of us can follow.

The technology for sustainable practices is available. Clear criteria for defining and guiding a path to sustainability, such as the Natural Step framework, are available. Successful change process models for how to systematically reorient to sustainable municipal and community practices are available. The challenges that remain are to increase awareness of the need to change and to generate the political will to carry out the process.

Appendix A:
Location Map

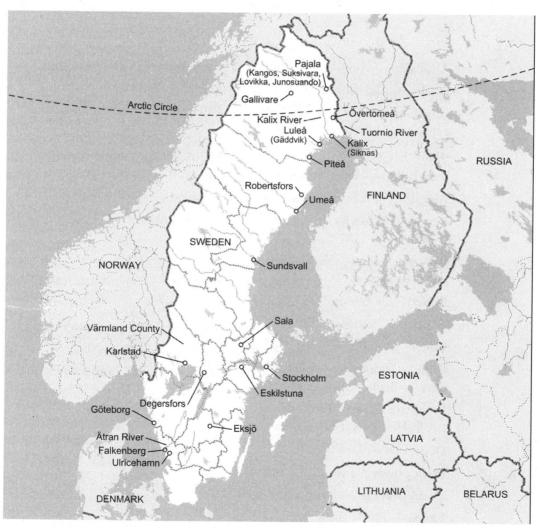

Figure A.1 Swedish cities, towns, and places described in this book.
Credit: Robin Harper, Knowledge Builder.

Appendix B:
Guide to Swedish Name Pronunciation

Åkullsjön — Auh'-kuell-sheun'

Aneby — Ah'-nehbee

Ängshagenskolan — Engs'-hah-gehn-skoo'-lahn

Ätran River — Eh' trahn

Baggböleri — Bugg-beuleree'

Bergsjön — Behryh'-sheun

Bergslagen district — Behryhs'-lah-ghen

Biskopsgården — Biss'-kopps-gohr'-dehn

Boden — Boo'-den

Boliden — Boo'-lee-dehn

Bollebygd —Boll'eh-bigd

Brandmästaren eco-condominiums — Brahnd'-meh-stahr-ehn

Bölebyns Garveri Tannery — Beuh'-leh-beens' Garr-veh-ree'

Degerfors — Deh'gehr-fosh

Dåva power plant — Doh'vah

Ekeby Wetlands — Eh'-keh-bih

Ekerö — Eh'-kehr-eu

Eksjö — Ehk'-sheu

Enköping — Ehn'-cheu-ping

Eskilstuna — Ess'kils-teu'-nah

Eslöv — Ehs'-leuv

Falkenberg — Fahl'kehn-behryh'

Filipstad — Filip-stahd'

FjällAgenda — Fyell'-Ah-ghen'-dah

Gotland — Gott'-lahnd

Gro Bruntland — Groo Breunt'-lahnd

Gäddvik — Yehdd'-veek

Gällivare — Yell'-ih-vah-reh

Göteborg — Yeu-teh-boryh'

Halland County — Hah'l-lahnd

Hallsberg — Hahlls'-behryh

Halmstad — Hahlm'-stahd

Haparanda — Hah-pahr-ahn'dah

Hedemora — Heh'deh-moo'-rah

Helsingborg — Hell-sing-boryh'

Huddinge — Heudd'-ing-eh

Hudiksvall — Heu-dicks-vahll'

Hylte — Hill'teh

Hällefors — Hell'eh-fosh

Härjedalen — Hehr'-yeh-dah'-lehn

Höglandskommunerna — Heug'-lahnds-komm-eu'-nehr-nah

Höör — Heuhr

Jokkmokk — Yokk'-mokk

Junosuando village — Yeu-nuh-suh-ahn'doh

Kalix — Kah'-lix

Kangos — Kahn'-gos

Karl-Henrik Robèrt — Kahrl-Hen'rik Robehr'

Karlskrona — Kahrls-kroo'-nah

Karlstad — Kahrl'-stahd

Klippan — Klipp'ahn

Kretsloppsföreningen — Kretts'-lopps-feuhr-eh'-ning-ehn

Kumla — Keum'lah

Kungsör — Keungs-eur'

Kungälv —Keung'-elv

Laholm — Lah-holhm'

Laponia — Lahpp-oh'-niah

Lappland — Lahpp'-lahnnd

Laxå — Lahx'-aw

Lovikka village — Loo'-vick-ah

Luleå — Leuh'-leh-aw

Maskringen — Mahsk'-ring-ehn

Mälardalen — Meh-lahr-dahl'en

Muonio Sámi — Mooh-oh'-nioh Sah'my

Mark — Marhk

Mats Fack — Mahtts Fahck

Miljöförskola — Mill-yeu'-feuhr-skoo'-lah

Mjölby — Myeul'-bee

Mulle — Meul'-leh

Munkfors — Meunk'-fosh

Mönsterås — Meun'-stehr-aws

Nacka — Nah'kah

NaturVärme — Nah-teur'Vehr'-meh

Nifsarpsmaden — Niffs'-ahrps-mah'-dehn

Norrbotten County — Norrh'-bohtt'en

Norrmejerier — Nohrr'-mehyeh-ree'-ehr

Norrtälje — Nohrr-tel'-yeh

Nynäshamn — Nee-nehs-hahmn'

Orsa — Ooh'shah

Östhammar — Eust'-hahm-mahr

Övertorneå — Eu-vehr-tawr'-neh-aw

Övre Bygd — Euh'vreh Bigd

Pajala — Pah'yah-lah

Piteå – Pee'–teh-aw

Pyramiden — Pee-rah-mee'-dehn

Returhuset — Reh-teuhr'-heu'set

Robertsfors — Roh-behrts-fosh'

Rosendal Garden — Roo-sehn-dahl'

Ruskola Ekoby — Reu'-skoo-lah Ehko-bih

Rönnskär Smelter — Reunn'-shehr

Sala — Sah'lah

Sámi — Sah'mi

Sápmi — Sahpp'mi

SeKom — Seh'-komm

Siknäs Framtid — Seek'-nehs Frahmm-teed

Sigtuna — Seeg'-teunah

Skara — Skah'rah

Smedjebacken — Smehd'-ye-bah'-kehn

Sorsele — Sosh'eh-leh

Sotenäs — Soo'teh-nehs

Stockholm — Stock'hohlm

Suksivara — Seuk'sih-vah'-rah

Sundbyberg — Seund-bee-behryh'

Sundsvall — Seunds'-vahll

Suomussalmi — Suh'-oh-muh'sahl'-mih

Sånga-Säby — Song'-ah Seh'-bih

Sävsjö — Sehv'-sheuh

Söderköping — Seu'dehr-cheu'ping

Södertälje — Seu-dehr-tel'yeh

Söderhamn — Seu-dehr-hahmn'

Tegelviken — Teh-'gehl-vee'-kehn

Timrå — Tim'-raw

Tranås — Trahn'-aws

Torbjörn Lahti — Toohr'-byeurn Lah'-tih

Trosa — Troo'sah

Tuggelite — Teugg'-eh-lee'-teh

Tuornio River — Tuh-ohr'-neh-aw

Tvärred school — Tvehr-'rehd

Ulricehamn — Eull-ree-seh-hahmn'

Umeå — Euh'-meh-aw

Understenshöjden — Eun-'dehr-stehns-heuy'-dehn

Uppsala — Eupp'-sah-lah

Vansbro — Vahns'-brooh

Varberg — Vahr'-behryh

Värmland — Vehrm'lahnd

Vingåker — Ving'-aw-kehr

Värmdö — Vehrmd'-eu

Värnamo — Ver'-nah-mooh

Ystad — Ee'-stahd

Appendix C:
National Association of Swedish
Ecomunicipalities (SeKom)
Members in 2005

Aneby	Härnösand	Sigtuna
Ånge	Höör	Skara
Boden	Karlskrona	Smedjebacken
Bollebygd	Klippan	Sollefteå
Degerfors	Kumla	Sorsele
Ekerö	Kungsör	Sotenäs
Eksjö	Kungälv	Stockholm
Enköping	Laholm	Sundbyberg
Eskilstuna	Laxå	Sundsvall
Eslöv	Luleå	Sävsjö
Falkenberg	Mark	Söderköping
Filipstad	Mjölby	Södertälje
Gotland	Mönsterås	Söderhamn
Hallsberg	Munkfors	Timrå
Halmstad	Nacka	Tranås
Haparanda	Norrtälje	Trosa
Hedemora	Nynäshamn	Varberg
Helsingborg	Orsa	Vingåker
Huddinge	Örnsköldsvik	Värmdö
Hudiksvall	Övertorneå	Värnamo
Hylte	Robertsfors	Ystad
Hällefors	Sala	

References and Sources

Bibliography

Alexander, Christopher, *The Timeless Way of Building*, Oxford University Press, 1979.

American Planning Association, *Planning for Sustainability Policy Guide*, April, 2000. <www.planning.org/policyguides/sustainability.htm>

Ander, Hans and Lars Berggrund, "Göteborg: From Dirty Old City to Environmental Capital," *Swedish Planning Towards Sustainable Development*, PLAN, the Swedish Journal of Planning, 1997.

Anderson, Ray, *Mid-Course Correction*, Peregrinzilla Press, 1998.

AtKisson, Alan, *Believing Cassandra: An Optimist Looks at a Pessimist's World*, Chelsea Green Publishing, 1999.

Benyus, Janine, *Biomimicry*, Quill William Morrow, 1997.

Boliden Company, "New Rönnskär," "Rönnskär 2001," and "Environmental Facts 2000: Rönnskär Smelter," Skelleftehamn, Sweden. See also <www.boliden.ca/index.htm>

Borchert, Nanna, in K.Fields, ed., *Land is Life: Traditional Sámi Reindeer Grazing Threatened in Northern Sweden*, Nussbaum Medien, 2001. <www.oloft.com/pressfolder.htm>

Brink, Torsten and Barbro Sundström, "Biskopsgården, Göteborg: A Process of Joint Action," *Swedish Planning Towards Sustainable Development*, PLAN, the Swedish Journal of Planning, 1997.

Burlington Electric Department, City of Burlington, Vermont, March, 2003. <www.burlingtonelectric.com>

Canada Office of Urban Agriculture, *City Farmer*, November, 1992. <www.cityfarmer.org>

Canadian Museum of Nature, "The Rideau River Biodiversity Project," August, 2002. <www.nature.ca/rideau/>

Cardinal Group, *The Eco-Industrial Advantage*, Vol.1, no.1, 2001. <www.cein.ca>

Carstedts, *A Road to Sustainability*, Sundsvall, 2000. This publication can be ordered from Carstedt's, Överstevägen 1, Umeå, Sweden. See also <www.greenzone.nu>

Coalition for Environmentally Responsible Economics (CERES), *CERES Principles, November, 2002.* <www.ceres.org/our_work/principles.htm>

Colburn, Theo, Dianne Dumanoski, and John Peterson Myers, *Our Stolen Future*, Penguin Books, New York, 1996.

Cole, Rick, Trish Kelly, and Judy Corbett, *Ahwahnee Principles for Smart Economic Development*, Center for Livable Communities, 1998.

Community Renewable Energy (CORE), "A Biomass District Energy Program," Essex Junction, n.d.

Dallas Area Rapid Transit Authority, "Newsroom," 2003, <www.dart.org.newsroom.asp>

District Energy Library, University of Rochester, "District Energy in Sweden," June, 2002. <www.energy.rochester.edu/se/>

District Energy Library, "District Heating Systems in the United States," Rochester, NY, June, 2002. <http://www.energy.rochester.edu /us/comdhlst.htm>

Economy and Energy, "Electricity Generation from Thermal Power Plants and Fuel Demand for Generation," No.23, December 2000-January 2001. <http://ecen.com/matriz/eee23/ger_elt_e.htm>

EcoTrust Canada, March, 2003. <www.ecotrustcan.org/projects/community/gbasin.shtml#ed>

Ekins, Paul, and Manfred Max-Neef, *Real-life Economics*, Routledge Publishing, April, 1997.

Eksjö, Municipality of, "Welcome to the Wetland Nifsarpsmaden," n.d. See also <www.eksjo.se>, March, 2003.

Environmental Defense Fund, *Scorecard*, "Chemical Profile for Acetone," CAS Number 67-64-1, 2003. <www.scorecard.org/chemical-profiles/summary.tcl?edf_substance_id=67%2d64%2d1>

Environmental Defense Fund, "Chemical Profile for Cadmium," CAS Number 7440-43-9, March, 2003. <www.scorecard.org/chemical-profiles/summary.tcl?edf_substance_id=7440%2d43%2d9>

ESAM (Human Ecological Corporation) and Torbjörn Lahti, "A Guide to Agenda 21." 1997. See <www.esam.se>

Eskilstuna Energi and Environment, "Our Name is Our Line of Work," n.d.

Eskilstuna Energi and Environment, "The Tandlaå Project: Constructing Wetlands in the Agricultural Landscape," 1999. See also <www.eskilstuna-em.se> (Swedish only).

Falkenberg, Municipality of, "Environment and Eco-cycling Program for the Municipality of Falkenberg: 2001-2005," April, 2001.

Falkenberg Tourist Information Office, "Falkenberg — the Swedish West Coast!" 2001 and "Salmon Fishing in the River Atran," Falkenberg. See also <www.falkenberg.se>

Ford Motor Company, "Rouge Renovation: An Icon of 20th Century Industrialism," 2003. <www.ford.com/en/dedication/environment/cleanerManufacturing/rougeRenovation.htm>

Ford, Bill Jr., Ford Motor Company. www.ford.com/en/ourCompany/environmentalInitiatives/cleanerManufacturing/rougeTurningA Monument.htm

Friends of Rosendal Garden, "The Rosendal Garden: An Introduction," Rosendalsterassen 12, Stockholm, Sweden, n.d.

Germany, Federal Environmental Agency Press Office, "Gas Filler in Sound Insulating Windows and Car Tires Adds to Greenhouse Effect," Berlin, April 16, 2002. <www.umweltbundesamt.de/uba-info-presse-e/presse-informationen-e/p4002e.htm>

Global Action Program, "Sustainable Lifestyles Campaign," March, 2003. <www.globalactionprogram.org>

Göteborg, City of, March, 2003. <www.goteborg.se>

Greiner Environmental, Inc., *Environmental, Health, and Safety Issues in the Coated Wire and Cable Industry*, prepared for the Massachusetts Toxics Use Reduction Institute, University of Lowell, April, 2002. <www.turi.org/PDF/Wire_Cable_TechReport.pdf>

Hawken, Paul, Amory Lovins, and L. Hunter Lovins, *Natural Capitalism: Creating The Next Industrial Revolution*, Little Brown, 1999.

Hermansson, Marianne, "Neighborhood Renovation in Bergsjön," *Swedish Planning Toward Sustainable Development*, PLAN, the Swedish Journal of Planning, 1997.

Herr, Philip B., "The Art of Swamp Yankee Planning: Making Plans That Work," unpublished paper, Newton, MA, revised October, 2002.

Ikonomou, M.G., S. Rayne, and R.F. Addision, "Exponential Increases of the Brominated Flame Retardants, Polybrominated Diphenyl Ethers, in the Canadian Arctic from 1981 to 2000," *Environmental Science and*

Technology, 36, pp.1886-1892.

International Organization of Standardization (ISO), March, 2003. ‹www.iso.ch/iso/en/ISOOnline.frontpage›

International Project Group on Solar Heating in Northern and Central Europe, "Solar Energy for District Heating: Here It Works — Sweden," March, 2003. <www2.stem.se/opet/solarheating/district/sweden.htm>

James, Sarah, "Moving Toward Sustainability in Planning and Zoning," Editor's Notes, *Planning Commissioner's Journal*, no. 47, Summer, 2002.

Jeyeratnam, J., "Acute Pesticide Poisoning: A Major Global Health Problem," *World Health Statistics Quarterly*, 43, pp.139-143, 1990.

Johns Hopkins School of Public Health and Center for Communications Programs, "Population and the Environment: The Global Challenge," Series M, no. 1, 2002.

Kemp, René and Jan Rotmans, "Managing the Transition to Sustainable Mobility," paper for workshop on Transitions to Sustainability through System Innovations Enschede, University of Twente, July 4-6, 2002.

Kemp, René and Jan Rotmans, "More Evolution than Revolution: Transition Management in Public Policy," Maastricht Economic Research Institute on Innovation and Technology (MERIT), Maastricht University, P.O. Box 616, 6200 MD Maastricht, The Netherlands, n.d.

Koepf, H.H., "The principles and practice of biodynamic agriculture," pp.237-250, in: B. Stonehouse, ed., *Biological Husbandry: A Scientific Approach to Organic Farming*, Butterworths, 1981. <http://attra.ncat.org/attra-pub/biodynamicap1.html>

KRAV, 2001 KRAV Annual Report, Uppsala, Sweden, 2001. <www.krav.se/arkiv/rapporter/AsredEngelska.pdf>

Kretsloppsföreningen Maskringen, "Basic Ideas and Practical Activities of the Maskringen Self-Sustainers." See also <www.grogrund.net/maskringen/main.html>, March, 2003.

Lahti, Torbjörn, *Eco-Municipality — a concept of change in the spirit of Agenda 21*, prepared for ESAM, November, 1996, revised March, 2000. See <www.esam.se>

Lilienfeld, Robert and William Rathje: *Use Less Stuff: Environmental Solutions for Who We Really Are*, 1998. In William McDonough and Michael Braungart, *Cradle to Cradle*, North Point Press, 2002.

Living Machines, Inc. <www.livingmachines.com>, March, 2003.

Malbert, Björn, "Sustainable Development, a Challenge to Public Planning," *Swedish Planning Towards Sustainable Development*, PLAN: Journal of Swedish Planning, Swedish Society for Town and Country Planning, 1997.

Massachusetts Technology Collaborative, *Green Schools Initiative*, February, 2003. <www.mtpc.org/RenewableEnergy/green_schools.htm>

McDonough, William and Michael Braungart, *Cradle to Cradle: Remaking the Way We Make Things*, North Point Press, 2002.

McDonough, William et.al, *Hannover Principles*, November, 2002. <www.mcdonoughpartners.com/principles.pdf>

National Association of Energy and Environmental Education Professionals, National Award for "A Child's Place in the Environment," October 27, 1998. < www.acpe.lake.k12.ca.us/awards.htm>

National Environmental Education and Training Foundation and Roper Starch Worldwide, *The National Report Card on Environmental Knowledge, Attitudes, and Behaviors: The Sixth Annual Survey of Adult Americans*, November, 1997, as reported by the U.S. EPA Office of Communications, Education, and Media Relations. <www.epa.gov/enviroed/pdf/19-keyfindings.pdf>

National Environmental Education Advancement Project, Status of State Level Environmental Education Programs in the United States, 1995, updated 1998. <www.uwsp.edu/cnr/neeap/statusofee/breakdow.htm>

Nattrass, Brian and Mary Altomare, *The Natural Step for Business*, New Society Publishers, 1999.

Nattrass, Brian and Mary Altomare, *Dancing with the Tiger*, New Society Publishers, 2001.

Newton, City of, "Sunergy Program." < www.ci.newton.ma.us/sunergy/>

North Carolina Triangle J Council of Governments, High Performance Guidelines: Triangle Region Public Facilities, September, 2001. <www.tjcog.dst.nc.us/hpgtrpf.htm>

Onstot, J., R. Ayling, and J. Stanley, "Characterizations of HRGC/MS Unidentified Peaks from the Analysis of Human Adipose Tissue", Volume 1: *Technical Approach*, Washington, DC: U.S. Environmental Protection Agency Office of Toxic Substances (560/6-87-002a), 1987.

Organic Trade Association, "Industry Statistics," Greenfield, MA, March, 2003. <www.atoexpo.com/industrystats.htm>

Paxton, Angela, "The Food Miles Report: The Dangers of Long Distance Transport," 1994, prepared for the Safe Alliance. *In Sharing Nature's Interest*, by Nicky Chambers, Craig Simmons, and Mathis Wackernagel, Earthscan Publications, 2000.

Pennsylvania Department of Education, *Environmental Assignment Scope for Certification*, 1987. <www.teaching.state.pa.us/teaching/cwp/view.asp?>

Physicians for Greater Social Responsibility, *In Harm's Way: Toxic Threats to Child Development*, Physicians for Social Responsibility, 1999.

Revenga, Carmen and Greg Mock, "Freshwater Biodiversity in Crisis," Summary, *EarthTrends*, World Resources Institute, October, 2000.

Robèrt, Karl-Henrik et al, "Strategic Sustainable Development — Selection, Design, and Synergies of Applied Tools," *Journal of Cleaner Production*, Volume 10, 2002.

Robèrt, Karl-Henrik, *The Natural Step Story: Seeding a Quiet Revolution*, New Society Publishers, 2002.

Robèrt, Karl-Henrik, et al., "The Natural Step to Sustainability," *Wingspread Journal*, The Johnson Foundation, Spring, 1997.

Robyn Van En Center for CSA Resources, March, 2003. <www.csacenter.org>

Roodman, David Malin and Nicholas Lenssen, *A Building Revolution: How Ecology and Health Concerns Are Transforming Construction*, 1995. <www.worldwatch.org/pubs/paper/124.html>

Santa Monica, City of, "Sustainable Development Program," 2002. <www.santa-monica.org/environment/policy/SCP2002.pdf>

Saunders, Tedd and Loretta McGovern, *The Bottom Line of Green is Black: Strategies for Creating Profitable and Environmentally Sound Businesses*, Harper, 1993.

SEEDS Foundation, Green School Program, March, 2003. < www.green-schools.ca>

Stockholm, City of, "Stockholm: Investing In Clean Vehicles," Environment and Health Protection Administration, n.d.

Stockholm, City of, "Stockholm: Clean and Green," n.d.

Stokes, C.S. and K.D. Brace, "Agricultural Chemical Use and Cancer Mortality in Selected Rural Counties in the U.S.A.," *Journal of Rural Studies*, 4, 1988. In *Living Downstream* by Sandra Steingraber, Vintage Books, Random House, 1998.

Sustainable Communities Network, "Sustainable Cobscook," March,

2003. <www.sustainable.org/casestudies/SIA_PDFs/SIA_maine.pdf>

Svensson, Sven-Åke, "Introduction to Sustainable Ideas in the Municipality of Eksjö," Eksjö, unpublished paper, August 9, 2001.

Swedish Waste Management 2000, "Towards Sustainable Development — the Implementation of Political Decisions," 2000. <www.rvf.se/avfall-shantering_eng/00/rub4.html>

Tallman, Janet, *An Inventory of the Flow of Energy Through a City Farm*, Luleå University of Technology, December, 1999.

The Nature Conservancy, "The Berkshire Taconic Landscape Program," 2002. <http://nature.org/aboutus/projects/berkshire/>

Thornton, Joe, *Pandora's Poison*, Massachusetts Institute of Technology, 2000.

Toronto, City of, "Idling Control Bylaw," 1998-2003. <www.toronto.ca/row/idling.htm>

Transport Canada, "ÉcoloBus — comparative evaluation of ecologically friendly buses," 2003. <www.tc.gc.ca/tdc/projects/road/>

Trivector Traffic, *Eskilstuna Mats: Program for an Environmentally Adapted Transportation System in Eskilstuna*, Report 2001:40, Eskilstuna, September, 2001. (Swedish only)

U.S. Department of Energy Boston Regional Office, "Making Energy is a Breeze in Hull," December, 2001. <www.eere.energy.gov/bro/hull.html>

U.S. Department of Energy Office of Power Technologies, "Consumer Guide to Renewable Energy," March, 2003. <www.eere.energy.gov/power/consumer/buycleanelec.html>

U.S. Department of Energy Smart Communities Network, *Green Buildings*, March, 2003. <www.sustainable.doe.gov/buildings/gbintro.shtml>

U.S. Department of Health and Human Services Agency for Toxic Substances and Disease Registry (ATDSR) *Public Health Statement for Vinyl Chloride*, CAS#75-01-4, September, 1997.

U.S. Department of Health and Human Services Agency for Toxic Substances and Disease Registry (ATDSR) Chromium Toxicity, *Case Studies in Environmental Medicine*, Course SS3048, October, 1992, revised July, 2000. < www.atsdr.cdc.gov/HEC/CSEM/chromium>

U.S. Department of Health and Human Services Agency for Toxic Substances and Disease Registry (ATDSR), <www.atsdr.cdc.gov/glos-sary.html>

U.S. Department of Health and Human Services Agency for Toxic Substances and Disease Registry (ATDSR), <www.atsdr.cdc.gov/toxpro-files/phs20.html>

U.S. Environmental Protection Agency Green Building Program, *Buildings and the Environment*, updated August 14, 2002. <www.epa.gov/greenbuilding/envt.htm>

U.S. Environmental Protection Agency Office of Pollution Prevention and Toxics, *Chemical Information and Data Development*. <www.epa.gov/opptintr/chemtest/index.htm>

U.S. Geological Survey, "Pharmaceuticals, Hormones, and Other Organic Wastewater Contaminants in U.S. Streams, 1999-2000: A National Reconnaissance," March, 2002.

U.S. General Accounting Office (GAO), *School Facilities: Condition of America's Schools Today*, GAO HEHS-95-61, June, 1996. <www.gao.gov-archive-1996-he96103.pdf>

Umeå Energi, *Dåva Combined Power and Heating Station Report*, Umeå, November, 2002. <www.umeaenergi.se>

Union of Concerned Scientists, *World Scientists' Warning to Humanity*, April, 1997.

Wackernagel, Mathis and William Rees, *Our Ecological Footprint: Reducing Human Impact On the Earth*, New Society Publishers, 1996.

West Start-Calstart, "Electric Buses in Transit Service," 1996. <www.cal-start.org/fleets/elbuses.html>

Westman, Bengt, "Local Agenda 21 in Sweden," *Swedish Planning Towards Sustainable Development*, PLAN: Journal of Swedish Planning, Swedish Society for Town and Country Planning, 1997.

Whistler, Resort Municipality of, "Comprehensive Sustainability Plan," April, 2003.

Wiklund, Lars, "Case Study No.12: Sala Eco-Municipality," *Stepping Stones*, No.20, United Kingdom Natural Step, December, 1998.

Williams, Ron, "Free Urea Based Fertilizer," 2002. <www.geocities.com/impatients63/FreeUreaBasedFertilizer.htm>

Wilson, E.O., *The Diversity of Life*, Belknap Press of Harvard University Press, 1992.

Wilson, E.O., *The Future of Life*, Borzoi Books, Alfred A. Knopf, 2002.

Wright, John W., ed. *The New York Times Almanac 2003*, Penguin Reference Books, 2002.

Wright, Richard T. and Bernard J. Nebel, *Environmental Science*, 8th ed., Pearson Education, Prentice-Hall, 2002.

Wulf, Margaret, "Is Your School Suffering from Sick Building Syndrome?" prepared for *PTA Today*, Nov/Dec 1993, revised 1997. <www.pta.org/programs/envlibr/sbs1193/htm>

Yang, R.S.H., ed., *Toxicology of Chemical Mixtures*, New York: Academic Press, 1994.

Talks and Presentations

Blomster, Rune, Technical Manager, Municipality of Övertorneå, Sweden, August 17, 2001.

Borgernäs, Ola, Managing Director, Carstedts, Umeå, Sweden, August 13, 2001.

Carlsson, Ulf, Principal, Tegelviken School, Eskilstuna, Sweden, August 6, 2001.

Douglas, Glenn, Kalix Kommun Fisheries Officer, August 18, 2001.

Eskilstuna municipal officials: Hans Ekström, Executive Committee Chair; Lena Sjöberg, Chief Information Officer; Tommy Hamberg; Lars Anderson, Managing Director, Eskilstuna, Sweden, August 6, 2001.

Eskilstuna Energi and Environment: Lynd, Leif, Anders Bjorklund, Eskilstuna, Sweden, August 6, 2001.

Fack, Mats, CEO, Sånga-Säby, Sweden, August 12, 2001.

Falkenberg Energi, Falkenberg, Sweden, August 9, 2001.

Falkenberg municipal officials: Andersson, Jan-Olof, Agenda 21 Coordinator; Environmental Health Office ecologist, Falkenberg, Sweden, August 9, 2001.

Friden, Bertil, Director, Center for Building Preservation (Byggnadsvård Qvarnarp), Eksjö, Sweden, August 10, 2001.

Frikvist, Eino, village association member, Lovikka village, Pajala, Sweden, August 16, 2001.

Ganslandt, Marie, Arkitekt, Björkelkullen Cultural Farm, Bråtadal, Sweden, August 9, 2001.

Helldorf, Nicke, Eskilstuna Nature School at Tegelviken, Eskilstuna, Sweden, August 6, 2001.

Karlstad Town Planner, Karlstad, Sweden, August 7, 2001.

Lindell, Rolf, National Agenda 21 Coordinator, Sånga-Säby, Sweden, August 12, 2001.

Linder, Erik, Övre Bygd Village Association Chairman, Kalix villages, August 18, 2001.

Luleå municipal officials: Lena Bengten, Eco-Coordinator; Bo Sundström, City Planner, Luleå, Sweden, August 15, 2001.

Lundgren, Eva, Lena Richard, and Anders Lund, Ekocentrum, Göteborg, Sweden, August 8, 2001.

Olsson, Anders and Jonas Lagneryd, Environmental Action Värmland, Degerfors, Sweden, August 7, 2001.

Robèrt, Karl-Henrik, Kalmar, Sweden, August 11, 2001.

Sandlund, Jan, Bölebyn Garveri, Piteå, Sweden, August 14, 2001.

Sannebro, Magnus, Agenda 21 Coordinator, Stockholm, Sweden, August 5, 2001.

Sundgren, Lisen, herbalist, Rosendal Garden, Stockholm, Sweden, August 5, 2001.

Tiberg, Nils, Maskringen Farm, Gäddvik, Sweden, August 15, 2001.

Ylvin, Sten and Lennart Wanhaniemi, Kangos village, Pajala, Sweden, August 16, 2001.

McDonough, William, Harvard Business School, April 14, 2003.

Endnotes

Chapter 1. Introducing and Using the Natural Step Framework

1. An analogy used by Dr. Karl-Henrik Robèrt.

2. Karl-Henrik Robèrt, *The Natural Step Story: Seeding a Quiet Revolution*, New Society Publishers, 2002, p. 32.

3. Ibid., p. 48.

4. Ibid., pp. 65-66.

5. Change in earth vegetated surface: *World Scientists' Warning to Humanity*, Union of Concerned Scientists, April, 1997.

    Species extinction: talk given by Dr. Jane Lubchenco, past president of American Academy for the Advancement of Science, November, 2000.

    Freshwater: "Freshwater Biodiversity in Crisis," Summary, Carmen Revenga, and Greg Mock, *EarthTrends*, World Resources Institute, October, 2000.

    Water contamination: "Pharmaceuticals, Hormones, and Other Organic Wastewater Contaminants in U.S. Streams, 1999-2000: A National Reconnaissance," U.S. Geological Survey, March, 2002.

6. Population and food supply: "Population and the Environment: The Global Challenge," Johns Hopkins School of Public Health and Center for Communications Programs, Series M, No. 1, 2002.

    Water supply: D. Hinrichsen, B. Robey, and U.D. Upadhyay, "Solutions for a Water-Short World." *Population Reports*, Series M, no. 14. Baltimore, Johns Hopkins School of Public Health, Population Information Program, December 1997.

7. Disproportionate consumption: World Wildlife Fund, as quoted by the Population Institute, n.d. See <www.population.newc.com/teampublish/71_234_1055.CFM>

    An ecological footprint is the estimated amount of land area associated with the averaged resource consumption and waste generation patterns of a defined population. Mathis Wackernagel and William Rees, *Our*

Ecological Footprint: Reducing Human Impact On the Earth, New Society Publishers, 1996.

Also, Mathis Wackernagel, Chad Monfreda, and Dana Deumling, "Geological Footprint of Nations," *Redefining Progress*, November 2002 <www.redefiningprogress.org/publications//ef1999.pdf>

8. The concept of a funnel as a metaphor for decreasing resources was introduced by Karl-Henrik Robèrt, John Holberg, et al., The Natural Step, circa 1996.

9. Robèrt, op. cit., pp. 64-74.

10. EPA (U.S. Environmental Protection Agency), *Chemical Information and Data Development*, <www.epa.gov/opptintr/chemtest/index.htm www.epa.gov/opptintr/chemtest/index.htm.>

11. Flame retardents in the Arctic: M.G. Ikonomou, S. Rayne, and R.F. Addison, "Exponential Increases of the Brominated Flame Retardants, Polybrominated Diphenyl Ethers, in the Canadian Arctic from 1981 to 2000," *Environmental Science and Technology*, 36, pp.1886-1892.

12. J. Onstot, R. Ayling, and J. Stanley, "Characterizations of HRGC/MS Unidentified Peaks from the Analysis of Human Adipose Tissue", Volume 1: *Technical Approach*, U.S. EPA Office of Toxic Substances (560/6-87-002a), 1987. As referenced by Joe Thornton, Pandora's Poison, MIT, 2000, p.43.

13. R.S.H.Yang, ed., *Toxicology of Chemical Mixtures*, New York: Academic Press, 1994, pp.99-117. As referenced by Joe Thornton, *Pandora's Poison*, MIT, 2000, p. 83.

14. Joe Thornton, op. cit., p. 83. Based upon R.S.H.Yang's asssertion that the number of experiments required to investigate the effects of all possible combinations of N chemicals is always 2 to the N^{-1}.

15. Loss of forest cover and species decline: Johns Hopkins School of Public Health, op. cit.

16. Manfred Max-Neef, a South American social scientist, has developed a typology of human needs that is sometimes used in deepening understanding of the Natural Step's System Condition #4. Max-Neef's typology of human needs are: subsistence, protection, affection, understanding, participation, leisure, creation, identity, freedom. Source: *Real-life Economics*, Paul Ekins and Manfred Max-Neef, Routledge Publishing, April, 1997.

Based upon the premise that all human activity is carried out to meet human needs, a human needs-centered approach for changing to sustainable behavior has been developed by Torbjörn Lahti and is found in the forthcoming English translation of "A Guide to Agenda 21." See <www.esam.se>

17. The American Planning Association has adopted a policy guide for planning for sustainability whose guiding objectives are essentially the same as these listed here. See *Planning for Sustainability Policy Guide*, American Planning Association, April, 2000. <www.planning.org/policyguides/sustainability.htm>

18. Diagram based upon "Hitting the Wall" diagram by Karl-Henrik Robèrt, Paul Hawken, & The Natural Step, as presented in "The Natural Step to Sustainability," *Wingspread Journal*, The Johnson Foundation, Spring, 1997.

19. For example, the U.S. federal government regulates water and air quality through the Clean Water Act (42 U.S.C.'7401-7671) and the Clean Air Act (33 U.S.C. s/s1251 et.seq.). The U.S. federal government plays a dominant role in transportation — location of highways — a major determinant of local development (23 U.S.C. and 49 U.S.C.)

20. The image of a tree is used by Karl-Henrik Robèrt to portray a complex system.

Chapter 2. Sustainability: The Trouble We Have Talking About It

1. World Commission on Environment and Development, *Our Common Future*, Oxford Universitiy Press, 1987, p. 43.

2. A clear delineation of the differing levels of sustainability principles, approaches, strategies, tools, measures, and actions can be found in: Karl-Henrik Robèrt et.al, "Strategic Sustainable Development — Selection, Design, and Synergies of Applied Tools," *Journal of Cleaner Production*, Volume 10, pp.197-214, 2002. The diagram "Sustainability and Levels of Approaches" is adapted from a diagram in this article.

3. Rick Cole, Trish Kelly, and Judy Corbett, *Ahwahnee Principles for Smart Economic Development*, Center for Livable Communities, 1998.

4. *Hannover Principles*. <www.mcdonoughpartners.com/principles.pdf>

5. *CERES Principles*, Coalition for Environmentally Responsible Economics (CERES). <www.ceres.org/our_work/principles.htm>

6. Alan AtKisson, *Believing Cassandra: An Optimist Looks at a Pessimist's World*, Chelsea Green Publishing, 1999.

Chapter 3. The Natural Step Approach: Why Is It Useful?

1. For more about Scandic Hotel's reorientation, see *The Natural Step for Business*, Brian Nattrass and Mary Altomare, New Society Publishers, 1999.

2. See *Dancing with the Tiger*, Brian Nattrass and Mary Altomare, New Society Publishers, 2001.

3. Karl Henrik Robèrt, *The Natural Step Story: Seeding a Quiet Revolution*, New Society Publishers, 2002, pp. 60-74.

Chapter 4. The Eco-municipalities of Sweden: A Little Background

1. In North America, municipal policy documents that guide land use, development, transportation, economic development, public facilities, among other elements are called master plans, comprehensive plans, or general plans, depending upon the region of the country. In Sweden, they are called general plans. (See preface and Chapter 14 for more about master plans and planning).

Chapter 5. Changing to Renewable Energy Sources

1. Karl-Henrik Robèrt, *The Natural Step Story: Seeding a Quiet Revolution*, New Society Publishers, 2002, p. 65.

2. "District Energy in Sweden." <www.energy.rochester.edu/se/>

3. Information about Falkenberg's wind farm and solar array from: a) talk given by Falkenberg Energi, August 9, 2001; b) "Solar Energy for District Heating: Here It Works — Sweden," n.d. <www2.stem.se/opet/solarheating/district/sweden.htm>

4. Jan-Olof Andersson, Agenda 21 Coordinator, Falkenberg, February 3, 2003.

5. Information about Eskilstuna from talks given by Hans Ekström, Executive Committee Chair; Lena Sjöberg, Chief Information Officer; and Tommy Hamberg, Eskilstuna, August 6, 2001.

6. "Electricity Generation from Thermal Power Plants and Fuel Demand for Generation," *Economy & Energy*, No. 23, December 2000-January 2001, <http://ecen.com/matriz/eee23/ger_elt_e.htm>

7. Information about Eskilstuna's CHP plant and heating system from presentations given by Anders Bjorklund, District Heating Manager, and Lars Anderson, Managing Director, Municipality of Eskilstuna, August 6, 2001.

8. Information about Övertorneå's fossil fuel reduction initiative and heat plant operation from a presentation by Rune Blomster, Technical

Manager, Övertorneå Municipality, August 17, 2001.

9. Baggböle (Bugg'-beuh'leh) was a village that large timber companies bought up forest land owned by small property owners at prices far below their market value, then brutally clearcut large swaths of forestland.

10. Umeå Energi, *Dåva Combined Power and Heating Station Report*, Umeå, n.d. <www.umeaenergi.se>

    Efficiency of conventional plants: see Economy and Energy <http://ecen.com/matriz/eee23/ger_elt_e.htm>

11. Umeå Energi. <www.umeaenergi.se>

12. "District Energy in Sweden." <www.energy.rochester.edu/se>.

13. Talk given by Rolf Lindell, National Agenda 21 Coordinator, to the 2001 Sustainable Sweden Tour, Sånga-Säby, August 12, 2001.

14. District Energy Library, University of Rochester, "District Heating Systems in the United States," June, 2002. <http://www.energy.rochester.edu/us/comdhlst.htm>

15. Ibid.

16. For more information about Burlington's biomass power plant, see <www.burlingtonelectric.com>

17. Community Renewable Energy (CORE), "A Biomass District Energy Program," Essex Junction, n.d.

18. Boston Regional Office, U.S. Department of Energy, "Making Energy is a Breeze in Hull," December, 2001, <www.eere.energy.gov/bro/hull.html>

19. City of Newton, "Sunergy Program," <www.ci.newton.ma.us/sunergy/>

20. Office of Power Technologies, U.S. Department of Energy, "Consumer Guide to Renewable Energy," <www.eere.energy.gov/ power/consumer/buycleanelec.html> <www.eere.energy.gov/consumerinfo/>

Chapter 6. Getting Away from Fossil-fueled Vehicles

1. Ray Anderson, *Mid-Course Correction*, Peregrinzilla Press, 1998, p. 77.

2. Paul Hawken, Amory Lovins, and L. Hunter Lovins, *Natural Capitalism: Creating the Next Industrial Revolution*, Little Brown, 1999, p. 40.

3. Philip B. Herr, Herr Associates, March, 2003.

4. Trivector Traffic, *Eskilstuna MATS: Program for an Environmentally Adapted Transportation System in Eskilstuna*, Report 2001, p. 40, Eskilstuna, September, 2001. (Swedish only)

5. Talks given by Lena Bengten, Eco-Coordinator, and Bo Sundström, City Planner, Municipality of Luleå, August 15, 2001.

6. For more information about eco-driving, see <www.ecodrive.org>

7. Magnus Sannebro, Stockholm Agenda 21 Coordinator, Stockholm, August 5, 2001.

8. City of Stockholm, *Stockholm: Investing In Clean Vehicles*, Environment and Health Protection Administration, n.d.

9. West Start-Calstart, "Electric Buses in Transit Service," 1996, <www.calstart.org/fleets/elbuses.html>

10. Transport Canada, "ÉcoloBus — comparative evaluation of ecologically friendly buses," 2003. <www.tc.gc.ca/tdc/projects/road/>

11. City of Toronto, "Idling Control Bylaw," 1998-2003. <www.toronto.ca/row/idling.htm>

12. Dallas Area Rapid Transit, "Newsroom," 2003. <www.dart.org.newsroom.asp >

Chapter 7. Ecological Housing

1. As quoted by Ray C. Anderson, *Mid-Course Correction*, opening page.

2. *Buildings and the Environment*, Green Building Program, U.S. Environmental Protection Agency. <www.epa.gov/greenbuilding/envt.htm> updated August 14, 2002.

3. David Malin Roodman & Nicholas Lenssen, *A Building Revolution: How Ecology and Health Concerns Are Transforming Construction*, Worldwatch Paper 124, the WorldWatch Institute, 1995, as quoted by Paul Hawken, Amory Lovins, and L. Hunter Lovins, *Natural Capitalism: Creating the Next Industrial Revolution*, p. 85.

4. *Green Buildings*, Smart Communities Network, U.S. Department of Energy. <www.sustainable.doe.gov/buildings/gbintro.shtml>

5. David Malin Roodman and Nicholas Lenssen, *A Building Revolution: How Ecology and Health Concerns Are Transforming Construction*, WorldWatch Paper 124, The WorldWatch Institute, 1995. <www.worldwatch.org/pubs/paper/124.html>

6. American Planning Association, *Policy Guide on Planning for Sustainability*, p. 3.

7. Editor's Notes, "Moving Toward Sustainability in Planning and Zoning," Sarah James, *Planning Commissioner's Journal*, no. 47, Summer, 2002, p. 10.

8. Mathis Wackernagel and William Rees, *Our Ecological Footprint: Reducing Human Impact on the Earth*, New Society Publishers, 1996, p. 104

9. For more about VOCs, see Chapter 8: Green Business; Green Buildings, "GreenZone: Big business pilots green development."

10. Based upon the work of Mats Wolgast, Professor of Medicine in the Department of Medical Physiology, Biomedicum, Uppsala University. See also Ron Williams, "Free Urea Based Fertilizer," 2002, at <www.geocities.com/impatients63/FreeUreaBasedFertilizer.htm>

11. Information about Pyramiden and Stockholm from talk given by Magnus Sannebro, August 5, 2001.

12. Talk given by Karlstad Town Planner, Karlstad, August 7, 2001.

13. Information about FaBo and Falkenberg council housing from "Environment and Eco-cycling Program for the municipality of Falkenberg: 2001-2005," Falkenberg Kommun, April, 2001.

Chapter 8. Green Businesses; Green Buildings

1. Tedd Saunders and Loretta McGovern, *The Bottom Line of Green is Black: Strategies for Creating Profitable and Environmentally Sound Businesses*, Harper, 1993.

2. Ray Anderson, *Mid-Course Correction*, Peregrinzilla Press, 1998, p. 16.

3. Brian Nattrass and Mary Altomare, *The Natural Step for Business*, New Society Publishers, 1999.

4. For more information about PVC toxicity, see *Public Health Statement for Vinyl Chloride*, CAS#75-01-4, Agency for Toxic Substances and Disease Registry, U.S. Department of Health and Human Services, September, 1997. <www.atsdr.cdc.gov/toxprofiles/phs20.html> For more information about risks of halogen and PVC in wire and cable coatings, see *Environmental, Health, and Safety Issues in the Coated Wire and Cable Industry*, prepared by Greiner Environmental, Inc., for the Massachusetts Toxics Use Reduction Institute, University of Lowell, April, 2002. <www.turi.org/PDF/Wire_Cable_TechReport.pdf>

5. "Volatile Organic Compounds (VOCs): Substances containing carbon and different proportions of other elements such as hydrogen, oxygen, fluorine, chlorine, bromine, sulfur, or nitrogen; these substances easily become vapors or gases. A significant number of the VOCs are commonly used as solvents (paint thinners, lacquer thinner, degreasers, and dry cleaning fluids)." Source: Agency for Toxic Substances and Disease Registry, U.S. Department of Health and Human Services.

<www.atsdr.cdc.gov/glossary.html>.

6. Chloroflurocarbons (CFCs) are ozone-depleting compounds used as refrigerants and solvents. For more information, see Joe Thornton, *Pandora's Poison*, MIT, 2000, pp. 301-305, 341.

7. ISO 14001 is an internationally recognized set of environmental management standards administered by a 140-country network called the International Organization of Standardization (ISO), with headquarters in Geneva, Switzerland. ISO developed the 14000 standards to support sustainable development as a response to the United Nations Conference on Environment and Development, in Rio de Janeiro, in 1992. See <http://www.iso.ch/iso/en/ISOOnline.frontpage>

8. Bill Ford, Jr., Ford Motor Company. <www.ford.com/en/ourCompany/environmentalInitiatives/cleanerM anufacturing/rougeTurningAMonument.htm>

9. Information about GreenZone from: 1). Talk given by Ola Borgernäs, Managing Director, Carstedts, Umeå, August 13, 2001; and 2). Carstedts, *A Road to Sustainability*, Sundvall, 2000. This publication can be ordered from Carstedt's, Överstevägen 1, Umeå, Sweden. See also <www.greenzone.nu>

10. ISO, <http://www.iso.ch/iso/en/ISOOnline.frontpage>

11. Information about Sånga-Säby from a talk given by Mats Fack, CEO, at Sånga-Säby, August 12, 2001. See <www.sanga-saby.se>

12. William McDonough and Michael Braungart, *Cradle to Cradle: Remaking the Way We Make Things Work*, North Point Press, 2002, p. 99.

13. For more information about chromium and its toxicity, see *Chromium Toxicity, Case Studies in Environmental Medicine*, Course SS3048, Agency for Toxic Substances and Disease Registry (ATSDR), U.S. Dept. of Health and Human Services, October, 1992, revised July, 2000. < www.atsdr.cdc.gov/HEC/CSEM/chromium/>

14. Information based upon talk by Inger Sandlund, co-owner of Bölebyns Garveri, Piteå, August 14, 2001. See <www.bolebyn-tannery.se>

15. Information about Värmland County's programs from talks given by Anders Olsson & Jonas Lagneryd, Environmental Action Värmland, Degerfors, August 7, 2001. See <www.hallbart.nu>

16. See "Volatile Organic Compounds" endnote 5, ATDSR.

17. From book title of *The Timeless Way of Building* by Christopher Alexander, Oxford University Press, 1979.

18. Information about Eksjö's Center for Building Preservation (Byggnadsvård Qvarnarp) from talk given by Bertil Friden, Director, Center for Building Preservation, Eksjö, August 10, 2001. See <www.eksjo.se>

19. Ford Motor Company, "Rouge Renovation: An Icon of 20th Century Industrialism," 2003. <www.ford.com/en/dedication/environment/cleanerManufacturing/rougeRenovation.htm>

    See also William McDonough and Michael Braungart, *Cradle to Cradle: Remaking the Ways We Make Things,* North Point Press, 2002, pp.157-165. Stormwater system costs from talk given by Bill McDonough, Harvard Business School, April 14, 2003.

20. For more information about the Interface Company, see: 1). Ray Anderson, *Mid-Course Correction,* and 2). Brian Nattrass and Mary Altomare, *The Natural Step for Business,* pp. 101-125.

21. The U.S. Green Building Council, a coalition of building industry leaders, has developed the LEED (Leadership in Energy and Environmental Design) building standards that are being used throughout the U.S. as criteria for green buildings. <www.usgbc.org >

Chapter 9. Journeys to Self-sufficiency: Community Eco-economic Development

1. Talk given by Erik Linder, Chairman of Övre Bygd Village Association, Kalix, August 18, 2001.

2. United Nations Conference on Environment and Development, June 3-14, 1992, Rio de Janeiro, Brazil, also known as the Earth Summit or Rio Summit. At this conference, more than 178 nations came together to develop strategies to halt or reverse the negative impact of human behavior on the environment. Out of this summit emerged an action blueprint, for local as well as national governments to move toward sustainable development that became known as Agenda 21.

3. Nanna Borchert, in K. Fields, ed., *Land is Life: Traditional Sámi Reindeer Grazing Threatened in Northern Sweden,* Nussbaum Medien, 2001, pp.20-21, 23. Publication also available at <www.oloft.com/pressfolder.htm>

4. Ibid., p. 2.

5. Ibid., p. 27.

6. Torbjörn Lahti, *Eco-municipality — a concept of change in the spirit of Agenda 21,* p. 16.

7. Sustainable Communities Network, "Sustainable Cobscook," <www.sustainable.org/casestudies/SIA_PDFs/SIA_maine.pdf>

8. EcoTrust Canada, <www.ecotrustcan.org/projects/community/ gbasin.shtml#ed >

Chapter 10. Ecological Schools; Ecological Education

1. Margaret Wulf, "Is Your School Suffering from Sick Building Syndrome?" originally published in *PTA Today*, Nov/Dec 1993, revised 1997. <www.pta.org/programs/envlibr/sbs1193/htm>

2. U.S. General Accounting Office (GAO), *School Facilities: Condition of America's Schools Today*, GAO HEHS-95-61, June, 1996, p. 1. <www.gao.gov-archive-1996-he96103.pdf>

3. Information about the Tegelviken School: Ulf Carlsson, Principal of Tegelviken School, August 6, 2001. Information about Televiken's ecological curriculum: Nicke Helldorf, Eskilstuna Nature School, August 6, 2001. <www.eslilstuna.se/tegelviken/> (Swedish only)

4. Based on a talk given by Ann Britt Aasa, teacher, Miljöförskola School, Övertorneå, August 17, 2001.

5. Information about the Kangos School based upon talks given by Sten Ylvin, Lennart Wanhaniemi, Kangos village, August 16, 2001.

6. Information about the Tvärred School renovation from talk by Marie Ganslandt, Arkitekt, Porten Ritare AB, designer for the Tvärred School renovation, at Björkelkullen Cultural Farm, Bråtadal, August 9, 2001.

7. Christopher Alexander, *The Timeless Way of Building*, Oxford University Press, 1979, p. 7.

8. For more about ISO 14001 environmental standards, see chapter 4: Green Businesses; Green Buildings.

9. Mathis Wackernagel and William Rees, *Our Ecological Footprint: Reducing Human Impact on the Earth*, New Society Publishers, 1996.

10. Benzene compounds accumulate in fatty tissue and can build up in concentration up the food chain. See Joe Thornton, *Pandora's Poison*, MIT, 2000, pp. 35-36.

11. For information about acetone risks, see Environmental Defense Fund, Scorecard, "Chemical Profiles, CAS Number 67-64-1, 2003. <www.scorecard.org/chemical-profiles/summary.tcl?edf_ substance_id=67%2d64%2d1>

12. Cadmium is a known carcinogen and toxicant to reproduction, fetus

and child development, blood, immune system, endocrine system, and kidneys. See Environmental Defense Fund, *Scorecard*, "Chemical Profiles," CAS Number 7440-43-9. <www.scorecard.org/chemical-profiles/summary.tcl?edf_substance_id=7440%2d43%2d9>

13. Federal Environmental Agency of Germany, Press Office, "Gas Filler in Sound Insulating Windows and Car Tires Adds to Greenhouse Effect," April 16, 2002. <www.umweltbundesamt.de/uba-info-presse-e/presse-informationen-e/p4002e.htm>

14. Ekocentrum information based upon talks given by Eva Lundgren, Lena Richard, and Anders Lund, Ekocentrum, Göteborg, August 8, 2001. See <www.ekocentrum.se>

15. *Green Schools Initiative*, Massachusetts Technology Collaborative. <www.mtpc.org/RenewableEnergy/green_schools.htm>

16. *High Performance Guidelines: Triangle Region Public Facilities*, North Carolina Triangle J Council of Governments, September, 2001. <http://www.tjcog.dst.nc.us/hpgtrpf.htm>

17. Green School Program, SEEDS Foundation, St. Albert. <www.greenschools.ca >

18. Ibid.

19. National Environmental Education Advancement Project, *Status of State Level Environmental Education Programs in the United States*, 1995, updated 1998. <www.uwsp.edu/cnr/neeap/statusofee/breakdow.htm>

20. Pennsylvania Department of Education, *Environmental Assignment Scope for Certification*, 1987. <www.teaching.state.pa.us/teaching/cwp/view.asp?>

21. National Association of Energy and Environmental Education Professionals, October 27, 1998. <http://www.acpe.lake.k12.ca.us/ awards.htm>

22. National Environmental Education and Training Foundation and Roper Starch Worldwide, *The National Report Card on Environmental Knowledge, Attitudes, and Behaviors: The Sixth Annual Survey of Adult Americans*, November, 1997, as reported by the U.S. EPA Office of Communications, Education, and Media Relations. <www.epa.gov/enviroed/pdf/19-keyfindings.pdf >

Chapter 11. Sustainable Agriculture: Growing Healthy; Growing Locally

1. Janine Benyus, *Biomimicry*, Quill William Morrow, 1997, p. 20.

2. Paul Hawken, Amory Lovins, and L. Hunter Lovins, *Natural Capitalism:*

Creating the Next Industrial Revolution, Little Brown, 1999, p. 192.

3. Angela Paxton, "The Food Miles Report: The Dangers of Long Distance Transport," 1994, produced for the Safe Alliance, as quoted by Nicky Chambers, Craig Simmons, Mathis Wackernagel, *Sharing Nature's Interest*, Earthscan Publications, 2000, p. 88.

4. Janine Benyus, op. cit., p. 19.

5. Ibid., p. 20.

6. Richard T. Wright and Bernard J. Nebel, *Environmental Science*, 8th edition, Pearson Education, Prentice-Hall, 2002, pp. 416-417.

7. J. Jeyeratnam, "Acute Pesticide Poisoning: A Major Global Health Problem," *World Health Statistics Quarterly* 43, pp.139-143, 1990, as referenced by Joe Thornton, *Pandora's Poison*, MIT Press, 2000, p. 300.

8. C.S. Stokes and K.D. Brace, "Agricultural Chemical Use and Cancer Mortality in Selected Rural Counties in the U.S.A.," *Journal of Rural Studies*, 4, 1988, pp.239-247, as referenced by Sandra Steingraber, *Living Downstream*, Vintage Books, Random House, 1998, p. 63.

9. Physicians for Greater Social Responsibility, *In Harm's Way: Toxic Threats to Child Development*, Physicians for Social Responsibility, 1999.

10. Theo Colburn, Dianne Dumanoski, and John Peterson Myers, *Our Stolen Future*, Penguin Books, 1996, p.140.

11. Richard Wright and Bernard Nebel, op. cit., p. 599.

12. Paul Hawken, Amory Lovins, and L. Hunter Lovins, op. cit., p. 191.

13. Janine Benyus, op. cit., p. 195.

14. Organic Trade Association, "Industry Statistics," <www.atoexpo.com/industrystats.htm>

15. KRAV, *2001 KRAV Annual Report*, 2001.

16. Organic Trade Association, op. cit.

17. For a comparison of biodynamic and conventional farming, see H.H. Koepf, "The principles and practice of biodynamic agriculture," pp. 237-250, in B. Stonehouse, ed., *Biological Husbandry: A Scientific Approach to Organic Farming*, Butterworths, 1981, as referenced at <http://attra.ncat.org/attra-pub/biodynamicap1.html>

18 Information about Rosendal Gardens from: 1). Talk given by Lisen Sundgren, Rosendal Gardens herbalist, at Rosendal Gardens, August 5, 2001; 2). "The Rosendal Garden: An Introduction," The Friends of the Rosendal Garden, Rosendalsterassen 12, Stockholm, Sweden, n.d. EcoPark information from "Stockholm: Clean and Green," City of

Stockholm, n.d.

19. <www.grogrund.net/maskringen/main.html>

20. Kretsloppsföreningen Maskringen, "Basic ideas and practical activities of the Maskringen self-sustainers," unpublished, n.d.

21. Janet Tallman, *An Inventory of the Flow of Energy Through a City Farm*, Luleå University of Technology, December 1999, using U.S. data from Hall, Cleveland, and Kaufman, *Energy and Resource Quality*, John Wiley and Sons, 1986.

22. For more about urine use as a fertilizer, see Chapter 7: Ecological Housing, "Understenshöjden Ecological Housing."

23. Information about the Maskringen Cooperative from 1). a talk given by Nils Tiberg, Maskringen Farm, Gäddvik, August 15, 2001, and 2). Kretsloppsföreningen Maskringen, "Basic Ideas and Practical Activities of the Maskringen Self-Sustainers." See also <www.grogrund.net/maskringen/main.html>

24. Information in this section from: KRAV, *2001 KRAV Annual Report*, 2001. See also <www.krav.se/arkiv/rapporter/AsredEngelska.pdf> or <www.krav.se>

25. For more information about community-supported agriculture cooperatives, see <www.csacenter.org>

26. Canada Office of Urban Agriculture, *City Farmer*, November 1992. <www.cityfarmer.org>

Chapter 12. Dealing with Waste

1. William McDonough and Michael Braungart, *Cradle to Cradle: Remaking the Way We Make Things Work*, North Point Press, 2002, p. 103.

2. Paul Hawken, Amory Lovins, and L. Hunter Lovins, *Natural Capitalism: Creating the Next Industrial Revolution*, Little Brown, 1999, p. 52.

3. Karl-Henrik Robèrt, *A Framework for Achieving Sustainability in Our Organizations*, Pegasus Communications, 1997, p. 9.

4. Robert Lilienfeld and William Rathje: *Use Less Stuff: Environmental Solutions for Who We Really Are*, 1998, as quoted by William McDonough and Michael Braungart, *Cradle to Cradle: Remaking the Way We Make Things Work*, North Point Press, 2002, p. 50.

5. Paul Hawken, Amory Lovins, and L. Hunter Lovins, op. cit., p. 81.

6. William McDonough and Michael Braungart, op. cit., p. 67.

7. Mathis Wackernagel and William Rees, *Our Ecological Footprint:*

Reducing Human Impact On the Earth, New Society Publishers, 1996.

8. Kansas City Star, May 9, 2000. <wwwpcdisposal.com/industrynews.htm>

9. Robèrt, op. cit., p. 65.

10. Information about the Rönnskär plant from 1). a tour of the facility, August 14, 2001, and 2). "New Rönnskär," "Rönnskär 2001," & "Environmental Facts 2000: Rönnskär Smelter," Boliden, Skelleftehamn, Sweden. See also <www.boliden.ca/index.htm>

11. Based upon talk given by Eino Frikvist, Lovikka village association member, Lovikka, August 16, 2001.

12. John W. Wright, ed., *The New York Times Almanac* 2003, Penguin Reference Books, 2002, p. 777.

13. For more about KRAV environmental labeling, see Chapter 11, Sustainable Agriculture: Growing Healthy; Growing Locally.

14. Eksjö eco-team information from "Introduction to sustainable ideas in the Municipality of Eksjö," Sven-Åke Svensson, Agenda 21 Coordinator, Eksjö, unpublished paper, August 9, 2001.

15. Eutrophication: a condition where the balance between nutrients in the water and the algae that feed on them is disrupted. Increasing nutrients brings about rapid algae growth. The excess of dead algae then sets off a rapid increase in the algae's decomposers — bacteria. Too many bacteria, that breathe using dissolved oxygen, then suffocate water creatures that also depend on dissolved oxygen to breathe — fish and shellfish, for example. Further particles suspended in water block sunlight penetration that fuels the natural photosynthesis process of water ecosystems. This system breakdown creates one form of water pollution.

16. Information about the Ekeby wetland based upon 1). a talk given by Leif Lynd, Eskilstuna Energi & Environment, Eskilstuna, August 6, 2001; and 2). "Our Name is Our Line of Work," Eskilstuna Energi and Environment, undated brochure; 3. "The Tandlaå Project: Constructing Wetlands in the Agricultural Landscape," Eskilstuna Energi and Environment, 1999. See also <www.eskilstuna-em.se> (Swedish only).

17. Information about Eksjö's Wetland Nifsarpsmaden and regional and Polish community collaborations from 1). "Welcome to the Wetland Nifsarpsmaden," municipality of Eksjö, unpublished paper, n.d; and 2). "Introduction to Sustainable Ideas in the Municipality of Eksjö," Sven-Åke Svensson. See also <www.eksjo.se>

18. *Swedish Waste Management 2000*, "Towards Sustainable Development — the Implementation of Political Decisions," 2000. <www.rvf.se/avfallshantering_eng/00/rub4.html>

19. Global Action Plan, "Sustainable Lifestyles Campaign," <www.global-actionprogram.org>

20. The Cardinal Group, *The Eco-industrial Advantage*, Vol.1, no.1, 2001. <www.cein.ca>

21. Living Machines, Inc., <www.livingmachines.com >

Chapter 13. Natural Resources: Protecting Biodiversity

1. As quoted by William McDonough and Michael Braungart in *Cradle to Cradle: Remaking the Way We Make Things*, North Point Press, Farrar, Straus, and Giroux, 2002.

2. Karl-Henrik Robèrt, *The Natural Step Story: Seeding a Quiet Revolution*, New Society Publishers, 2002, p. 71.

3. E.O. Wilson, *The Diversity of Life*, Belknap Press of Harvard University Press, p. 182.

4. "We must be careful not to justify preserving wild species and biodiversity with predictions of disasters. However, it is possible to lose what ecologists call keystone species — species whose role is absolutely vital for the survival of other species in an ecosystem ... greater biodiversity will make the presence of key species more likely in an ecosystem. Thus, biodiversity is an insurance policy against environmental variability." Richard T. Wright and Bernard J. Nebel, *Environmental Science*, 8th edition, Pearson Education, Prentice-Hall, p. 281.

5. Ibid.

6. Information about Falkenberg's salmon biodiversity protection project from talk given by the municipal ecologist, Environmental Health Office, Municipality of Falkenberg, August 9, 2001. Information about Falkenberg from "Falkenberg — the Swedish West Coast!" 2001 and "Salmon Fishing in the River Atran," Falkenberg Tourist Information Office. See also <www.falkenberg.se>

7. Based upon talk given by Glenn Douglas, Fisheries Officer, Kalix, August 18, 2001.

8. Municipality of Falkenberg, "Environment and Recycling Program for the Municipality of Falkenberg," April, 2001, p. 12.

9. Canadian Museum of Nature, "The Rideau River Biodiversity Project," August, 2002, < www.nature.ca/rideau/>

10. The Nature Conservancy, "The Berkshire Taconic Landscape Program", 2002, <http://nature.org/aboutus/projects/berkshire/>

11. As quoted by E.O. Wilson, *The Future of Life*, Borzoi Books, Alfred A. Knopf, 2002, opening page.

Chapter 14. Sustainable Land Use and Planning

1   American Planning Association, "General Policy Objectives," *Planning for Sustainability* Policy Guide, p. 6.

2. Information about Göteborg from 1). an article by Hans Ander and Lars Berggrund, "Göteborg: From Dirty Old City to Environmental Capitol," *Swedish Planning Towards Sustainable Development*, PLAN, the Swedish Journal of Planning, pp. 73-75; and 2). City of Göteborg Web Site, <www.goteborg.se> Information about Biskopsgården from article by Torsten Brink and Barbro Sundström, "Biskopsgården, Göteborg: A Process of Joint Action," *Swedish Planning Towards Sustainable Development*, pp. 47-50. Information about Bergsjön from an article by Marianne Hermansson, "Neighborhood Renovation in Bergsjön," *Swedish Planning Toward Sustainable Development*, pp. 87-89.

3. Information about Sala planning from an article by Wiklund, Lars, "Case Study No.12: Sala Eco-municipality," *Stepping Stones*, no.20, United Kingdom Natural Step, December, 1998.

4. For information about Santa Monica's sustainable development program see <www.santa-monica.org/environment/policy/SCP2002.pdf>

5. Brian Nattrass and Mary Altomare, *Dancing with the Tiger*, New Society Publishers, 2002, pp.140-188. For more information about Whistler's comprehensive sustainability plan, see

6. Bengt Westman, Swedish Association of Local Authorities Agenda 21 Coordinator, "Local Agenda 21 in Sweden," *Swedish Planning Towards Sustainable Development*, PLAN: Journal of Swedish Planning, Swedish Society for Town and Country Planning, 1997, pp. 82-86.

7. Björn Malbert, Senior Researcher, Chalmers University of Technology, "Sustainable Development, a Challenge to Public Planning," *Swedish Planning Towards Sustainable Development*, p. 71.

8. Ibid., p. 70.

Chapter 16. Three Change Processes That Work

1. Sven-Åke Svensson, Eksjö Agenda 21 Coordinator, "Introduction to Sustainable Ideas in the Municipality of Eksjö," Eksjö, August 9, 2001.

2. Karl-Henrik Robèrt, in a talk given to the 2001 Sustainable Sweden Tour in Kalmar, Sweden, August, 2001.

3. Karl-Henrik Robèrt, *A Framework for Achieving Sustainability in Our Organizations*, Pegasus Communications, 1997, p. 102-104.

4. Ibid., p. 106.

5. Information about Sånga-Säby from a talk given by Mats Fack, CEO, at Sånga-Säby, August 12, 2001. See <www.sanga-saby.se>

6. Philip B. Herr, "The Art of Swamp Yankee Planning: Making Plans That Work," unpublished paper, revised October, 2002, Newton, MA.

7. René Kemp and Jan Rotmans, "Managing the Transition to Sustainable Mobility," paper for workshop on Transitions to Sustainability through System Innovations Enschede, University of Twente, July 4-6, 2002. Transition management is more fully described in the article "More Evolution than Revolution: Transition Management in Public Policy," Jan Rotmans, René Kemp, and Marjolein Van Asselt, Maastricht Economic Research Institute on Innovation and Technology (MERIT), n.d.

Chapter 17. Steps to Change

1. One method of identifying community priorities in a public forum used in Swamp Yankee planning processes is called red-dot-voting. Action proposals from the range of topic groups are written on strips of paper and put up on the walls. Forum participants are given a strip of four or five sticky red dots, and instructed to place these dots on their highest-priority action proposals. Participants can chose to put all their dots on one proposal or disperse their dots among several proposals. These red dot votes can then be counted to tally forum participant priorities for action proposals. If forum participation includes people from all community interests, these priorities can give a good indication of community-wide priorities.

Chapter 18. Inside the Head of a Process Leader

1. Robertsfors and the Environmental Forum were able to secure funding of US$2.5 million over five years from the European Union.

Index

About the Authors

Credit: Edward Mason

Sarah James has worked with local communities for more than twenty years in the areas of urban and town planning, community development, and sustainable development. She has worked as a regional planner, consulting planner, and also was founder of a non-profit community development corporation. Since 1986, she has operated a consulting practice in planning and community development that specializes in community participatory approaches to planning. She has worked closely with Philip Herr, originator of the Swamp Yankee planning approach, for over a decade. She is a co-author of the American Planning Association's Policy Guide *Planning for Sustainability*. She has taught workshops, written articles, and lectured on planning and sustainability at conferences and institutions across the United States. She has taken advanced training in the Natural Step approach to sustainability, and holds a master's degree in city planning from the Harvard Graduate School of Design.

Born and raised in Cooperstown, New York, Sarah has lived in the Boston, Massachusetts area for over three decades. She also has longstanding ties to outer Cape Cod. She has traveled around the world by herself, and lived for some time at the Findhorn commmunity in Scotland. She presently lives in a cohousing community. She enjoys roller-blading, watercolor painting, cross-country skiing, golf, kayaking, hiking, and has a cat named Persephone who loves dogs.

About the Authors

Torbjörn Lahti is a planner and economist based in Umeå, Sweden. He worked as the Town of Overtorneå's planner during the 1980s, helping that community to become Sweden's first eco-municipality. Since that time, he has assisted scores of other cities and towns to become eco-municipalities, and has led sustainability education programs and workshops in over 160 communities — half of all municipalities in Sweden. He co-founded Esam AB, a consulting firm in human ecology. He was instrumental in founding Sweden's national association of eco-municipalities during the 1990s. He has received national foundation awards in Sweden for his work in promoting a human ecology approach in community development. He has authored several publications about community sustainability, including a guide for community change and a history of the eco-municipality movement in Sweden. He is one of the original trainers of the Natural Step framework for sustainability. He holds a master's degree in planning and coursework for a doctorate degree in economics from the University of Umeå. He is presently directing the Sustainable Robertsfors initiative in Sweden, an international sustainable community demonstration project.

A lifelong native of northern Sweden, with Swedish and Finnish ancestry, Torbjörn has a wife and three children. He plays jazz piano, and has been known to be formidable on the basketball court.

If you have enjoyed *The Natural Step for Communities*,
you might also enjoy other

BOOKS TO BUILD A NEW SOCIETY

Our books provide positive solutions for people who want to
make a difference. We specialize in:

**Sustainable Living • Ecological Design and Planning
Natural Building & Appropriate Technology • New Forestry
Environment and Justice • Conscientious Commerce
Progressive Leadership • Resistance and Community • Nonviolence
Educational and Parenting Resources**

New Society Publishers

ENVIRONMENTAL BENEFITS STATEMENT

New Society Publishers has chosen to produce this book on Enviro recycled
paper made with 100% post consumer waste, processed chlorine free, and
old growth free.

For every 5,000 books printed, New Society saves the following resources:[1]

47	Trees
4,239	Pounds of Solid Waste
4,664	Gallons of Water
6,084	Kilowatt Hours of Electricity
7,706	Pounds of Greenhouse Gases
33	Pounds of HAPs, VOCs, and AOX Combined
12	Cubic Yards of Landfill Space

[1]Environmental benefits are calculated based on research done by the Environmental Defense Fund and
other members of the Paper Task Force who study the environmental impacts of the paper industry.

For more information on this environmental benefits statement, or to inquire about environmentally
friendly papers, please contact New Leaf Paper – info@newleafpaper.com Tel: 888 • 989 • 5323.

For a full list of NSP's titles, please call **1-800-567-6772** *or check out our web site at:*

www.newsociety.com

NEW SOCIETY PUBLISHERS